Richard Meier

Foreword and acknowledgments by
Richard Koshalek and Dana Hutt
Introduction by Dana Hutt
Essays by Stan Allen, Kenneth Frampton,
Jean-Louis Cohen, Lisa J.Green
Designed by Massimo Vignelli

THE MONACELLI PRESS

THE MUSEUM OF CONTEMPORARY ART
LOS ANGELES

Richard Meier Architect

First published in the United States of America in 1999 by
The Monacelli Press, Inc.
10 East 92nd Street, New York, New York 10128
and The Museum of Contemporary Art, Los Angeles
250 South Grand Avenue
Los Angeles, California 90012

This publication accompanies the exhibition "Richard Meier Architect,"
organized by Richard Koshalek and Dana Hutt on behalf of The Museum
of Contemporary Art, Los Angeles (MOCA).

"Richard Meier Architect" is made possible in part by a generous
gift from The J. Paul Getty Trust. Additional support has been
provided by Max Weishaupt GmbH, D-Schwendi; Lisette and Norman
Ackerberg; Hathaway Dinwiddie Construction Group; Christie's;
and The Broad Art Foundation.

Editor: Lisa J. Green
Book Design: Massimo Vignelli
Design Coordinator: Letizia Ciancio
Translator ("Creative Repetition"): Christian Hubert

Library of Congress Cataloging-in-Publication Data
Meier, Richard, date.
Richard Meier architect / foreword by Richard Koshalek ;
introduction by Dana Hutt ; essays by Stan Allen . . . [et al.].
  p.   cm.
Catalog accompanying an exhibition organized by The Museum of
Contemporary Art, Los Angeles.
Includes bibliographical references.
ISBN 1-58093-044-1. — ISBN 1-58093-061-1 (pbk.)
1. Meier, Richard, date, Exhibitions. 2. Architecture, Modern—
20th century—United States Exhibitions. 3. Architectural practice,
International—Europe Exhibitions. I. Allen, Stan. II. Title.
NA737.M44A4 1999
720'.92—dc21   99-35830

Illustration Credits

Contents

Foreword and Acknowledgments

Richard Koshalek and Dana Hutt

In a century characterized by an overwhelming confusion of styles, trends, and attitudes—and controversies over the very meanings of these words—a few creative individuals stand apart for their single-minded commitment to a purity and clarity of vision. Rather than changing mercurially from one decade to the next, their work is a sustained virtuosic performance that continually refines itself.

More than any architect today, Richard Meier embodies the virtues of this clarity of vision. Paradoxically, his adherence to a single visual aesthetic reflects not only the basic tenets of modernist abstraction, making him thoroughly an architect of our time, but also the centuries-old line of classical thought and imagery in architecture and urban design. In their seeming austerity, his buildings convey the alienation of the late twentieth century. Yet at the same time, these structures embody the serenity of another age—a quality increasingly coveted in our tumultuous era. These subtle dualities have made Meier's work so valued not only in his native United States, but throughout the world. His architecture is not only for and of our time, it will endure for the centuries to come.

As with all architecture of true importance, Meier's work can only be truly understood through directly experiencing his buildings. Even though this exhibition—or any once-removed viewing of spatial structures—cannot fully re-create this experience, it will, we believe, convey the unique qualities of Meier's built environments and present his continuing search for the ultimate refinement of three-dimensional abstraction. Most importantly, we hope that this assembly of extraordinary work from the past four decades will enhance the public's sensitivity to the powerful achievements of architecture and urban design at the highest level.

The essential character and scope of "Richard Meier Architect" would not have been possible without the support and cooperation of certain institutions and individuals. We wish to express our deepest gratitude to the sponsors of "Richard Meier Architect," who gave generous support to realize this project. First and foremost, the exhibition has been made possible by The J. Paul Getty Trust. Under the leadership of Harold Williams, former President, Barry Munitz, President, and Stephen D. Rountree, Executive Vice President, The J. Paul Getty Trust contributed a major gift to enable substantial research and the implementation of this exhibition.

Significant support was also provided by Max Weishaupt GmbH, D-Schwendi. For their additional support we also thank Norman and Lisette Ackerberg; Hathaway Dinwiddie Construction Group; Christie's; and The Broad Art Foundation.

The Museum of Contemporary Art, Los Angeles, was given unrestricted access to the archives of Richard Meier & Partners, an invaluable resource from which the core of the exhibition was assembled. Major thanks are extended to Richard Meier's associates and staff in New York and Los Angeles, who assisted with preparing the objects in the exhibition for display. We would like to recognize the singular contribution by the indefatigable Lisa Green, assisted by Nadia Khan and Donald Cox. In Los Angeles, we are indebted to Michael Palladino, Partner, who provided us with considerable insight and support; Michael Gruber, who oversaw the conservation of the many Getty Center models; and Lori East, who assisted us with miscellaneous arrangements.

We are equally grateful for the participation of the other lending institutions and their staff members who assisted with these loans: Arnold Feinsilber, Marilyn Farley, Robert Peck, and Keith Lew, General Services Administration of the United States Government, Washington, D.C.; Manuel J. Borja-Villel, Director, and Antònia M. Perelló, Curator for the Permanent Collection, Museum of Contemporary Art, Barcelona; Terence Riley, Chief Curator, Department of Architecture and Design, The Museum of Modern Art, New York; and Professor Gunter R. Standke, Siemens Immobilien Management GmbH & Co., Munich; and Hochbauamt, Stadt Frankfurt am Main.

We also thank the directors, curators, and other colleagues at the museums that are hosting the exhibition during its international tour, and appreciate their hospitality and assistance in realizing the site-specific installation that Meier has designed for each venue.

To understand architecture, the most experiential and substantial of the arts, is to visit the building in situ. While many Meier buildings are open to the public, his residential buildings are not, and we express particular appreciation to the Meier homeowners who opened their doors to us: Norman and Lisette Ackerberg, Joel and Anne Ehrenkrantz, Howard Rachofsky, Sondra and David Mack, J. Paul and Penny Beitler, Richard Maidman, Anita Hoffman, and Susan Loren and Geoffrey Wharton. We would also like to thank everyone who assisted with our visits to the public buildings, including Jane Owen, C. A. Weinzapfel, and Julie Rutherford, Historic New Harmony; M. Jessica Rowe, Associate Director, Des Moines Art Center; Ned Rifkin, Director, and Marjorie Harvey, Manager of Exhibitions and Design, High Museum of Art; and Tony Pirraglia of Swiss Air Transport Co. Ltd. For facilitating our visits to the Meier buildings in Europe, we extend our thanks to Marc-André Feffer, Vice President Delegue General, Canal+; Miquel Molins, former director, the Museum of Contemporary Art, Barcelona; P. R. Ruytenbeek, Communications Adviser, The Hague; Thomas Notermans of ENDEMOL Entertainment; Bernd Janietz and Barbara Fischer-Fuerwentsches of Hypobank International S.A.; Hans-Peter Vollmer of Daimler-Benz AG; Herbert Hennefarth of Max Weishaupt GmbH; and architect Bernhard Lutz.

We have benefited from conversations and information gleaned from many sources. In addition to the above individuals and institutions, we would like to thank the writers, architects, historians, and others who have assisted us in the research and administration of the project, including Julia Bloomfield, Françoise Cachin, Tim Christ, Francesco Dal Co, Dominique de Menil, Adri Duivesteijn, Kurt Forster, Mickey and Martin Friedman, Frank Gehry, Joseph Giovannini, Paul Goldberger, Thomas S. Hines, Craig Hodgetts, Robert Hughes, Arata Isozaki, Anne and Betty Koshalek, Sylvia Lavin, Pierre Lescure, Jose Rafael Moneo, Richard Oldenburg, Nicolai Ouroussoff, Thomas Phifer, André Rousselet, Frank Stella, Rose Tarlow, Billie Tsien, John Walsh, and Tod Williams.

This book was copublished by MOCA and The Monacelli Press. Our sincere thanks to Gianfranco Monacelli, Editor Andrea Monfried, and Associate Editor Ron Broadhurst, who worked closely with both the architect and the authors throughout the realization of the book. We are most grateful to Massimo Vignelli, who contributed his signature design of supreme elegance, and to Letizia Ciancio, who executed his concepts, as well as to the authors of the catalog essays—Stan Allen, Jean-Louis Cohen, Kenneth Frampton, and Lisa Green—whose special insights into Meier's work are of inestimable value.

Numerous members of the MOCA staff have contributed immeasurably to the successful realization of this exhibition and publication. Stacia Payne, Exhibitions Coordinator, became involved in the project at an important stage and oversaw the tour arrangements with tenacity and enthusiasm. John Bowsher, Exhibitions Production Manager, thoughtfully directed the physical presentation, coordinating with Richard Meier's staff and museum staff to customize the installations for each tour venue. Robert Hollister, Chief Registrar, skillfully coordinated all aspects of the transportation of the exhibition. David Bradshaw, Media Arts Technical Manager, worked closely with Meier's office on the creative design of the exhibition's technical component. Erica Clark, Director of Development, oversaw the funding for the exhibition and helped negotiate key arrangements in Paris with panache. Kathleen Bartels, Associate Director, and Alma Ruiz, former Exhibitions Coordinator, played key roles in the planning, guidance, and organization of the exhibition tour. Katherine Lee managed the public relations program. We would also like to recognize Paul Schimmel, Chief Curator, for his advice and acumen, and Jack Wiant, Chief Financial Officer, for his expert counsel. In addition, special thanks are due to Sheila Low, Assistant to the Director; Stephanie Emerson, Editor; Zazu Faure, Exhibitions Production Associate; Danny Yee, Designer; Russell Ferguson, Associate Curator; and Susan Jenkins, Research Associate, for their invaluable assistance with other aspects of exhibition and catalog preparation.

We are deeply grateful to the Board of Trustees of The Museum of Contemporary Art, Los Angeles, for their encouragement and support. In particular, we would like to acknowledge Audrey Irmas, Chair; Gilbert B. Friesen, President; and Lenore S. Greenberg, Vice Chair, who has been a vital force in the advancement of the museum's art and architecture programs.

Finally, we would like to thank Richard Meier, whose steadfast vision and commitment to design excellence is an inspiration to us all.

Introduction: Richard Meier, Light + Space Architect

Dana Hutt

*Abstraction allows architecture to express
its own organizational and spatial consequences,
it permits the creation of space without confusing
its volume with any superimposed system
of meaning or value. It allows architecture to be
what it needs to be, namely tectonic form
expressing anti-tectonic concepts.*

Richard Meier, interview, 1987[1]

*Fundamentally, my meditations are on space,
form, light, and how to make them. My goal is presence,
not illusion.*

Richard Meier, Pritzker Architecture Prize
acceptance address, 1984[2]

For well over three decades, Richard Meier has engaged in an architecture of abstraction. Beyond the programmatic requirements of a given commission, his fundamental concerns are the essences of "space, form, light, and how to make them." Germane to Meier's design process is a geometrical analysis of the site and of the building's program, entrance, circulation systems, structure, and enclosure. His planning strategies distill cues from the context: the angle of the nearby freeway for the Getty Center (1984–97); the module of an existing villa and skewed angle of the riverbank for the Museum for the Decorative Arts in Frankfurt am Main (1979–85); and a module derived from the Ulm Cathedral for the Exhibition and Assembly Building in Ulm, Germany (1986–93). While each project is also inflected by the historic and cultural particularities of its site, the tremendous consistency of form and materials in Meier's oeuvre reflects his abiding interest in abstraction as a means of process, and expression through an emphasis on light and space.

A concern with abstraction, to a greater or lesser extent, was shared by artists working in all forms and genres since the early decades of the century, and architects were no exception. In *Towards a New Architecture* Le Corbusier proclaimed "Architecture has nothing to do with the 'styles.' It brings into play the highest faculties by its very abstraction."[3] For Le Corbusier, this abstraction principally resided in the plan as generator of form. For others, including the Russian Constructivists and the architects of the Bauhaus in Germany and the de Stijl movement in the Netherlands, it defined a new attitude. Inspired by technological and sociopolitical transformations in the first decades of the century, a Zeitgeist emerged to make visible the meaning of the time—to reveal abstract form in a universal character, thereby rejecting historicist styles and orders, eliminating figurative ornament, reducing the appearance of structure, and increasing transparency and planarity. The de Stijl movement, for example, provided important precedents for the new modern architecture, as the works of Theo van Doesburg, J. J. P. Oud, and Gerrit Rietveld translated the pure language of painting into a new spatial conception. They reimagined buildings as abstract sculptures, favoring asymmetrical compositions over Beaux-Arts axial planning, and replacing applied ornament with a dynamic spatial plasticity and a formal vocabulary of intersecting planes, light and shadow, masses and voids.

With a keen awareness of architectural history, Meier draws upon and extends the spatial and formal investigations of this early-twentieth-century modernism. The early masters Meier acknowledges as primary influences—Le Corbusier, Alvar Aalto, Ludwig Mies van der Rohe, Louis I. Kahn, and Frank Lloyd Wright[4]—each developed an individual language of form, space, and structure, demonstrating diverse routes to modern architecture. Meier's work is informed not only by the spirit and example of these architects, but also by specific motifs and strategies in their work, which, on occasion, he addresses directly. He discusses the Smith House (1965–67), for example, in terms of Le Corbusier's Maison Citrohan and Dom-ino skeleton; the design for the

Dormitory for the Olivetti Training Center (1971) alludes to Aalto's Baker House; the High Museum of Art (1980–83) is inspired by and a commentary on Frank Lloyd Wright's Guggenheim Museum.[5]

Meier's designs are further inflected by his interactions with the art world and his interest in collage as form and process. Early on he produced abstract paintings and became involved in the design of exhibition installations, galleries, and artists' studios in New York City. He has since collaborated with Frank Stella, experimented with cast metal sculpture, and built museums in the United States and Europe. In the early 1960s Meier began to create books of collages, a medium that is particularly important to him, connecting a personal pastime to the larger body of work: collage as a formal exercise, diaristic expression, organizing device, plan generator, and urban design strategy.

His design language, which abstracts and reinterprets "pure" architectural forms, is an updated version of the classical orders; it is a set of principles and precepts about construction methods, details, materials, and aesthetics. The units of his distinct syntax—the white metal panels, large expanses of glazing, pipe railing, glass block, piano curves, brise-soleils—serve as the basis of his architectural concepts. Inherent to his design process is a collage sensibility that integrates geometrical site analyses, the overlay and application of grids and modular systems, and the recombining and reconfiguration of his form language, regardless of building typology. "I am interested in spatial elements, not elements of construction," he has said. "I want the wall to be a homogeneous plane."[6] A Meier building in essence redefines the function of architectural structure and form, as the tectonic is abstracted into the nontectonic as a means of creating a space that becomes art.

Central to Meier's abstraction is the use of light as a material. The deployment of natural and artificial light activates the interior of each building and creates pure space that heightens, dazzles, and, on occasion, confuses perception. In each design, Meier demonstrates his control and mastery of the material: light from seen and unseen sources, light that dematerializes, light that reflects off curved and extended planes of white surfaces, light that creates abstract space. "I have always been preoccupied with the filtration and reflection of natural light, with chiaroscuro effects, and with the way in which a building becomes animated through the movement of the subject in space,"[7] he has said. This preoccupation expands on the work of Le Corbusier, who had stated, "Architecture is the masterly, correct, and magnificent play of masses brought together in light."[8]

In Meier's architecture, the magnificent play of light occurs both externally and internally. The use of white throughout the work is crucial to amplify the contrast between light and shadow, as well as solid and void. Continuous planes and fractured geometric forms—which are canvases for light—also function as screens for structural and mechanical systems. Meier has fully developed light as an integral material in his buildings. Consider, for example, the

1

1. Museum of Contemporary Art, Barcelona, Spain

central light well of the Douglas House, the dematerialized window wall adjacent to the ramp of the Atheneum, the illuminated altar in the chapel of the Hartford Seminary, the cascading shadow patterns in the atrium of the High Museum of Art, the layers of filtered light in the main circulation space of the Museum of Contemporary Art in Barcelona, the colossal composition of white grids and catwalks in the atrium of the City Hall and Central Library, The Hague. These spaces provoke visceral yet cerebral reactions to what is experienced.

Meier's meditations on space, form, and light, as well as his goal of "presence," dovetail with the work of the California Light and Space artists of the mid-1960s, who sought to make light palpable.[9] Artists working in this field—among them, Robert Irwin, James Turrell, Douglas Wheeler, Maria Nordman, Larry Bell, and Eric Orr—examined realms of perception and phenomenology through site-specific spaces, installations, and environments that manipulated artificial and natural light in distinct ways. Light is a material and has a physical presence in these diverse works. As historian Jan Butterfield noted, the participant in a work of Light and Space slips into an altogether different perceptual state in which "the *presence* of light, the *sense* of color, and the *feel* of space merge, becoming far more real than any literal representation of them could be."[10]

Concerned with the perception of color, not color itself, some Light and Space artists—like Meier—used white extensively in their work: for example, James Turrell's *Lunette* installation (1974); Robert Irwin's spun aluminum discs (begun in 1965) and scrim installations of the early 1970s; and, in particular, Douglas Wheeler's environments *Light Wall* (1970) and *RM 669* (1969). About *Light Wall*, Peter Plagens wrote: "The room 'is' white ('is' only because white material—flooring, paint, etc., has been used); the color of the room during the Wheeler installation is something else, but 'white' is enough to acknowledge its starting point."[11] Wheeler's own description of the room environment suggests an affinity with Meier's stated objectives of "presence not illusion": "I wanted to effect a dematerialization so that I could deal with the dynamics of the particular space. It was a real space—not illusory—it was a cloud of light in constant flux."[12] Meier, who has cited Colin Rowe and Robert Slutzky's essay "Transparency: Literal and Phenomenal" as an important influence, had begun to dematerialize wall planes in the mid-1960s. Of his early houses, he explained, "They are not intended to look like concrete, as some English critics assume; rather they are dematerialised, planar and linear."[13]

Meier's work fully encompasses the myriad requirements of the discipline of architecture, far from the focused investigations of the Light and Space artists. Yet, for Meier, creating architecture has always entailed designing beyond function, and his manipulation of light supersedes the requirements of most commissions. "As far as I'm concerned, there can never be enough light," he has stated.[14] For Meier, light intensifies the architectural experience and is instrumental to "the expressive making of space, an architecture that is perceptible."[15] At its best, the work of Meier is an architecture of abstraction and transcendence, an architecture that embodies one dream of modernism in a trajectory toward a nonobjective art of pure perception.

Endnotes

1 Interview with Charles Jencks in *Richard Meier* (New York: St. Martin's Press, 1990), p. 31.
2 Richard Meier, acceptance address, The Pritzker Architecture Prize 1984 (Hyatt Foundation, 1984).
3 Le Corbusier, *Towards a New Architecture*, trans. Frederick Etchells (New York: Praeger Publishers, 1960), p. 45.
4 Richard Meier, *Building the Getty* (New York: Alfred A. Knopf, 1997), p. 12.
5 Richard Meier, "My Statement," *A+U* 64 (April 1976); Michele Costanzo, Vincenzo Giorgi, and Maria Grazia Tolomeo, eds. *Richard Meier/Frank Stella: Arte e Architettura* (Milan: Electa, 1993), pp. 45–46.
6 Colin Davies, "Meier Joins the Gold Chain Gang," *Architects' Journal* 188: 44 (November 2, 1988), p. 15.
7 Richard Meier, *Building the Getty*, pp. 12–13.
8 Le Corbusier, *Towards a New Architecture*, p. 31.
9 It is interesting to note that when commissioning artists to develop site-specific works for the central garden of the Getty Center, the Getty Trust selected James Turrell and Robert Irwin, two leading figures of Light and Space.
10 Jan Butterfield, *The Art of Light + Space* (New York: Abbeville, 1993), p. 10.
11 As quoted in Butterfield, p. 121.
12 Butterfield, p. 121.
13 Davies, p. 15.
14 Yukio Futagawa, ed. *Richard Meier: GA Document Extra 8* (1997), p. 31.
15 Futagawa, p. 30.

6

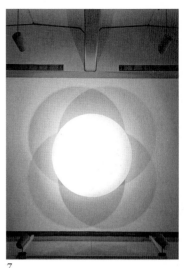

7

8

9

10

11

6. James Turrell, Sky Window 1 (vista diume), *1974; fluorescent light and open sky*
7. Robert Irwin, Untitled, *1965–1967; Acrylic automobile lacquers on prepared, shaped aluminum with metal tube, four 150 watt floodlights; 60" diameter x 3¹/₂" Collection: Walker Art Center, Minneapolis. Purchased with matching grant from Museum Purchase Plan, the National Endowment for the Arts and Art Center Acquisition Fund, 1968.*
8. Eric Orr, Light Space, *installed 1985, Haags Gemeentemuseum, The Hague*

9. Robert Irwin, Untitled, *1971; synthetic scrim, wooden frame, double-stripped fluorescent lights, floodlights; approx. 96 x 564" (size of scrim may vary) Collection: Walker Art Center, Minneapolis, Gift of the artist, 1971.*
10. Douglas Wheeler, RM 669, *1969; vacuum-formed Plexiglass and white UV neon light; 96 x 96"*
11. *Museum of Contemporary Art, Barcelona, Spain*

Richard Meier's Working Space: The Uses of Abstraction

Stan Allen

*It seems to me that architecture is radiated
by the building and does not clothe it,
that it is an aroma rather than a drapery;
an integral part of it and not a shell.*

Le Corbusier, "Concerning Architecture and Its
Significance," 1926[1]

Dilemmas of Formalism

Richard Meier belongs to a generation of modern architects
whose working careers bridged a major paradigm shift.
Trained under the canons of late modernism, Meier's early
career unfolded during the period of the massive
reassessment of the modern movement in the late 1960s
and 1970s. As a result, all of his working principles—the
clarity of basic geometrical forms, white surfaces free of
ornament, a feel for abstract form cultivated through
contact with painting, and the idea of technical perfectibility
based on progressive modernist principles—were subject
to intense critique while his own architectural language
was still being formed. To situate Meier's work it is
therefore important to revisit the terms of that critique
and Meier's response to it.

To accomplish this it is necessary to explore the theoretical
framework of Meier's early work, in particular his debt to
Colin Rowe, although Rowe's influence alone cannot
account for the long-term evolution of Meier's work.
If the unfolding course of modernity in the twentieth
century describes a double trajectory—at once toward ever
increasing abstraction, the substitution of immaterial
ciphers for concrete things; and, at the same time, toward
an all-pervading instrumentality—Meier has insisted on
a difficult synthesis: critical of Rowe's disembodied
formalism, he turns instrumentality into a positive value.
Skeptical of the dominant means-ends rationality
of contemporary society, he employs abstraction as a
countervalue to mere functionalism. For Meier, abstraction
is not a stylistic veneer laid over building's materiality,
but is instead an integral aspect of architecture's concrete,
material expression. Nor is it simply a property of graphic
expression that disappears in the realized building.
In Richard Meier's architecture, abstraction is not a vague
concept floating over the work; rather, it thrives in
and through contact with all of architecture's matter.

Educated at Cornell in the late 1950s, Meier apprenticed
with Marcel Breuer in New York for two years before
establishing his own practice in 1963. His first independent
works reflect modernist principles of tectonic clarity,
layered composition, and an abstract conception of space
that is still present in his work today. At the same time,
these early works built upon existing diversity in the late
modernism that Meier inherited from Breuer and other
sources. In the Smith House of 1965–67 or the Saltzman
House of 1967–69, the abstraction of the European
avant-garde is crossed with American building traditions
to create taut, singular compositions that work with
surface and space. These works affirmed that the strident
newness of the modernism of the 1920s still had meaning
in the present. Between the American mythology
of architecture as nature and the European construct of
architecture as culture, Meier had carved out his own
identity. Within a decade he had extended these working
principles to institutional buildings, large-scale public
housing, and exhibition spaces. However, it is important
to remember that during these same years, the architects
and critics later associated with postmodernism were
conducting a sustained critique of the abstract modernism

that had been so instrumental to Meier's early work. Already identifiable as a rigorous and consistent modernist practitioner, Meier was launched into the polemics of "whites" (the neomodernists whose work had been collected in the 1972 publication *Five Architects*)[2] versus "grays" (the emergent postmodernists, associated with Yale University and the University of Pennsylvania, and gathered around Robert Stern).[3]

The traditional account of Meier in this period is of a figure who keeps the faith, stubbornly holding the modernist line in the face of opposition and critique. But this does justice neither to the complexity of the shuffled alliances that characterize this period, nor to the subtlety of Meier's response. Meier's early career bridges the postmodernist turn in architecture, and although he emerges from this period a committed modernist, his work is undoubtedly marked by the polemic surrounding these debates. Although it is convenient to think in terms of the simple opposition of white versus gray, that is, abstract modernism versus realist postmodernism, it was actually far more complex.

The most incisive critique of architectural modernism was developed by architect Robert Venturi in the mid-1960s,[4] and later elaborated with his partner, Denise Scott Brown.[5] Taking cues from pop art and the vernacular landscape of mainstream America, Venturi and Scott Brown argued for a populist architecture having accessible meanings and legible historical references: a thin architecture of surface and sign, dumb and ordinary, where modernism had been heroic and original. Their approach was pragmatic, and it looked for new forms in the messy reality of the American city.[6] On the other hand, the publication of Aldo Rossi's *The Architecture of the City*[7] signaled the rise of an interest in typology and the traditional space of the historical European city. Despite this implicit realism, Rossi's identification with an "autonomous" architecture (that is, an architecture vested in its own disciplinary limits) and the reductive formal vocabulary of his architectural work sponsored an affiliation with the more abstract practitioners of the New York Five, in particular Peter Eisenman and John Hejduk. Finally, in the influential book *Collage City*, Colin Rowe (onetime mentor and advocate of the Five) and Fred Koetter (one of the most cogent critics of Venturi and Scott Brown's *Learning from Las Vegas*),[8] argued for an open, democratic urbanism based on traditional forms held together through a series of compositional checks and balances derived from cubist collage.[9] Rowe and Koetter explicitly criticized modern architecture's tendency toward isolated objects and implicitly questioned its reductive formal bias.

These architectural debates were played out in an atmosphere of intense interdisciplinary awareness—at least around the Institute for Architecture and Urban Studies in New York, where Meier was elected to the board of trustees in 1972. Pop art, minimalism, and conceptual art all figured prominently in these debates, which were conducted under the shadow of an increasingly sophisticated theoretical discourse, the origins of which were in the historical and

1

2

3

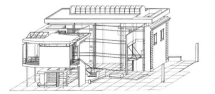

4

1. *Smith House,
Darien, Connecticut*
2. *Smith House,
Darien, Connecticut*
3. *Twin Parks Northeast Housing,
The Bronx, New York*
4. *Villa Strozzi, Florence, Italy*
5. *Villa Strozzi. Axonometric*

5

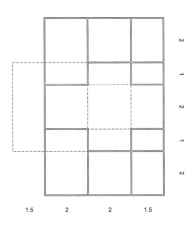

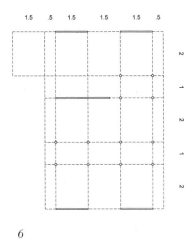

6

6. Analytical diagrams:
(top) Palladio, Villa Foscari/
La Malcontenta, Gambarare di
Mira, Italy, c. 1560;
(bottom) Le Corbusier and Pierre
Jeanneret, Villa Stein-de-Monzie,
Garches, France, 1927.

critical work of Manfredo Tafuri and the school of Venice as well as in French structuralism and poststructuralism. For architecture, as for other disciplines, 1966–76 was a decade of inquiry, during which the field of what could be called properly architectural was substantially broadened, and many of modernism's underlying assumptions were called into question.[10]

For a thoughtful architect like Meier, who affirmed his commitment to abstract modernism in the face of this questioning, the force of this critique would appear to be double. On the one hand, modernism could no longer be accepted innocently or unselfconsciously. It is true, as Joseph Rykwert has observed, that "Meier has always worked as if no possible alternative existed."[11] Yet it is also true that during this period Meier was working in an atmosphere of critique and contingency. As a result, his approach to architecture has to be a decision defended from within, rather than an imperative mandated or institutionally sanctioned from outside. If Venturi rejected the progressive modern project as utopian in favor of the banal landscape of everyday life, and if Rossi wanted to return to the traditional architecture of the European city, Meier was unwilling to give up on the possibility of a progressive modernity located in the present. He knows, however, that this is a reality that can only be gained with difficulty. On the other hand, this questioning of canonical modern architecture also represents permission to depart from orthodoxy and to create, within the terms of modernism, new and unprecedented hybrids and transformations. Against the either/or logic of modernity, Venturi opted for the postmodern pluralism of both/and. But Meier accepts the rigorous discipline of the either/or, and internalizes it as a productive tension within modernism. Instead of opening architecture to interdisciplinary flux, Meier critiques it from within. And in Meier's case, the modernism that emerges is all the more robust for having been subjected to such a critical examination. For Meier modernism—if accepted at all— had to be accepted with all of its contradictions intact.

It was Colin Rowe who articulated these contradictions most forcefully, and in so doing established the critical terms for subsequent understanding of the work of Meier and others. Rowe is best known for his ability to link formal themes across history, using modern architecture as a heuristic device with which to reexamine classical architecture, and vice versa. He was among the first to describe the ways in which the multiple languages of modern architecture were at odds not only with one another, but with the theoretical propositions of orthodox modernism. In the justifiably famous "Mathematics of the Ideal Villa" (1947), "Mannerism and Modern Architecture" (1950), and the two-part "Neo-'Classicism' and Modern Architecture" (1956–57)[12] Rowe mapped a series of compositional themes that joined modern architecture to a wider and continuing humanist project. But this new reading of continuity, in turn, undermines the avant-garde's claim to continual innovation and a total break with the past.

Rowe's critique takes two paths. First, in an argument that

he hinted at in these earlier essays and fully developed in his later writings, the social and political ambitions of early modernism are portrayed as naive, suspiciously utopian, and perhaps even totalitarian. It was evident, he wrote in 1972, that "the central and socialist mission of modern architecture had failed—or alternatively, that this mission had become dissolved in the sentimentalities and bureaucracies of the welfare state."[13] And if its original social basis is flawed, it follows for Rowe that the architectural programs that depend on it (mass production, social housing, and rationalized urbanism), as well as their formal corollaries (reductive geometries, unornamented surfaces, and asymmetrical composition) must themselves be deeply suspect. The only way to rescue modernism, then, is to divest it of its flawed social baggage and to reinscribe it in an unfolding history of formal research on timeless architectural problems. Thus questions of central versus peripheric composition, abstract geometrical armatures of number and grid, the frontal layering of enclosing facades, and the intricacies of phenomenal transparency become the distinguishing themes of Rowe's analysis.

Second, and more complexly, Rowe suggested that modern architecture built its theoretical foundation on an accidental convergence. Modern architecture was to be at once objective and rational (the index of programmatic and technical facts), and at the same time it was to express the spirit of the age. With tongue characteristically in cheek, Rowe spelled out what that might have implied in the 1920s: "The spirit of the age was an enthusiast for speed, mass production, airplanes, reinforced concrete, sociology, sunbathing, heavy machinery, simple life, factories, grain elevators, Atlantic liners, hygiene, and the classic automobiles which were created in its own image; and so long as it could be believed that the creature was aesthetically neutral, rationalism was not eager to discourage such discriminating excess."[14] In other words, as long as the will of the epoch could plausibly be made to align with the dictates of rationalism, there was little difficulty in reconciling modernist theory and practice. But by mid-century, the suspicion arose that what had appeared objective might be nothing more than a series of formal prejudices and shifting fashions—in short, the product of something like taste: "By the late 1940's, so much could be intuited. For by then it had become evident . . . that the spirit of the age was not to be entirely trusted."[15] Moreover, modernism's own stated project of continual innovation would, by definition, guarantee that these enthusiasms (which were already taking on a patina of nostalgia) would become outmoded. As Rowe has repeatedly pointed out, the ideal of architecture as an objective registration of programmatic or technical facts (which are always changing) is at odds with the development of a coherent and repeatable catalogue of formal solutions—in short with the idea of a style, International or otherwise.[16] For Rowe, it comes down to honestly recognizing taste rather than stubbornly adhering to outmoded ideals of objectivity. In a statement that seems to anticipate the historicist postmodernism of the 1970s and 1980s, Rowe pointed out that as soon as the link between objectivity and the spirit of the age is shown to be more or less accidental, the door is open to all kinds of eclectic variation: "If the spirit of the age could show a taste for peripheric composition, it might equally well develop one for Corinthian capitals and/or pointed arches." The internal coherence of modern architecture's theoretical propositions were beginning to fall apart. "Rationalism," he remarked, "was distinctly embarrassed."[17]

It is therefore not surprising that in his introduction to the 1972 publication of the architects who then came to be called the New York Five (Peter Eisenman, Michael Graves, Charles Gwathmey, John Hejduk, and Richard Meier), Rowe posed the question in terms of a choice between the formal program of the avant-garde and its rhetorical claims: *"The* physique *and the* morale *of modern architecture, its flesh and its word, were (and could) never be coincident; and it is when we recognize that neither word nor flesh was ever coincident with itself, let alone with each other, that, without undue partiality, we can approach the present day. For under the circumstances what to do? If we believe that modern architecture did establish one of the great hopes of the world—always in detail ridiculous, but never, in toto, to be rejected—then do we adhere to the* physique-*flesh or to the* morale-*word?"*[18]

It was an ambivalent and preemptive defense: stipulate the formalism of this work as a given, but then argue, with great subtlety, that the accomplishments of modern architecture have never been anything else; make no claims for innovation, but rather identify the work as "belligerently second hand."[19] The totalizing project of progressive modernism—by now ideologically suspect—is held securely at arm's length. But if such a defense is effective at warding off potential criticism, it also leaves these architects vulnerable to co-optation by the very postmodernist arguments they were aligned against. Robert Stern, among others, argued in the mid-1970s that these architects were simply involved in another form of historical eclecticism, with its point of reference in twentieth-century modernism rather than in eighteenth- or nineteenth-century classicism. Rowe's surgical separation of the modernist *physique*/flesh from its *morale*/word, and the consequent description of the neomodernist project as a rewriting of canonical modernist themes under the shadow of postmodernist repetition has become the accepted critical mode in regard to this work. If defended, it is on the basis of its formal brilliance; if attacked, it is on the basis of social irresponsibility.

Two things seem left out of this calculation. First, could such a narrow program ever actually sustain an architectural practice such as Meier's, which has addressed such a wide range of urban and institutional programs? Everything that can be deferred in a small single-family house will come back to haunt the architect faced with commissions for larger-scale work. And all of these issues—complex questions of representation, context, procession, and scale—demand some kind of theoretical address. Meier remains close to the *morale*/word of modern architecture—not as an academic posture, but incorporating it into the working equipment of a practicing architect in the twentieth century. Secondly, the rhetorical separation of *physique*/flesh from

7

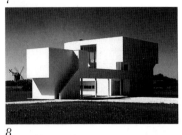

8

9

10

7–10. Saltzman House,
East Hampton, New York

morale/word is one of those double binds that tends to make
the intricate dilemmas of formalism invisible.[20] For is not
the very decision to prefer a robust *physique*/flesh over a
suspect *morale*/word itself a deeply moral decision, fully
engaged in theoretical speculation? As Rowe understands
very well, any architectural work—formal or otherwise—
requires theoretical speculation. Without some sense of
architecture's place in the social order, the architect is the
passive servant of political or economic forces. In Meier's
case, the modern movement's rather naive idea that
architecture could construct a better world is not rejected
outright, but pragmatically reinterpreted. Meier, I would
suggest, understands his own deeply felt commitment to
the art of architecture as a kind of social mandate. By
innovative work within the limits of his own discipline, he
contributes something that in modest ways might make
the world a better place. Through a disciplined research on
architectural form, he is able to give back to society the
very best products of his own activity as an architect.

Radical Instrumentality
If Rowe emphasized a shared ethos of the New York Five,
the Italian critic and historian Manfredo Tafuri was more
interested in identifying differences. "Should anyone wish
to challenge the consistency of the Five, Meier's work
would offer the best proof," wrote Tafuri in his 1976 article
"American Graffiti: Five x Five = Twenty-five."[21] Although
a similar metaphysical or magical overtone is recognizable
in this early work, Tafuri points out that Meier refuses
the linguistic play that is dominant in Hejduk, Graves,
or Eisenman. In its place is an emphasis on the functional
character of the sign: "Geometry is no longer cruelly
chained to its own harrowing silence, nor is there a search
for 'deep structures' or any attempt to extract multiple
meanings from signs, as Graves attempts to do. Meier's use
of geometry also excludes any attempt to regain semantic
values: the articulation of his signs is but a testimony
to the presence of objects which display their function in
absolute clarity."[22]

This attention to functional value and the practical
consequences of formal decisions places Meier closer
to the philosophical tradition of American pragmatism
than to European structuralism or poststructuralism.
It is an attitude characteristic of an architect who is
a practitioner first and a theorist only so far as practice
requires it. Meier is less concerned with the consistency of
modern architecture's theoretical precepts than with their
utility. What Meier is reluctant to let go of in modernism is
precisely its instrumentality—the ability to organize space
through the abstract instruments of plan and section, the
ability to engage issues of building technology, functional
prediction, and the logistics of implementation through
architecture's technical devices. Instrumentality is not
simply a tool, but a value in and of itself, connected to
the work that architecture performs in the world as well as
to elegance and economy of means.[23] Far from a narrow
professional convenience (and, in fact, highly critical
of the shortcuts and conventions of standard professional
practice), this commitment to a radical instrumentality
is deeply philosophical, connected to a way of being in the

world as much as to a way of making architecture. It is no accident that of the New York Five architects, Tafuri is most positive about Meier. Tafuri here follows philosopher Theodor Adorno in looking for an uncompromising, technically perfect modernism that partakes of the means-ends rationality of modern life in order to criticize it from within. For Adorno, the modern life-world is so thoroughly penetrated by abstraction and by instrumentality that any attempt to escape it would be sentimental and naive. Among architects, Meier is one of the few who has faced this pervading instrumentality head on and made it thematic to his work, looking for a dialectic in which something positive, hopeful, and progressive can be constructed out of the abstract character of modern life.

Such a point of view also serves as a key to understanding the gradual evolution of Meier's architecture. His is, of course, an oeuvre characterized above all by consistency. As he goes deeper and deeper into modernism's material and operative basis, refining and sharpening its tools with an almost hallucinatory precision, he also incrementally extends its limits. Rykwert, for example, writing about the High Museum of Art in Atlanta (where explicitly referential forms begin to appear), explained that "the reference is not, as may be suspected by a superficial observer, self-reference. On the contrary, it shows Meier attempting an exposition of the traditional forms of modern architecture. These forms are in no sense canonical, they have no fixed meaning, nor even a clearly circumscribed range of reference; they are merely types: shapes and formal devices which have a refractive power dependent on their context . . ."[24] For Meier, it is not a question of adding new "words" to an already tested vocabulary; rather, his primary work is on the system of language itself. Meier's architectural language has an internal logic that dictates its own limits. But that same logic also indicates those places where the system is incomplete, and hence where new elements might be introduced. Thus in Meier's recent work, local symmetries, axial relationships, baroque curves, highly textured materials, and figural forms have appeared. But all of these exist in the larger web of Meier's architecture, and each one is tested for a specific usefulness within the limits of that architectural language. Thus we can say that everything in Richard Meier's work has at once an *instrumental* value—a specific position within the system—and an *expressive* value, which is intelligible in more general terms.

Surface and Space: The Saltzman House and the High Museum of Art

Another important claim Tafuri made is that Meier's small projects, which allow intensive work on form, are a proving ground for larger projects where the limits of those formal constructs are further tested: "In other words, Meier seems to go back over, though in a deeply critical manner, some of the stages already traveled by the classical 'masters' of the Modern Movement: from the self-sufficiently perfect configuration of objects rich in metaphorical reference, to the institutional values of technology, and finally to their reconfiguration within the urban fabric."[25] Tafuri's assertion might be tested by examining two projects in detail: the Saltzman House (1967–69) and the High Museum of Art

in Atlanta (1980–83). While superficially similar— to the extent that a quarter circle appears as a dominant plan figure in each—the two buildings are otherwise entirely dissimilar. Program, organization, structure, and section are all distinct. What they do share is more general: a highly abstract technique of space-making based on the plastic modeling of interior spaces, and also a corresponding feel for taut surfaces stretched over active interior volumes.

Meier is close, in his early houses, to Le Corbusier in the sense that the "plan is the generator." But in the case of the Saltzman House, which has a highly developed sectional concept, the plan, like Le Corbusier's Dom-ino frame, is an armature for complex plasticity created from two interlocking oppositions: one, the opposition of space and surface; and two, compact massing versus aggregate form. As an object, the house is highly ambiguous. Tafuri used the phrase "suspended tonality" to characterize the work of Meier and the other New York Five architects. Here it suggests that the forms are between states, like bodies not fixed in one pose or another, but temporarily arrested in a state of transition. The flatness of the site contributes to this: it makes the scale and distance difficult to judge and renders the sky an active element of the composition.

At least three other design decisions contribute to the ambiguous character of the Saltzman House. The first is the small guest pavilion, pulled away from the main house. Not quite distant enough to read as independent, it is connected as part of the entry sequence. Its mass is calibrated to act as a volumetric counterpoint to the main house from the sweeping south lawn, whereas it extends the plane of entry on the north. Second is the sweeping, quarter circle curve that encloses the main living space. Curves in Meier's other early works often appear as incidents or quotations in an otherwise regular fabric, but this curve is fully integral and distorts the fabric itself. However, it does not undermine the essentially cubic form of the house: the massing reads as a cube with rounded corners rather than a quarter circle joining two arms. The plan is compact, not an aggregation of parts. Finally, in the handling of the base, which is eroded in layers, he achieved an effect of weightlessness without relying on the more obvious, or referential, strategy of pilotis.

The house is entered informally by means of a small zigzag movement off the axis of the driveway. This jogging movement is immediately taken up in the diagonal staircase and curved wall that brings one to the second-floor living space. Here the movement of the visitor is incorporated into the organizational logic of the house: the curving trajectory of the stair carves the boundary between the public and private precincts of the house. As a result, the primary diagonal of the house (perpendicular to the view, as indicated in the architect's diagrams), is answered by a virtual diagonal, extending from corner to corner. Looking back on this axis, the outside edges of the space flatten and press forward toward the viewer, like the distorted view in a wide-angle lens.

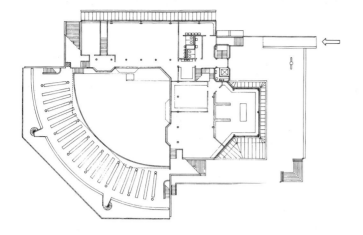

11

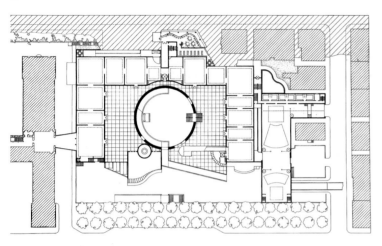

12

13

14

15

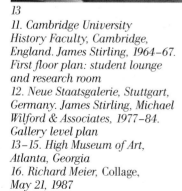

16

*11. Cambridge University
History Faculty, Cambridge,
England. James Stirling, 1964–67.
First floor plan: student lounge
and research room
12. Neue Staatsgalerie, Stuttgart,
Germany. James Stirling, Michael
Wilford & Associates, 1977–84.
Gallery level plan
13–15. High Museum of Art,
Atlanta, Georgia
16. Richard Meier, Collage,
May 21, 1987*

Inside, the double-height spaces and the stepping terrace to the west create an interlocking spatial block, and generous openings link the interior volume to the site beyond. But here the ambiguity of surface and space comes into play. The interior space of the house reads at once as a dense plastic mass, swelling the walls outward, but at the same time it is allowed to flow continuously out into the translucent air and space of the site itself. Meier has created this effect in part through his arrangement and detailing of the exterior openings. Looking at the south elevation, the first element on the left is the rounded, planar enclosure of the spiral staircase, floating above the base and pressing slightly forward. To its immediate right is the recessive void of the terrace/balcony, more or less solid above and open below. Next to this, an enormous glass plane runs the full three-story height. In this sequence of solid/void/plane, Meier has taken full advantage of the changeable character of glass as a material. By detailing the glass without intermediate mullions, and by framing it very close to the enclosing skin, he has created a shifting scrim. Charged to near opacity by reflection of the sky, it continues the stretched surface of the enclosing skin, but at other times it nearly disappears, creating the visual effect of dissolving large chunks of the exterior skin, leaving the interior vulnerable and exposed.

The placement of these openings in plan is also critical. The edge of this large window nearly coincides with the beginning of the curve, whereas the other large opening (on the east elevation) is placed half a column bay back from the beginning of the curve, and not—as might be expected—symmetrically across the diagonal. The reason for this is clear in the elevation. It is as if the second opening has been displaced by the linear extension of the strip window. This element, although recognizable, has little to do with quotation; rather, it is an example of Meier's painterly sense of the importance of negative space in a composition. In this case, the solid wall surface above and below registers the gentle outward push of the space within at the same time that the strip window marks a cut in the membrane that separates the interior from the exterior.

Finally, another feature demonstrates the fundamentally three-dimensional character of this house. In the traditional reading of the modernist free plan, a regular grid of columns acts as a fixed counterpoint to the flowing movement of space. Here this does not appear to be the case. The columns, which in plan have a somewhat awkward relationship to the enclosing walls, nearly disappear in the three-dimensional experience of the architecture. Placed very close to the walls, they read as an event on the surface rather than a linear counterpoint to the space. This confirms that for Meier the plan is not an end in itself but a step toward the finished work. Meier's plans are not reduced pictures of the completed building, but are notational schemas, scores that require interpretation and performance. The notated architecture will necessarily be transformed—and usually improved—along the way to the realized building.

Among other significant differences of scale and program, as Meier made the transition from single-family houses to institutional buildings, he has had to contend with implicit representational mandates. With the Saltzman House, Meier feels himself under little obligation to represent the domestic program. All of the familiar icons (pitched roof, chimney, etc.) are absent, and the scale is highly ambiguous, indicated mainly by functional rather than by symbolic elements.

The formal type of the museum was in a state of transition in the early 1980s. At the High Museum of Art in Atlanta Meier chose to represent the museum as an open, public institution, clearly distinguished as a unique building—even a monumental building in the context of Atlanta's slack urban fabric—and he does so without recourse to any of the traditional devices of classical architecture. The site, of course, is very different from that of the Saltzman House, but there is a similar ambiguity at the High Museum between a reading of the building as a compact object versus an aggregate of elements penetrated by a continuous spatial field. This is in part the result of organizational decisions Meier made early in the design process. For functional as well as expressive reasons, the galleries are discrete rectilinear volumes forming an L-shaped block that embraces the curved public atrium. Elements of the public program—for example the auditorium and the entry pavilion—are arrayed at the perimeter of the curve. This makes the High Museum the distant typological cousin of such classical examples as Karl Friedrich Schinkel's Altes Museum in Berlin. But here the enclosure is fragmented, as if Schinkel's closed form has been blown apart. Instead of hiding the public atrium behind a representational screen, the internal organization of the museum's public spaces is evident on the exterior. From this we can draw an interesting series of comparisons. The plan schema of Meier's building recalls James Stirling's 1964 Cambridge History Faculty, which has a similar public atrium nested between the arms of a rectilinear L. Meier, however, has treated that type in a more dynamic and figural manner, closer to Stirling's more or less contemporary Staatsgalerie in Stuttgart (1977–84), which in turn is a more or less explicit homage to the Schinkel original. The comparison is telling in that Stirling at Stuttgart is involved in a highly self-conscious game of repetition and commentary. In Meier's building, however, the reference is veiled. It is filtered through the instrumentality of his own space-making techniques, and hence closer to the 1964 Stirling building, where technique was still a primary concern.

The shift in scale and complexity occasioned by Meier's move to museum projects also required different compositional techniques. At the High Museum, instead of the curves being a counterpoint to the regular grid (two orders superimposed), radial geometries organize the curved atrium space, while rectilinear geometries are maintained in the adjacent gallery blocks (two orders juxtaposed). The radial geometry of the public spaces necessarily sets up a dynamic push/pull of centrifugal forces that works against the relative stability of the L-shaped gallery blocks that are nested into the corner of the site. This is also driven by programmatic considerations: the radial geometries allow the static form to be opened up at its perimeter, introducing movement and tension to the public field of the building while preserving the rectilinear form of the gallery blocks. This creates new axes of movement, but they are glancing, oblique, or tangential rather than frontal and symmetrical. Meier establishes the entry sequence on an extended diagonal path that runs from the corner of the site toward the center of the building. The entry ramp directs the visitor to the space between the hooded volume of the auditorium and the curved block of the entry pavilion. The obvious axial movement is redirected at this point, in an about-face that leads the visitor through the entry pavilion to the sweeping curve of the atrium ramps. Here, as anticipated on a small scale at the Saltzman House, the movement of the visitor in space is actively incorporated into the composition. However, at the High Museum the radial geometries of the plan direct this movement outward, creating a complex layered boundary at the outside edge of the public space—recalling more explicitly the Corbusian notion of a *promenade architecturale*.

This spatial layering continues inside the museum and is used as a device to modulate the transition between the contained space of the galleries and vertiginous space of the atrium. A series of blank white panels sits forward from the structural frame on the two straight sides of the atrium. These panels are used for exhibition on the gallery side, forming an intermediate-scale transition zone. Although they have been used to great effect for temporary installations (of works by Sol Lewitt, for example), they serve on the atrium side to reflect the pattern of light and shadow cast by the radial beams of the skylight above. As such they are typical of the painterly effects of surface that Meier achieves with architectural means of structure, light, and the organization of space. As Stephan Barthelmess has observed, "In this context, the surface becomes the decisive intermediary that makes it possible to demonstrate the relation between art and architecture."[26]

To speak about surface in these two projects is also of course to speak about the metal panel cladding system, which Meier has used consistently since the mid-1970s. As Meier pointed out in a 1990 interview, the panel system implies a complete three-dimensional organizing matrix: "The gridding exists in plan and section. The use of the panels is simply an expression of an aspect of that grid, which not only comprises the cladding system, the division of window mullions and the interrelationship of all these linear elements, but also has to do with the structure and organization of spaces."[27] This implies the presence of a three-dimensional spatial armature, which is registered on every available surface (including soffits and paving patterns), and also structures the enclosed space. The grid lines materialize as the visible traces of this abstract ordering system where they intersect with the surface of the enclosing envelope. At the same time, the grid lines create a surface effect that maintains continuity across the inflected volumes and distinctive materials of Meier's more figural late work.

17

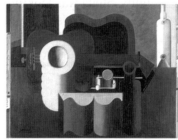

18

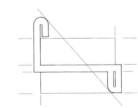

19

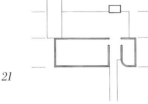

20   *21*

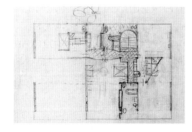

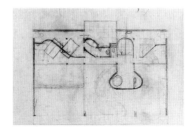

22

One of the persistent misconceptions about Meier's work is that its whiteness creates a neutral condition, designed to minimize the importance of surface in favor of massing and space.[28] I would argue that white here is not a neutral ground. It is not, as Meier himself often insists, the absence of color, but the presence of all colors. As such, it becomes a surface charged with potential, constantly being changed by the environment or by the life of the building within. Hence, while these complementary surface effects—white walls within and gridded volumes outside—are both fundamentally abstract and immaterial, they undergo a similar transformation: they are activated by light and produce complex material effects, activating the space of the museum and the experience of the viewer.

Transparencies and Working Spaces

There is no doubt that Meier's feeling for abstract form is connected to his deep involvement with painting. This includes his long-standing personal affiliations with artists—Frank Stella and Robert Slutzky, for example— as well as his frequent engagement with artists' materials and procedures. Meier's torn-paper collages are more than a simple design exercise; they are his technical link to the painterly means of space-making by the use of color, surface, line, and contour. While on the surface one might identify some of Meier's plans as collagelike, what is actually involved is more complex. Through the intermediary of abstract architectural notations he achieves analogous spatial effects in the collages and in his buildings.

Here, as with other aspects of Meier's early work, the mandatory starting point is Colin Rowe, specifically his essay "Transparency Literal and Phenomenal," written with painter Robert Slutzky in 1955–56.[29] Rowe and Slutzky elaborated a distinction between literal transparencies— the optical or physical properties of transparent materials such as wire mesh or glass curtain walls—and phenomenal transparencies—effects of simultaneity, interpenetration, and spatial overlap achieved by two- and three-dimensional organization.[30] Their analysis is not based on a loose analogy between cubist painting and the compositional devices of modern architecture; rather, they identify a specific catalog of spatial effects within a limited historical context, specifically analytical cubism of the early 1910s and two projects by Le Corbusier from 1927. Their emphasis on the abstract character of phenomenal transparencies provides a potential point of contact between architecture and painting. For Rowe and Slutzky, phenomenal transparency is not found in the deep space of perspectival illusion, but in cubism's shallow fluctuating space, that is, exactly where painting already most closely resembles architecture in its material expression: "Literal transparency . . . tends to be associated with the trompe l'oeil effect of a translucent object in deep, naturalistic space; while phenomenal transparency seems to be found when a painter seeks the articulated presentation of frontally aligned objects in a shallow abstracted space."[31]

Phenomenal transparency in architecture turns on two characteristic compositional devices present in Le Corbusier's early work. The first is the facade that, within its own relatively shallow depth, registers the organization of the space located behind it. The second is the *promenade architecturale*, the extended route of pedestrian movement through the space that brings the viewer into contact with a series of "frontally aligned objects" that can in turn be reconstructed into an imaginary picture of the building's structure simultaneously appercieved. In other words, over time and through an effort of mental reconstruction, what is not immediately available to the senses can be made concretely perceptible. In this way, the tension between frontality and rotation, identified by Kenneth Frampton as a common compositional principle for the New York Five, has its origin in Le Corbusier's own painterly reconstructions of cubist spatial principles. As Rosalind Krauss wrote, elaborating on Frampton's reading, "For Le Corbusier, the counterpoint between frontality and rotation equals the contrast between ideation and experience. And what Le Corbusier demands of architectural composition is that it should acknowledge the mutual interdependence of the one on the other."[32]

While Rowe and Slutzky insisted that their article was never intended as a prescription for architectural design, it is hard not to see the tendency toward frontally layered spatial organizations, especially in the early work of Eisenman and Meier, as specifically dependent upon their readings of phenomenal transparency. Meier, however, developed the idea of the *promenade architecturale* more explicitly. In his Atheneum in New Harmony, Indiana (1975–79), for example, the movement of the viewer through the building transforms the reading of the space. The Atheneum is a sculptural object constructed almost entirely by articulated planes, and hence visually related to cubist composition. But more importantly, from an architectural point of view, these planes are presented to the viewer sequentially, and the movement of the viewer causes them to fluctuate ambiguously in space. As the visitor moves through the building on the carefully choreographed route, deep vistas alternatively open up or collapse into shallow tableaux. The latent tension between frontality and rotation identified by Frampton and Krauss is here converted into a compositional principle that makes perceptible an abstract spatial order that is distinct from the visible compositional mechanisms of the architecture.

At the same time that Meier and other architects were exploring the spatial implications of early-twentieth-century painting, the painters and sculptors who are their contemporaries were moving away from what they saw as the limited scope of cubist composition. Minimal artists such as Carl Andre, Dan Flavin, Robert Morris, and Donald Judd sought to go beyond formal or compositional variation to produce compact, singular objects that could engage the space of the gallery and the body of the viewer. As Morris wrote in 1968, "European art since Cubism has been a history of permuting relationships around the general premise that relationships should remain critical. American art has developed by uncovering successive premises for making itself."[33] Donald Judd was less concerned with process but equally dedicated to moving away from composition based on assembling parts.

In 1965 he wrote, "In the new work the shape, image, color and surface are single and not partial and scattered. There aren't any neutral or moderate areas or parts, any connections or transitional areas."[34] His famous characterization of the "specific object"—"The order is not rationalistic and underlying but is simply order, like that of continuity, one thing after another"[35]—in fact referred to the shaped canvases of Meier's close friend and sometime collaborator Frank Stella. The affiliation between painting and architecture becomes more complex as Meier's own career develops beyond the Corbusian principles that informed his early work, and as the scale and ambition of his projects change.

Stella's paintings from the mid-1960s onward are dedicated to the reintroduction of a more generous, even illusionistic, sense of space that is nominally at odds with Judd's reductive sensibility. Stella was looking for a revived sense of painting's potential to engage space, and he finds it in terms that might seem opposed to a reductive, teleological modernism. In this period, Meier and Stella seem to have pursued a parallel course. Within their respective disciplines each opened up the spatial and expressive possibilities of their objects while rigorously respecting the limits of modernism.

The ambitions of Stella's project are conveniently laid out in his 1983–84 Norton Lectures, published as *Working Space*.[36] Stella's propositions (though they sometimes run counter to conventional art-historical interpretation), offer a useful counterpoint to both Rowe and Slutzky's architectural reading of cubism and to Judd's reductionism. In his lectures Stella revisits, among other things, the question of the continuing viability of cubism. In this context, he explained, "it is worth reconsidering one of the biggest misapprehensions of current art criticism, one that first appeared in the late sixties or early seventies— the notion that the best abstract painting defined itself by being post-Cubist."[37] Stella's own work has traced an inverse course through the possibilities of abstraction. His black paintings of the late 1950s seem to shut space out. They worked through the principles of abstraction that had been defined by the previous generation of painters— including Barnett Newman and Ad Reinhardt—but with a more radical sense of painting's materiality. But sensing, at the very beginning of his career, that in this abstraction he might have already arrived at an end point, he progressively opened up the canvas to a revitalized sense of space. Stella's early canvases insisted on the reality of the painting as an object in space, whereas the later work sets out to activate and occupy that viewing space.

One important point of reference for Stella is Picasso's own development in the decade following his first cubist experiments. The appearance of "unabashed rendering of volume" in Picasso's paintings of the 1920s, Stella notes, proved to be difficult to reconcile with cubism's fragmented space—a space usually constructed out of faceted planes. Yet without volume, Stella asserts, abstract painting is weak and impoverished: "abstraction must have a viable sense and expression of volume, because without them the space available to abstraction is simply too closed, too dull, too

23

24

25

26

23–24. Atheneum,
New Harmony, Indiana
25. Frank Stella,
Diavolozoppo, 1984;
oil, urethane enamel, fluorescent
alkyd, acrylic, and printing ink
on canvas, etched magnesium,
aluminum and fiberglass;
139¹/₈ x 169³/₄ x 16¹/₈"
26. Frank Stella,
Maha-lat (maquette for Indian
Bird Series), 1977;
printed metal alloy sheets,
wire mesh, and soldered and
welded metal scraps with crayon,
15¹/₂ x 20"

unimaginative."[38] In his paintings of the 1970s and 1980s, Stella creates volume in two ways. On the one hand he literally shapes the canvas, testing the boundary between painting and sculpture even more assertively than he had done in the 1960s. He builds up complex three-dimensional configurations and utilizes transparent materials to make the painting a porous object through which space flows. He also makes volume illusionistically, by rendering curved surfaces and incorporating warped forms that imply volume in the field of his painting. This play between real and virtual space forms the tension that animates Stella's work and marks him as a late modernist, aware that in the expanded field of artistic activity in the late twentieth century the boundaries between disciplines are increasingly fluid. He explained, "Volume and mass—things that seem so real, and things, not so incidentally, that seem so natural to sculpture, need to be rediscovered, reinvented, or perhaps even reborn for abstract figuration."[39]

For Stella, it is not painting's planar character that connects architecture to painting, but the deep space of baroque illusion. His points of reference are Michelangelo and Caravaggio: "Painting before [Michelangelo's] Last Judgment was painting you could look at, or at least into; after the Last Judgment painting became something one could walk through. Michelangelo dissolves the end wall of the Sistine Chapel so that we can exit the church toward heaven and hell, moving out of the Renaissance toward Caravaggio's world, a world of sensuality and spatial incongruity beyond even Michelangelo's imagination."[40] This lush illusionism seems very distant from the blunt materiality of his early work. As he described, "My painting is based on the fact that only what can be seen there is there."[41] It is useful to remember that Stella, as Meier, is a latecomer to modernism, beginning his career late in the century, and inheriting an already historical sense of modernism. Although he feels subject to its imperatives, he is not inclined to consider them as being categorical. His are not outright rejections but expansions and revisions of the modernist canon. Stella seems to be declaring that after cubism's destruction of perspective, the production of illusion is simply one of the things that it is now possible to do with paint.

One of the first things that Stella's propositions in Working Space provides is a renewed sense of the importance of volume in Meier's work. This goes back as far as the difference between the Smith House, which is almost exclusively planar, and the Saltzman House, which is aggressively volumetric. In the later work, the characteristic figure of an extruded, curved plan form takes on greater importance. In the Atheneum, for example (earlier identified as a planar construction), curved volumes also play an important role. Seen from the lawn beyond the building, the swelling form of the piano curve sets up a volumetric counterpoint to the large canted plane to the right and to the intricate linear quality of the exposed stairway to the left. The calm, apparent solidity of this space contrasts to the excited interpenetration of the space immediately behind: a dense volumetric figure nested in a matrix of planes and lines. And on the entry elevation, the curved corner of the auditorium block recalls the stretched volume of the Saltzman House, establishing continuity across the 90-degree turn of the facade. Even the linear trajectory of the ramp is given volumetric expression. The extraordinary night views of this building published in Meier's 1984 monograph testify to the copresence and interdependence of deep illusionistic space and shallow cubist surfaces: a complex spatial artifice that is the architectural analog to Stella's painterly construction of spatial illusion.

Notational Abstractions: The Getty Center and the Museum of Contemporary Art, Barcelona

There is a final and important way in which abstraction figures in Meier's work: the functioning of architectural representation as a notational code. Le Corbusier's assertion that "the plan is the determination of everything; it is an austere abstraction, an algebrization, and cold of aspect," retains an important place in Meier's thinking.[42] Although present throughout his career, the "austere abstractions" of architectural representation become more evident in the larger-scale projects, where complex programs and difficult urban settings needed to be addressed. The Getty Center (1984–97), for example, has been criticized for its physical and symbolic separation from the city of Los Angeles. Its formal language has alternatively been described as lacking coherence or as overly uniform. But none of these criticisms takes into account the strengths of the building, which have little to do with its formal character, but a great deal to do with the architect's ability to reconfigure the given site and to adjust its performance over time.

The Getty has turned out to be an enormously popular site, and its public spaces are intensively used. This is at least in part due to the way a number of architectural and urbanistic strategies have been employed, creating an interlocking series of interior and exterior spaces. These spaces have a compact, urbane character, recalling some of the best spaces of the traditional European city, yet at the same time they are part of a fluid spatial continuum opening out to the landscape and the city beyond. For example, the airy drum that gives access to the plaza around which the exhibition pavilions are arrayed is at once a showy demonstration of Meier's architectural vocabulary and an urbanistic set piece: a void space that links other voids in sequence. In order to unify the distinct elements of the complex formally, Meier employs both a collage syntax, where interlocking profiles and juxtaposed volumes cohere through a field of differences, and a more conventional series of axial relationships and local symmetries. The surfaces, too, are treated as a kind of collage, with the dense textures of the unpolished travertine juxtaposed against the smooth white of aluminum panels.

But the elements are also unified experientially. The individual exhibition pavilions are accessible separately on the ground floor and linked together by a continuous series of connections on the second floor (as well as by a continuous service concourse below). The experience of the viewer is one of constantly moving from inside to outside, always aware of the site and the city beyond. The spatial experience of the museum, Meier has stated, "should allow for the contemplation of works of art from close up, from a distance, but also there has to be a periodic interval allowing the viewer to see nature, to see natural light, and to have a syncopated rhythm of experience as one moves through the museum. Otherwise museum fatigue takes over."[43] This "syncopated rhythm" is introduced to the visitor's movement by means of the sequence of bridges and terraces at the second level, and by the constant movement in and out at the ground level.

Unlike the typical museum experience of being immersed in a realm of passive, interior contemplation, at the Getty the viewer is always actively connected to the landscape beyond, which dominates the viewer's experience. Moreover, this experience of moving from place to place allows the visitor to understand the spatial organization and orientation of the building from both inside and out. Another highly effective organizational device is the exploitation of the *poché* spaces formed by the difference between the rectilinear form of the galleries and the curvilinear shell of the pavilions. These spaces, treated as terraces on the second level, accommodate visitor services and form an effective architectural buffer between the controlled environment of the galleries and the raw presence of the landscape beyond (and incidentally, they offer relief from the decorator sensibility of Thierry Despont's gallery interiors). Finally, on the western edge of the plaza, the architectural volumes are lifted up and the ground plane is terraced down, creating a remarkable sense of architectural openness and spatial interpenetration. These become some of the complex's most heavily used spaces, functioning as terraces, outdoor cafés, and a passage to the garden beyond.

These aspects are neither purely programmatic interventions nor purely formal devices. Each is a calibration of event, behavior, and potential in relation to the formal configurations of spaces and objects. The simultaneous articulation of social, programmatic, technical, and formal variables that constitutes architectural design at its highest level is only possible by way of a complex and highly developed notational language. By this I mean that Meier's drawings—plans, sketches, and working drawings—are not simply reduced pictures of the proposed architecture, scalar analogs that serve to visualize or predict the experience of the architecture, but instead are highly abstract notational scores that, like traditional musical notation, condense massive amounts of information—both visual and nonvisual—into a codified language of symbols.[44] Architectural plans are very familiar, and we sometimes forget how radical their abstraction is from everyday visual experience. A line on a plan may mark the separation of inside and outside, but it can also signify the edge of a volume, a change in material or level, or the presence of something above or beyond. Or it may indicate something not physical at all: axis of view, an alignment in space, or a trajectory of movement. Solid, void, or glazing can all be noted with a limited catalog of linear marks. In part the clues to read these marks are contextual, that is to say, fixed by the local syntax, and in part they are conventional, that is to say, based on architecture's accumulated memory. We read Meier's plans with the knowledge of Meier's previous buildings in mind. Two final properties of notation should also be mentioned. First is the capacity of an abstract notational language to function as a filter for information from other disciplines. This can range from the calculations of the structural engineer to spatial notations borrowed from painting. Second is the special capacity of notations to address issues of program and time. Notations deal less with objects than with the occupation of architecture's void spaces.

If we examine Meier's own drawings for the Getty complex or for the Museum of Contemporary Art in Barcelona (1987–95), it is evident that he is able to work with such fluidity because he takes full advantage of the notational character of architectural drawings. These are almost exclusively plan drawings—there are few perspectives, or sections. In these drawings, Meier is free to make a series of marks on paper—a curved profile, a dotted line, a smudged block—and to put various forms into various relationships with one another, governed sometimes by regulating grids, at other times by axes of movement or view, or the interplay of edges and borders. There is an implied system that seems to order the marks and relates the composition to structural, programmatic, or spatial concerns. Out of these abstract marks on paper, he and his collaborators can imagine a whole series of potential architectural experiences. Just as a composer reading a score hears music, Meier's architectural intuition is such that a highly reduced code of two-dimensional marks can suggest the complex three-dimensional realities and sensations of the built architecture. There is of course nothing new about this. It is a traditional property of architectural representation.[45] But Meier has the advantage of a thirty-five-year career in which he has not only sharpened his ability to read plans (and has seen numerous times what happens when those abstract marks are transformed into physical construction), he has also developed an extensive shorthand of figures, ciphers, favored sequences, and preferred relationships that can be deployed to address specific functional, urbanistic, or formal problems.[46]

I would even suggest that this aspect of Meier's architecture has an impact not only in the process of its making, but in the realized building itself. The high degree of abstraction in the Barcelona Museum of Contemporary Art has often been noted; it is, of course, a condition accentuated by the contrast between the building and its urban context. However, I think certain moments in the building can be identified where the abstract character of the notation imposes itself on the physical reality of the building. The most compelling of these occur where exterior elements are finished not in metal panels but in stucco. The abstract character of the floating entry screen, the cylinder housing the stair behind it, the drum that marks the entry itself, and the articulated volume projecting from the front elevation is emphasized by the material choice. Scaleless and neutral, the stucco finish promotes a more abstract reading of these elements. But the use of stucco here also works notationally to signify that these elements belong to a different system than those clad in metal panels.

It places them in material and perceptual continuity with the abstract character of the interior spaces, as if the building has undergone a topological inversion. Moreover, the tectonic character of these elements makes them seem to float in space. They are at once explicit references to the represented spaces of cubist—or better, purist—painting, yet they are also assertively present as real, three-dimensional elements.

To say that the notational character of architectural representation impacts the constructed building is not to argue that the building is just another representational device, or paper architecture made real. Rather, it signals the elusive character of abstraction, which resides in the physical, yet cannot be fully accounted for in the crude physical properties of things. It also signals the changeability of the physical and the way Meier's abstract architecture reacts with its surroundings—the changing light, the activities of the people—to take on different qualities.

In the Barcelona Museum, this backdrop status is particularly significant in relationship to the urban context. First, the building itself, for all its apparent objectlike character, operates urbanistically as a fourth wall to the open plaza in front. This is an abstract condition that allows the building to function as a blank slate upon which new information or content can be imprinted. Second, the role of the building as backdrop is an integral part of the program of an art museum. In the Barcelona building this is expressed as a dialogue between the layered front facade and the projected drum, as well as in the internal layering back through the glazed elevation, the ramp, the three-story void slot, and the galleries. These multiple layers establish complex arrangements of foreground and background that reframe the artworks displayed within.

One of the Barcelona Museum's most compelling spaces is an in-between space: the highly figural extension of the paseo past the entry drum, then through the building to the plaza behind. The inflected wall opposite the drum creates a space obviously reminiscent of the twisted streets of El Raval, but rendered here in white stucco, obliquely catching the Mediterranean sun, which in its reflective afterglow gives the space an otherworldly light. It is this ability to exist simultaneously in the world of recognizable things, and at the same time to capture the most ephemeral aspects of experience in abstract form, that distinguishes Meier's architecture. As such, the Barcelona Museum of Contemporary Art stands as a summation: absolute clarity of functional relations, the aspiration to technical perfection, formal complexity with inherent rigor, the delicate choreography of interlinked interior and exterior spaces, and an abstraction touched with painterly figuration. These appear to be the limits of Meier's working space. Although they have shifted, incrementally, over time, Meier has remained remarkably true to his beginnings. From our perspective at the end of the twentieth century, it would not be an exaggeration to say that the limits of Meier's working space are modern architecture's own limits.

27. The Getty Center,
Los Angeles, California.
Floor plan sketch,
April 2, 1987

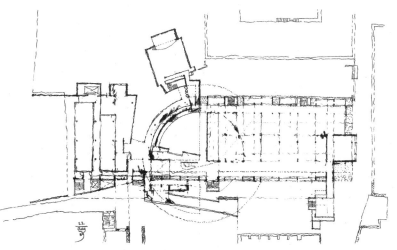

28. Museum of Contemporary Art,
Barcelona, Spain.
Floor plan sketch,
July 22, 1989

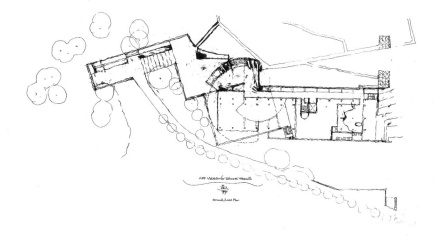

29. Arp Museum,
Rolandseck, Germany.
Ground level plan sketch,
April 10, 1990

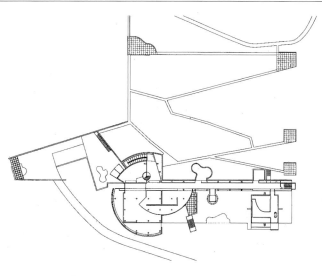

30. Arp Museum,
Rolandseck, Germany.
First level plan

31

32

33

31–33. Museum of Contemporary Art, Barcelona, Spain

Endnotes

1 Le Corbusier, "Concerning Architecture and Its Significance," *Almanach de l'architecture moderne* (Paris, 1926), p. 138; cited in Larissa A. Zhadova, *Malevich: Suprematism and Revolution in Russian Art, 1910–1930* (London: Thames and Hudson, 1982), p. 97.
2 *Five Architects: Peter Eisenman, Michael Graves, Charles Gwathmey, John Hejduk and Richard Meier* (New York: Wittenborn, 1972).
3 See Robert A. M. Stern, "Gray Architecture as Post-Modernism, or, Up and Down from Orthodoxy," in K. Michael Hays, ed., *Architecture Theory since 1968* (Cambridge, Mass.: MIT Press, 1998), pp. 242–45. Hays's introduction (pp. 240–41) gives some of the chronology of this debate.
4 Robert Venturi, *Complexity and Contradiction in Architecture* (New York: Museum of Modern Art, 1966).
5 Robert Venturi and Denise Scott Brown, with Steven Izenour, *Learning from Las Vegas* (Cambridge, Mass.: MIT Press, 1972).
6 "Inspirational sources for a new, socially-based formalism might include the Pop artists and the city around us, particularly sprawl city and the commercial strip . . . This pragmatist's way of going, where possible, with the grain of the problem is preferable to the confrontational techniques of revolutionary Modern architecture, because it is socially more responsible and aesthetically more successful." Denise Scott Brown, "On Architectural Formalism and Social Concern: A Discourse for Social Planners and Radical Chic Architects," *Oppositions 5*, summer 1975, pp. 111–12.
7 Aldo Rossi, *The Architecture of the City* (Cambridge, Mass.: MIT Press, 1966).
8 Fred Koetter, review of *Learning from Las Vegas, Oppositions 3*, May 1974.
9 Colin Rowe and Fred Koetter, *Collage City* (Cambridge, Mass.: MIT Press, 1978). The text for this book was completed in 1973 and was widely circulated before publication.
10 These dates coincide with the period covered in Meier's first monograph: *Richard Meier Architect: Buildings and Projects 1966–1976* (New York: Oxford University Press, 1976).
11 Joseph Rykwert, introduction to *Richard Meier Architect* (New York: Rizzoli, 1984), p. 11.
12 In Colin Rowe, *The Mathematics of the Ideal Villa and Other Essays* (Cambridge, Mass.: MIT Press, 1976).
13 Rowe, introduction to *Five Architects* (New York: Wittenborn, 1972), p. 7.
14 Rowe, *Mathematics*, p. 131.
15 Rowe, *Mathematics*, pp. 131–32.
16 "The *sense* of what was said some fifty years ago prohibits repetition; but then the *repetition* persists." Rowe, in *Five Architects*, p. 6.
17 Rowe, *Mathematics*, p. 132.
18 Rowe, in *Five Architects*, p. 7. See also R. E. Somol, ed., *ANY 7/8: Form Work: Colin Rowe*, 1994, especially Somol's essay "Oublier Rowe."
19 See the erratum, submitted to the second edition, published in K. Michael Hays, ed., *Architecture Theory since 1968*, p. 84.
20 See the discussion of this issue in Somol, "Oublier Rowe," p. 9. Somol refers to Gilles Deleuze and Félix Guattari, who refer in turn to Louis Hjelmslev: "Hjelmslev was able to weave a net out of the notions of *matter, content* and *expression, form, substance.* These were strata, said Hjelmslev. Now this net had the advantage of breaking the form-content duality, since there was a form of content no less than a form of expression." Gilles Deleuze and Félix Guattari, *A Thousand Plateaus*, trans. Brian Massumi (Minneapolis: University of Minnesota Press, 1987), p. 43.
21 Manfredo Tafuri "American Graffiti: Five x Five = Twenty-five," *Oppositions 5*, summer 1976, p. 68.
22 Tafuri, p. 68.
23 Instrumentality as used here should also be distinguished from functionalism. Functionalism was concerned above all with minimum standards and repeatable types. Instrumentality, on the other hand, concerns not only technical perfection and efficient planning, but also the ability to synthesize, order, and calibrate complex programmatic, logistical, and political matters. Meier's architecture, for example, always operates in excess of minimum functional requirements. This helps to clarify Meier's own assertions that architecture begins once structure and function have been taken care of. "I think function for an architect is like structure; you take it for granted that it works, that it stands up and that it's built well. That's a given. It's what happens beyond that which makes a building meaningful as a work of architecture." Richard Meier, "The Art of Abstraction," in Lois Nesbitt, *Richard Meier: Collages* (London: Academy Editions, 1990), p. 8.
24 Rykwert, in *Richard Meier Architect* (1984), p. 23.
25 Tafuri, p. 68.
26 Stephan Barthelmess, "Transparency and Perspective," *AV Monographs 59*, May–June 1996, p. 23.

27 Meier, "The Art of Abstraction," p. 9.

28 One is reminded of Le Corbusier's famous characterization of architecture as the "masterly, correct and magnificent play of masses brought together in light." Le Corbusier, *Towards a New Architecture*, trans. Frederick Etchells (New York: Praeger, 1960), p. 31.

29 Colin Rowe and Robert Slutzky, "Transparency Literal and Phenomenal," in Rowe, *Mathematics*. The essay was written in 1955–56 and first published in 1963.

30 "At the beginning of any inquiry into transparency, a basic distinction must perhaps be established. Transparency may be an inherent quality of substance—as in wire mesh or glass curtain wall, or it may be an inherent quality of organization . . . and one might, for this reason, distinguish between a real or *literal* transparency and a *phenomenal* or seeming transparency." Rowe, *Mathematics*, p. 161. The relation between painting and architecture, with specific reference to Rowe and Slutzky's article, is discussed in Stan Allen, "Conditional Abstractions," *Abstraction: The Journal of Philosophy and Art*, March 1995.

31 Rowe, *Mathematics*, p. 166. Robin Evans has also noted that many of the compositional devices of synthetic and analytical cubism (projection of simultaneous views, depiction of hidden facets through virtual transparencies, etc.) are drawn from the principles of mechanical drawing and description geometry. See the chapter "Persistent Breakage"in *The Projective Cast* (Cambridge, Mass.: MIT Press, 1994).

32 Rosalind Krauss, "Léger, Le Corbusier and Purism," *Artforum*, April 1972, p. 52. The reference to the interplay of frontality and rotation refers to Kenneth Frampton's introduction to *Five Architects*.

33 Robert Morris, "Anti Form," *Artforum*, April 1968, p. 34.

34 Donald Judd, "Specific Objects," *Arts Yearbook 8*, 1965; republished in Donald Judd, *Complete Writings 1959–1975* (Halifax, N.S.: Nova Scotia College of Art and Design, 1975), p. 183.

35 Judd, "Specific Objects," p. 184.

36 Frank Stella, *Working Space* (Charles Eliot Norton Lectures, 1983–84) (Cambridge, Mass.: Harvard University Press, 1986).

37 Stella, *Working Space*, p. 155.

38 Stella, *Working Space,* p. 77.

39 Stella, *Working Space*, p. 77.

40 Stella, *Working Space*, p. 10.

41 William S. Rubin, *Frank Stella* (New York: Museum of Modern Art, 1970), p. 41.

42 Le Corbusier, *Towards a New Architecture*, p. 166.

43 Richard Meier, "The Art of Abstraction."

44 See Nelson Goodman, *Languages of Art*, (Indianapolis, Ind.: Hackett Publishing, 1976): "Thus although drawing often counts as sketch, and a measurement in numerals is a script, the particular selection of drawing and numerals in an architectural plan counts as a digital diagram and as a score" (p. 219). "[T]he more we are startled by this, because we think of such diagrams as rather schematized pictures, the more strongly we are reminded that the significant distinction between the digital or notational and the non-notational, including the analog, turns not upon some loose notion of analogy or resemblance but upon the grounded technical requirements for a notational language" (p. 171).

45 See Stan Allen, "Mapping the Unmappable: On Notation" in *Practice: Architecture, Technique and Representation* (New York: G+B Arts International, 1999).

46 It should also be noted that the presence of this codified language of forms also allows Meier to work on a large scale and complete many projects in a given period of time (in two separate offices), which necessarily involves numerous collaborators. Because he has formulated a language that is more or less repeatable and coherent, he can guarantee the consistency of the office construction.

34

35

34–35. Museum of Contemporary Art, Barcelona, Spain

Figures in an Urban Landscape: Meier at the Millennium

Kenneth Frampton

A boundary is not that at which something stops, but, as the Greeks recognized, the boundary is that at which something begins its presencing.

Martin Heidegger
"Building, Dwelling, Thinking," *Poetry, Language and Thought*[1]

Somehow or other, there has always been a latent dimension of the unexpected in Meier's career, particularly when one considers that in every other respect his expression has remained so exceptionally predictable and consistent. The shift in orientation always seems to come about when one least expects it and from a quarter hitherto unforeseen. Starting his practice some thirty-odd years ago, as a member of the so-called New York Five, and designing houses for an emerging middle class, Meier began to establish a reputation as a public architect, most notably in the field of housing for the Urban Development Corporation, with a project known as Twin Parks Northeast in The Bronx, New York (1969–74), and in the aluminum-clad Bronx Developmental Center, completed nearby in 1977. These initial public works led, in one way or another, to a sixteen-year stretch of activity when he was continually involved in building civic institutions in major European cities, from the Museum for the Decorative Arts in Frankfurt am Main (1979–85) to the Museum of Contemporary Art in Barcelona (1987–95). Aside from endless urban projects covering a wide range of applications, from sensitive insertions into historic centers to fairly large urban renewal schemes, such as his plan for revitalizing the core of Aix-en-Provence (1990), he would also realize a number of set pieces in European capitals, including a large television headquarters on the banks of the Seine (1988–92) and a city hall and library for the center of The Hague (1986–95). He would not only become a leading public architect, but also, notwithstanding his nationality, a major European architect—so much so that when he came to design the Getty Center campus in Los Angeles, he would instinctively assume the paradigmatic European hill town as a parti for what was destined to become the ultimate humanist institution of our time.

Now, in the aftermath of the Getty, a quieter, more discreet dimension is beginning to emerge in Meier's architecture. We see this in certain tropes that may be regarded as "figures in an urban landscape." They are deft, relatively small, catalytic gestures that, because of their size, content, shape, and latent anthrogeographic implications, have the capacity to transform our reading and experience of the urban environment.[2] However, it is not only what these works imply by their presence and form, but also their specific programmatic character that assures them their impact, not only on the immediate environment but also on the extended urban fabric.

We might note that all these works are essentially reparatory. I shall start with the Swissair Headquarters, located in the suburban hinterland surrounding Manhattan (the only one of the four that is presently realized), and follow with two spiritual works, the Church of the Year 2000 and Ara Pacis. Finally, I shall touch on one of the latest projects in the office, a bridge for Alessandria, Italy.

Set within the slightly sunken confines of a rectangular bermed earthwork in order to meet local height restrictions while simultaneously shielding the building from the continual noise of the Long Island Expressway, the three-story Swissair Headquarters realized at Melville, New York,

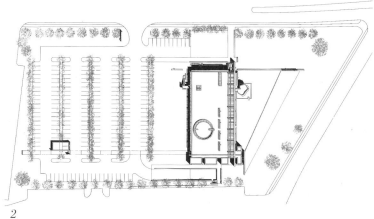

1

in 1995 is a kind of motopian redoubt that creates its own place-form within the placelessness of the suburban megalopolis. In so doing it not only provides a discernible pristine "otherness" amid the dreary, infinite proliferation of ill-related, freestanding objects, but it also claims a number of carefully selected views over the surrounding landscape.

In the first instance there is the intimate prospect from the general office space over a recreational forecourt comprising a tree-studded parterre interwoven with parking, while in the second, partial views of the expressway are provided through narrow horizontal windows let into the closed, southeastern facade. A berm and a line of trees is also deployed in order to screen the main northeastern entry from the nearby suburban access road while still preserving elevated views out over what is generally a greenfield site.

The official Meier description of the project is so informative about the basic intention as to make it worth repeating here: *"The orthogonal circulation, open-plan workspace (designed on a module for flexible subdivision), and location of the cafeteria on the lower ground floor promote efficiency without sacrificing environmental quality or access to light, air and surrounding views. The southeast elevation facing the highway is closed in order to isolate the offices from the noise of the expressway. Its internal circulation is lit by a roof light, and a long window in the facade permits distant views.*

"The northeast end of the building overlooks a narrow sunken patio, while the southwest end accommodates services, the elevator and lavatories, which are housed in three solid prisms separated by full-height glazing. The double-height glazed northwest elevation faces a parking lot with demarcated bays that is treated like a parterre. This building may be seen as an emergent exurban office type that has been given a particular identity in keeping with the client's prestige."

There is not much that one can usefully add to this except to note the subtlety of the language employed that puts this diminutive structure into a class apart within Meier's general production. Thus while the parti is oddly formalistic in that it echoes to some degree elements that appear in Meier's designs for both the Barcelona Museum and the law courts now under construction in Phoenix, it also deploys a delicate rhythmic language of its own. This is particularly noticeable on the entry facade and the curtain wall facing onto the parterre/parking lot. Where the former activates, in a very subtle way, Meier's familiar neo-Corbusian repertoire— an $a/b/a/b/a$ syncopation of brise soleil set within an overriding structural frame—the latter iterates an equally syncopated filigree rhythm in front of the freestanding columns of the office space, an expression that seems to evoke the work of Arne Jacobsen rather than Le Corbusier.

In some respects the Church of the Year 2000 (now under construction) is equally Scandinavian in its oblique reference to the overlapping shells of Jørn Utzon's Sydney Opera House. Its departure from the usual vocabulary of

1. Swissair North American Headquarters, Melville, New York
2. Swissair North American Headquarters. Site plan

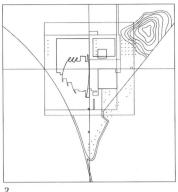

3

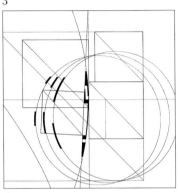

4

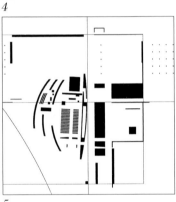

5

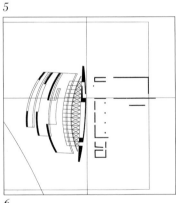

6

*3–6. Church of the Year 2000,
Rome, Italy. Diagrams:
site/landscape, geometry,
figure/ground, structure*

Meier's office is possibly in part due to the fact that Meier has never designed a church before. However, unlike Utzon's shells, Meier's overlapping spherical segments are derived from shifted circles of the same diameter. Conceived as a "city crown"[3] for the displaced center of a somewhat isolated housing scheme on the eastern outskirts of Rome, this parish center is divided into sacred and secular zones, with the sacred church precinct being situated to the south and the secular community precinct being situated to the north. The dividing east-west line between these two zones is paralleled by the east-west axis of the nave, which is inclined slightly toward the southeast. Along with the rhythm established by the concentric shells, this axial inclination appears as a response to the topography, above all to a small hill situated to the northwest of the church and to the spatial "contours" of the cranked housing blocks that flank the sides of the paved sagrato on its southern and northern boundaries. This inflected arrangement is reinforced by a roadway and parking to the south and a tree-lined boundary to the north, culminating in a square, formal cluster of fifteen trees to be planted adjacent to the *sagrato* entrance. The hierarchical ramifications of this organization in section and plan are evident from the following description:

"The paved sagrato *to the east of the church extends into the heart of the housing complex, providing an open plaza for public assembly. The northern half of the site is divided into two courts. The east court is sunken a full story to provide light and access to the lowest floor of the community center. The elevated western court is separated from a meditation court behind the church by a paved walkway that leads to the parking area."*

A double lenticular truss of welded tubular steel serves as the ultimate crown of the church. It is situated within the apex of the nave, where it helps to sustain a canted roof light coming off the highest, innermost shell as it slopes down onto the roof of the community building below.

As with the "visual acoustics" of Le Corbusier's Ronchamp, one can well imagine the spherical forms of this church radiating out from the crest of the high ground over the landscape to the west, while maintaining its serrated mass-form as the terminus of an axis passing through the center of the housing from the east. However, it is the elongated parking court to the west of the *sagrato* that finally relates the church to the wider domain of the megalopolis that surrounds it on every side—thus serving to remind us that, as in the case of Louis Kahn's Kimbell Art Museum, we live in an age in which any monument is constantly undermined by the automobile.[4]

Although cars do indeed continually sweep past the site, parking is not an issue in the case of Meier's project to reencase the Ara Pacis altar stone on the banks of the Tiber. This monumental stone, dating to A.D. 9, has been housed inadequately in a relatively rudimentary, ferro-vitreous structure ever since its removal from the Campo Marzio in 1938. Symbolically situated on the virtual axis of the mausoleum of Augustus, Meier was asked to re-present this relic to tourists and visitors, while protecting it from further deterioration. His strategy has been to simulate a pagan temple by enclosing the stone altar in a glazed prism on a narrow strip of land separating the Piazza Augusto Imperatore from the causeway running along the embankment of the Tiber. The "figure" in this instance could hardly be more minimal and transparent, affording views through its prismatic form of the Lungotevere in Augusta, while maintaining its own dematerialized presence.

Brilliantly orchestrated in section and plan, one ascends onto the narrow monumental podium of the pavilion through a sequence of spaces, moving across a covered threshold into a paved foyer that doubles as a small exhibition volume. From this second threshold one may survey the immediate context, looking in one direction toward the embankment and in the other toward the mausoleum, while immediately on axis there lies a short flight of steps bringing one into intimate contact with the altar. An elevated exhibition space, accessed by a short stair and a passerelle, continues behind the altar. Beyond this, a ramp and a stairway lead down to the double-height foyer of the 150-seat lecture theater below; the auditorium has a separate access from the Via Ara Pacis to the north. This level also houses supporting functions—workshops, storage, lavatories, a series of offices, a meeting room—all of which may be approached independently by a stair leading down to a staff entrance from the south.

In terms of its architectonic syntax, the whole piece seems to lie suspended between a reference to the rationalist language of Giuseppe Terragni's Asilo Sant'Elia of 1935 and the interpenetrating planar abstractions of Mies van der Rohe's Barcelona pavilion of 1929. At the same time a central axis running north-south through the Ara Pacis virtually intersects with the obelisk in the center of the Piazza del Popolo, while an east-west axis passing through the altar focuses on the center of the cylindrical mausoleum. These "near misses" are more than enough to relate the entire piece to the site in symbolic, historical, and topographic terms, let alone the more abstract regulating lines with which the architects have sought to tie the work to its ancient context, including a freestanding obelisk situated on the podium forecourt, serving as a southern point from which the north-south axis passes through the altar.

In terms of achieving the maximum catalytic potential from the most minimal of gestures it is hard to think of anything more effective than a bridge, although, at the same time, it is equally difficult to imagine a commission that could be more atypical for an architect of Meier's caliber. Projected for the small Italian city of Alessandria, Meier's Cittadella Bridge over the Tanaro River will link the historic core of the city to an eighteenth-century citadel on the opposite bank. At the heart of this citadel, surrounded by the landscaped terraced remains of bastions and contrescarpes, are the disused confines of a Napoleonic barracks that is now about to be relinquished by the military. Thus the primary reason for building the bridge is to facilitate access to this historic complex from the city center, enabling it to be more readily reused for cultural or other civic purposes.

7

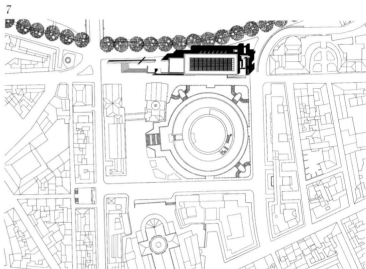

8

7–8. Ara Pacis Museum, Rome, Italy. Photomontage and site plan

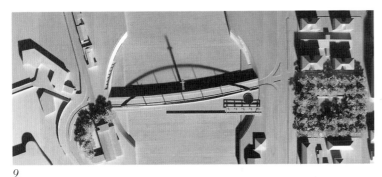

9

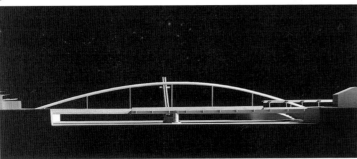

10

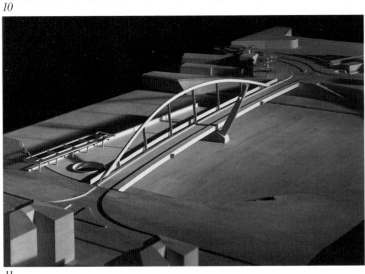

11

9–11. Cittadella Bridge,
Alessandria, Italy.
Model

This access is a fairly simple requirement, but the design of the crossing itself is complicated by the fact that the river has recently been subject to flooding. A severe inundation in 1994 spread beyond the riverbed largely because of debris that became lodged in the mid-span supports and abutments of a number of bridges. Aside from requiring the eventual reconstruction of these bridges, this experience has had a major impact on the design criteria for the Cittadella Bridge, including keeping the deck as thin as possible and reducing the mid-span support to a single pylon. As currently projected, the three-lane road bed of the bridge, arced in plan, is intended to be carried by the combination of an arch and cables suspended from an arm cantilevered off the central pylon. A pedestrian sidewalk of varying width is cantilevered off the road bed on the opposite side of the crossing.

As in the bridges of Santiago Calatrava, this entire structure is being exploited as an occasion to create an urban place-form rather than being merely conceived as a span linking two sides of a river. Thus, curving stairs off the left and right banks connect the upper embankment walks to riverside quays twenty-six feet below the deck level, close to the mean level of the river. In addition to this, the pedestrian crossing widens out toward the eastern abutment, forming a generous promenade that has been conceived as an extension of a tree-lined square on the right bank of the river. This links the pedestrian crossing to the residential fabric of the city and accounts for the slight shifting of the eastern bridgehead toward the north, providing a clear pedestrian axial connection between the square and the causeway. There are two further topographical nuances: first, short lines of trees on the left and right banks bond the bridge into the immediate context on both sides of the crossing; second, a loggia and a circular light well cut into the pedestrian deck, illuminating the quay beneath.

It is curious and, paradoxically, encouraging that an architect who has attained such acclaim—with over ten major works in both Europe and the United States, not to mention the enormous achievement of the Getty Center— should now suddenly pass through a period in which a number of his more recent commissions have a decidedly modest character. Even the Church of the Year 2000, while it is surely of considerable symbolic importance, is nonetheless a rather small building.

I have focused on these four structures because they typify so precisely the catalytic potential of discreet works, so that a small, judiciously sited, and rationally planned suburban office building may be seen as having as much of an impact in an urbanized region as a major public monument in a dense urban core. The first two buildings in the sequence reflect the megalopolis in which they are situated, not only through the parking to which they are symbiotically attached and which assures them a regional cast, but also through their outlook either toward the horizon or to the zenith that in both instances serves to inflect their respective forms toward the cosmos as a whole.

Conversely the tight inlaid character of the Ara Pacis pavilion and the Cittadella Bridge reveal themselves as tesserae within a historic urban fabric that is at once both long since finished and forever incomplete. It is Martin Heidegger who reminds us of the gathering character of the bridge:

"[The bridge] does not just connect banks that are already there. The banks emerge as banks only as the bridge crosses the stream. The bridge designedly causes them to lie across from each other. One side is set against the other by the bridge. Nor do the banks stretch along the stream as indifferent border strips of dry land. With the banks, the bridge brings to the stream the one and the other expanse of the landscape lying behind them. It brings stream and bank and land into each other's neighborhood. The bridge gathers the earth as landscape around the stream . . ."[5]

It is perhaps this special "gathering" potential that each of these works have in common. Thus the pavilion that separates the Tiber from the mausoleum in fact brings the two monuments even closer together, just as it attracts into its axial form the Piazza del Popolo and hence the city of Rome as a whole. To a similar end, the Swissair headquarters, bermed up against the Long Island Expressway, gathers into its form both the ceaseless automotive movement and the entire parkway system that extends from Manhattan to Montauk, at the extreme eastern tip of Long Island. These works are equally grounded in that they are patently not freestanding objects. They are each earthworks that are carefully inscribed into their respective sites—the office building through its berms, the church through its paved *sagrato*, the pavilion through its podium, and the bridge by virtue of the stairs linking its abutments to the quays beneath. Appropriately enough, to a greater degree than the other works, Meier's church in Rome pulls into its orbit not only the Autostrada del Sol and the Via Appenine, but also beyond the immediate topography of site the Heideggerian fourfold of earth, sky, mortals, and divinities.

Endnotes

1 Martin Heidegger, "Building, Dwelling, Thinking" in *Poetry, Language and Thought* (New York: Harper Colophon, 1975), p. 154.
2 The term anthrogeographic refers to the work of German proto-ecological geographer Friedrich Ratzel; see his *Anthropo-Geographie* (1882).
3 See Bruno Taut, *Die Stadtkrone* (1919). For Taut the "city crown" was the vertical crystalline religious building, whether a pagoda or cathedral.
4 See my chapter on Louis Kahn in *Studies in Tectonic Culture* (Cambridge, Mass.: MIT Press, 1995), pp. 243, 246. Despite the fact that the main entrance to the museum is patently from the park, only 15 percent of visitors actually enter through this portico; the remainder come from the parking lot to the rear.
5 Heidegger, p.152.

Creative Repetition

Jean-Louis Cohen

Only a few bodies of architectural work have managed to establish identifiable configurations in the jungle of late-twentieth-century cities. If, over the past thirty-five years, Richard Meier has been able to construct a recognizable constellation of work, it is because of his ability to pursue a methodical rather than a dogmatic course in the face of contradictory contexts and functional expectations. A coherent continuity runs through his work, similar to the one he pointed out himself in the oeuvre of Le Corbusier, in a commentary he made on the Villa Savoye in 1972.

The terms by which Meier's production can be analyzed have undoubtedly shifted since he arrived in the Old World and broke ground for the Museum for the Decorative Arts in Frankfurt in 1979. Up until that moment, Manfredo Tafuri could still invoke the "desperate attempt" of the New York Five to recover the traces of the avant-garde that America had never known. Since that moment, however, the terms of the discussion have changed. Although Richard Meier has in no way renounced his initial orientation, formulated in the 1960s, the "coming of age" of critical reflection, as Hubert Damisch noted in 1979, has served instead to justify and consolidate a posteriori Meier's early choices.

What was, then, the initial orientation of his work? From the outset, his freer but no less functionally and structurally ordered geometry distinguished him from his colleagues in the New York Five. Less literal in his readings and rewritings of Corbusian Purism than Michael Graves, less Talmudic in the use of self-referential geometries than Peter Eisenman, Meier's first projects pursued a course midway between John Hejduk's coded reminiscences and the smooth professionalism of Charles Gwathmey and Robert Siegel. While successive generations of Le Corbusier's disciples struggled to disengage themselves from the vocabulary that the master had elaborated in his postwar work, Meier's critical freedom allowed him to find the resources to enrich and surpass the Corbusian language, primarily through contact with programs essentially devoted to habitation.

In order to perceive the breadth of typological variation that is present even in Meier's early work, a barrier must be crossed. His tenacity in constructing a completely coded graphic and photographic universe, begun in the 1960s, has resulted on occasion in masking and flattening out the complex reality of the models and buildings. The refinements of Esto-style photography and the graphic rigor of Massimo Vignelli's design have played no small part in giving visual order and power of communication to the representations of Meier's work. But, at the same time, they have tended to smooth out any of its rough edges.

The rationalization of a building's published image, inscribed in a tradition which did not start with the *Oeuvre complète* of Le Corbusier, the *stylization* of the work conceived from the outset as a visual unity, is reinforced by the immediate appearance of the built work. Meier appears progressively to have diluted the specificity of each successive building, creating instead a continuous sequence of projects. Instead of the tectonic diversity of the earlier work, where concrete, metal, or brick retained some legibility, the buildings of the later period are each wrapped in the same gridded skin. But the reality is nonetheless more complex, and the apparent homogeneity of Meier's work is an indication of the coherence of thought that is at stake in any methodical intellectual operation.

Meier's buildings and projects constitute an ensemble of multiple variations within a voluntarily limited thematic register. This way of conceiving work belongs to a school of thought shared by several groups of European and American architects, who, starting in the mid-1960s, began to reflect on the capacity of architecture to find and maintain an identity during a period when the rapid obsolescence of forms and doctrines was to be expected. A fundamental split occurred between those who based their pursuits on a historical or urban paradigm and those who sought to validate the critical pursuit of what Jürgen Habermas hypothesized as the "unfinished project of Modernity," now detached from its historical links to projects of social reform. If Meier was part of the New York culture that sought to rehabilitate the formal strategies of the European artistic avant-gardes of the 1920s, including the Russian Constructivists, his exploratory program coincided with the emergence of new theoretical questions on the aesthetics of seriality and repetition.

Reluctant to produce texts, Meier has not appropriated Le Corbusier's taste for manifestos and proclamations of doctrine. He belongs more to the species of architects who express themselves, like Mies van der Rohe, either through quasi-aphoristic declarations or by way of apparently bland project descriptions. In the absence of texts, it is only through a comparative reading of his architectural strategies that one can distinguish between the persistence of his references and the displacements of his methodological tools. In his lecture of 1980, "On Architecture," one of his few remotely programmatic texts, Meier pointed out the extent to which the plan is the key to any project, echoing Le Corbusier's slogan of the plan as "generator."

This insistence on the plan is a postulate that even Julien Guadet, the theoretician of the Beaux-Arts, could have subscribed to without reservation. Meier's originality resides not in the mere emphasis on plan, however, but in his determination to base the study of his plans on the extensive use of regulating lines. Le Corbusier had first formulated the notion of regulating lines in the 1920s and gave it a somewhat mechanical final shape in his Modulor system. The new meaning that Meier gave to this idea unquestionably derives from the initial demonstrations of Le Corbusier, seen not through the Modulor, however, but through the prism of Colin Rowe's interpretations. In addition to abandoning the obsession with the golden section, Meier also offered a critique of the continued craving for modules and grids determined only by narrow considerations of use or construction on the part of the architects of vulgarized postwar modernism.

Much more than a system for carving up the interior of buildings and their parts, the gridded network through which each of Meier's buildings is conceived allows him,

1

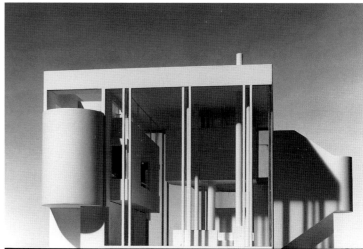

2
1. Smith House,
Darien, Connecticut
2. House in Pound Ridge,
Pound Ridge, New York.
Model

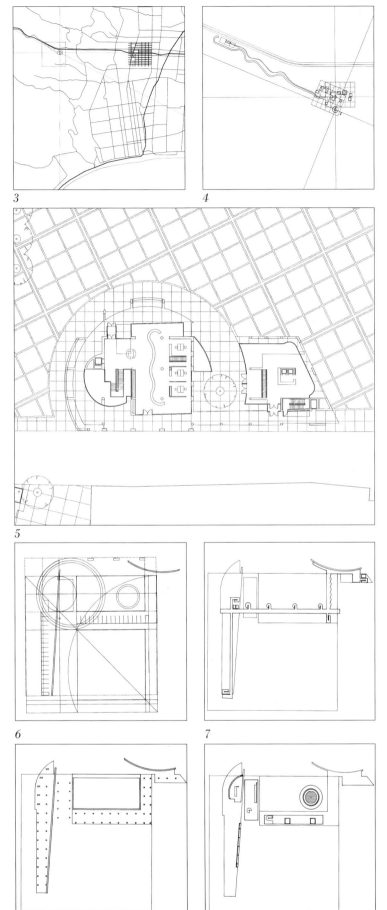

3. *The Getty Center,*
Los Angeles, California.
Context diagram
4. *The Getty Center,*
Los Angeles, California.
Geometry diagram

5. *Exhibition and Assembly Building,*
Ulm, Germany.
Ground floor plan
6-9. *Canal+ Headquarters,*
Paris, France.
Diagrams: geometry, circulation,
structure, elements

it is true, to treat materials—such as cladding panels—as repeatable units. However, this is not the essential feature of Meier's grid. Rectangular or square, depending on the urban circumstance, the regulating grid allows him to lay out the entire building on the ground and sets into place a matrix that permits the negotiation of the internal geometries of the project with those of the space in which it is inscribed. The grid becomes an ordering device capable of coordinating the two systems through which Meier conceives of the relation between his buildings and their space of inscription: the relation of *figure/ground* and *object/texture*.

The regulating grid is not necessarily a material one. It is both figure, when the overall configuration of the building is to be measured in the city, and ground, when the place of each element is to be fixed inside the building without defining the element itself, particularly in the case of curved or circular volumes. In fact, the grid serves more to clarify the syntax according to which Meier assembles the figures of his repertory than to specify their dimensions or volumes. Thus, because established geometrically, the syntax is itself regulated according to another order. Here again, the origin of this order is Corbusian—the *promenade architecturale*, which was introduced in the Parisian villas of the 1920s and based, as we now know, on an interpretation of the analyses of the nineteenth century, most notably Auguste Choisy's work on the Acropolis of Athens.

The particular syntax of each of Meier's buildings can be specified through a prefiguration of one's movement through spatial sequences. Here Meier opens a vast register of spatial dilations and contractions that lead the eye and body from one discovery to another. The result is in some ways an architecture of kinetic pleasure, in which circulation space is not the "servant," according to Louis Kahn's terminology, but is instead itself almost "served" by the spaces to which it leads and from which it derives value. The definition of the major circulation path is not regulated, as it is in the Beaux-Arts tradition, by the *marche* through the project, nor does it cut through the built mass of the building like a void hollowed out from a preestablished volume. Nonetheless, the major circulation path remains a *full* presence. One is reminded of Luigi Morandi's studies of the great spaces of architectural history and the models of the "voids" of Hadrian's Villa or of Saint Peter's in Rome. Because of this full presence, the circulation elements find a fertile relation to the exterior envelope of the building. Kenneth Frampton has justly remarked that they tend to "gravitate towards the skin," as is clearly demonstrated by the High Museum of Art in Atlanta (1980–83).

This working method—consolidated over the years and often explicated through the confection of analytic schemata relating the plan (a posteriori of course) to simplified representations of the program, the envelope, circulation, access, and structure—is inflected by differences in building type and scale. Thus the Bronx Developmental Center (1970–77) plays a pivotal role in the sequence of Meier's projects, for it established a new equilibrium between the different programmatic scales within a single ensemble and adopted new solutions for their distribution. Meier finds fertile ground in the play between serial programmatic elements, such as offices or living quarters, and singular ones, such as auditoriums or lobbies. This differentiation between the repetitive and the unique was the basis of Le Corbusier's research in the 1920s. However, unlike Meier, Le Corbusier always sought to maintain the primacy of the orthogonal volumes over the more plastic ones, as can be seen in the Cité de Refuge or the Centrosoyuz projects. This reassuring mode of classification is subverted and even sometimes inverted in Meier's buildings. In any case, it is reinvented on the basis of the itinerary described above.

This sort of typological invention reaches its high point in complex programs such as museums, where use and lighting requirements are extreme, and which join closed spaces lit from above with auditoriums, storage, and offices. Most important, however, is the fact that museums are institutionally committed to providing, through a kind of inverted metaphor of architecture or the city, an itinerary through culture, or at least through the works in a collection. This analysis, in my opinion, explains the extraordinary affinity between the basic strategies of Meier's projects in general and the mission of museums in particular, just as well as the problematic of natural light of which Meier is an acknowledged master.

The primacy of the itinerary, based on a programmatic necessity in the case of museums or of certain public institutions, is subject to rational and occasionally picturesque decisions, but rarely arbitrary ones. The itinerary always reinforces, in a certain way, the institutional narcissism of buildings that constantly offer themselves for their own viewing. This is not always the case for Meier's work with grids, which relates to his particular manner of reading the sites and projects. The plan of the Museum for the Decorative Arts in Frankfurt (1979–85) is regulated by the outline of the preexisting building and the angle it forms with the river, while the grid of Canal+ (1988–92) is determined primarily by the square form of an underground telephone exchange, which may be less exciting but nonetheless exists. This game between the given, between the *already there* and the geometry of volition introduced by the project, gives rise to an architecture that is certainly not contextual, but which acts to reveal both the regularities and singularities of the site, even if they occasionally need to be coaxed out into the open. Deformed and reflected in the curved outlines of Meier's buildings, the contemporary urban landscape thus becomes a more powerful regulator of his work than some imaginary museum of the avant-garde of the 1920s, and this literal approach to the site breaks with the strategies of late Purism. Meier's success in enriching what Le Corbusier, in *Précisions*, called his *propos architectural*, ultimately lies more in the capture of local circumstance than it does in the collection of machine age emblems, still to be found in the Bronx Developmental Center.

It might seem that dwelling places afford fewer possibilities for developing extraordinary itineraries. Nonetheless, the single-family residences of the 1960s, starting with the

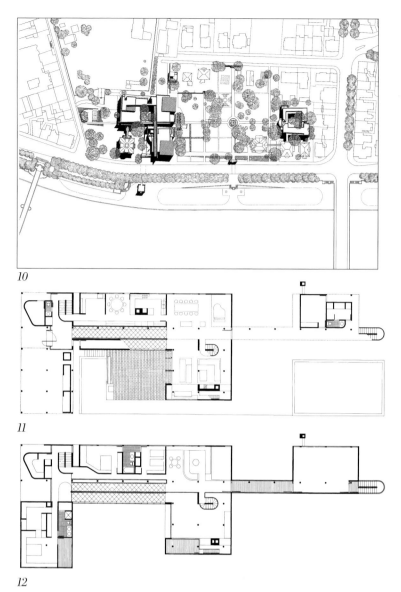

10. Museum for the Decorative Arts, Frankfurt, Germany. Site plan
11–12. House in Old Westbury, Old Westbury, New York. First and second level plans

13

14

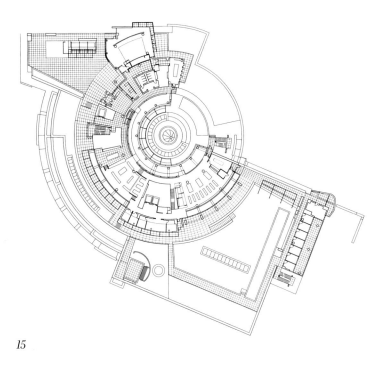

15

13–14. The Getty Center, Los Angeles, California
15. The Getty Research Institute for
the History of Art and the Humanities.
Entry level plan

Smith House (1965–67) and Saltzman House (1967–69) and the House in Old Westbury (1969–71), although they remain compact volumes, allowed Meier to give form to a procedure that he later extended to more complex programs. Even at this scale the differentiation of public and private spaces allowed him to juxtapose the dominant mass of the major living room element with the minor, but nonetheless serial, string of bedrooms. In addition, by controlling the privileged views to the outside or toward other parts of the house on the inside, Meier framed the openings to reveal the horizon of the site through successive punctures in the whiteness of the walls.

From the mid-1980s on, Richard Meier's strategy of invention did not abandon the single-family dwelling altogether, as the Ackerberg House (1984–86) and Grotta House (1985–89) attest, but was redeployed through the encounter with a new series of challenges. Ten years after a first—and unfruitful—project for the extension of the Villa Strozzi in Florence (1973), a series of European projects led to a confrontation between Meier's design method and highly structured urban sites. He was unable to convince the officials in charge to build his large-scale propositions for the area known as Sextius-Mirabeau in Aix-en-Provence (1990) or for the grounds of the Potsdamer Platz in Berlin (1992). Instead, he had to wrestle with sites in Paris, The Hague, Ulm, and Barcelona that were not only charged with a history that he generally considered with care but also with an elaborate baggage of regulations and technical requirements that he had to take into account before finally being able to achieve the same level of precision in plastic form and construction.

The greatest challenge that Richard Meier has faced in the third cycle of his work is, of course, the Getty Center project, opened in 1997 in Los Angeles. Instead of the multiple tensions inherent in the European sites, which sometimes undermined the very possibility of building a project, as in the case of the parvis of the Ulm Cathedral, the difficulties posed by the Getty Center site derive not from dense historicity but rather from a certain absence of context. Of course, this absence is relative. As Reyner Banham so convincingly argued in 1971 in *Los Angeles: The Architecture of Four Ecologies*, the freeways take on the role of thresholds and points of reference for the city of Los Angeles. As a result, it is precisely the 22.5-degree angle between the San Diego freeway and the urban fabric below the Getty site that provides the underlying basis for the organization of the ensemble, the articulation of which is particularly complex. The defining feature of the project consists more in the fabrication of a virtual urban fabric than in the combination of monumental buildings to form a sort of Acropolis—or fortress.

Here there is no itinerary proper to the whole of the complex, and each element of the ensemble is subject to different logics of organization. Without question, the J. Paul Getty Museum is subject to the hegemony of a route that runs through a tentacular assemblage of exhibition spaces and around a somewhat chopped-up exterior court. This is not the case for the building housing the Getty

Research Institute, whose library stacks are rolled with more clarity around a column of air. Framed by these two edifices, the landscape of Los Angeles spreads out in the distance below, stretching to the west toward the Pacific Ocean, shining like the luminescent waters of a painting by Claude Lorrain; and to the east toward downtown's renascent skyline. It is in the handling of these interstices and of the access sequence leading from the bottom of the hill to the slow discovery of the center's site that its most exciting spatial experiences reside.

The final articulation of the project, carried out through the construction of dozens of successive models of the complex as well as of its details, was accompanied by ongoing negotiations with the different programs of the Getty organization. Far from having diluted the initial project, these adjustments instead more rigorously inscribed it in the landscape, specifying the distribution and exterior skin of each constituent element and ultimately serving to eliminate some of the more questionable initial decisions. The circular ramp leading from the tramway stop to the museum, for example, was replaced by a more generous stairway that clarifies the hierarchy of the buildings for the public, a hierarchy otherwise difficult to discern, since the museum has been cut up into so many small parts. Problems emerge however, for instance with the use of travertine. Pleasant and logical as a rough epiderm in the lower parts of the structures, the Roman stone is more embarrassing used on large wall surfaces and vertical edges and on square pillars, as it soon appears as mere wrapping. The circulations are also problematic throughout the center. As in Barcelona's Museum of Contemporary Art, they are inflated to the point of crushing exhibition, collection, and staff spaces, manifesting the presence of an architectural will sometimes contradictory with the requirements of daily usage.

While Richard Meier's first projects proposed a critical reading of the architecture of Le Corbusier, the Getty Center is based on a retrospective reading of Meier's own lexicon and syntax, source of parallel strengths and weaknesses. Comprising a perhaps temporary point of culmination, the center can be seen as a reflection on the whole of Meier's work. It inevitably leads one to ask whether his largest projects are taking his previously formulated principles to a point of critical mass beyond which they undergo an irreversible fission. On the other hand, the Los Angeles complex also leads one to recognize that the formal repetition for which Meier is often criticized is tempered by its flexibility and its capacity to accommodate changes of scale and formal torsion.

The nostalgia that Manfredo Tafuri could correctly point out in Meier's first works was overcome once and for all in the successive large-scale projects of transatlantic reconnaissance, although it is true that an encounter with Japanese cities never took place. Nonetheless, these successive generations of studies and buildings that constitute the body of Meier's work still pursue the questions initially formulated twenty years ago. More so than the work of many of his contemporaries who came together in the celebration of "modern space," Meier's architecture illustrates the notion of "articulation" that Theodor Adorno identified in his *Ästhetische Theorie* as the distinguishing feature of the work of art. This is particularly the case when the structure of each fragment reflects the organization of the whole, which the Getty Center does without a doubt. Meier's work can thus be read as the ongoing displacement of the border between the order of repetition—of the lexicon of forms and the details of construction—and the order of differentiation— of itineraries, vistas, and the surfaces that envelope a building. In his book *Différence et Répetition* of 1968, the French philosopher Gilles Deleuze reflected on the meaning of these two terms in the fields of philosophy, biology, and art. He distinguished "the superficial repetition of identical exterior elements" from "the critical repetition of internal totalities." These two phenomena coexist in contradiction within Richard Meier's *propos architectural*, which continues to communicate an optimistic vision of a world still capable of transformation through the creative repetition of an architectural itinerary that modifies our perception of the cities and landscapes of today.

Smith House

Darien, Connecticut
1965 – 1967

Meier's most succinct essay on modern architecture,
the Smith House is the first of his pristine white buildings.
As early as 1965, the key elements associated with his work
were present: the brilliant white exterior, expanses of plate
glass framed by finely proportioned piers and mullions, distinct
circulation features, minimal interiors, and programmatic
separation between public and private spaces. Accordingly,
Meier considers the Smith House his first building. Earlier
work, including a house for his parents, helped him work
through influences—Frank Lloyd Wright's Fallingwater,
for instance—that he would soon reject, focusing instead on
architecture that clearly differentiates between exterior and
interior space. Indeed, the Smith House's hard-edged
geometries are set in opposition to the rugged coastline
of Long Island Sound. To minimize blasting costs, Meier
designed a small footprint and a vertically oriented parti.
From the front walkway, which establishes the major site axis,
visitors approach an almost solid facade before crossing the
front ramp and entering the second floor of what Meier terms
a "180-degree explosion." The living room, dining area,
and terraces all open to the waterfront view, while the
family's private realm is contained in the enveloped core.
In addition to exploring the dialectic of enclosure
and openness, the house reflects concerns with direction and
movement, and with planar abstraction, attained through
white paint on redwood siding. Meier later acknowledged the
house as an investigation of Colin Rowe and Robert Slutzky's
notions of literal and phenomenal transparency.

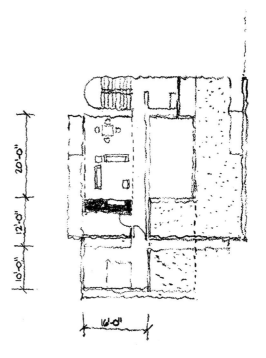

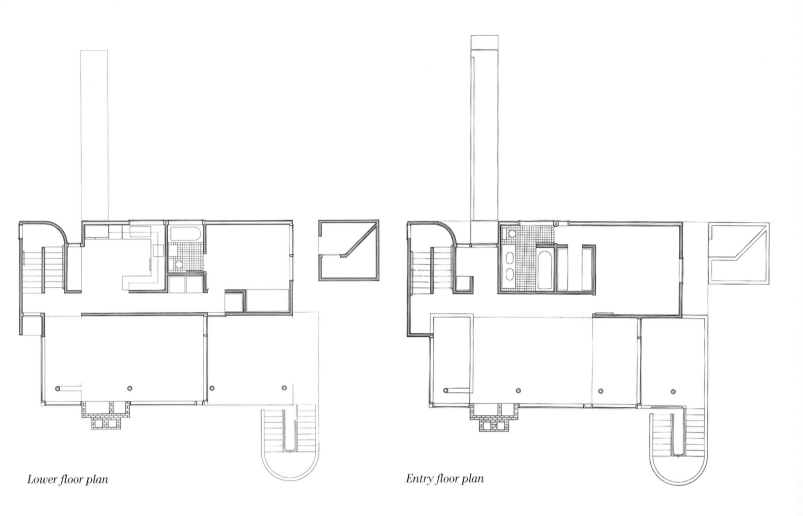

Lower floor plan

Entry floor plan

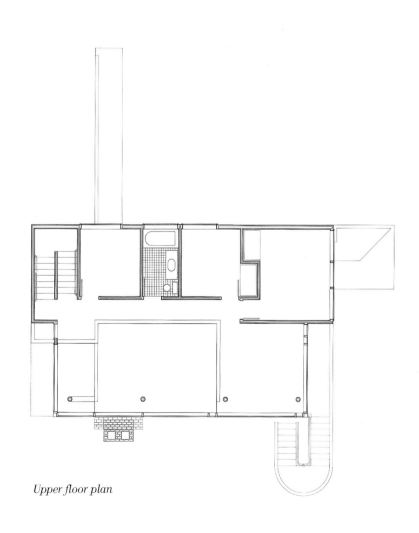

Upper floor plan

45

Bronx Developmental Center

The Bronx, New York
1970–1977

Meier's late-1960s research into metal-panel wall systems
led to the use of rolled-sheet aluminum panel construction
for the Bronx Developmental Center. This construction
method—which had been used primarily for industrial
buildings—was highly utilitarian and inexpensive
and until then lacked detail complexity and sophistication.
Meier, however, was able to manipulate the system's flat
and curved panels to express the various spaces throughout
the complex, providing him with a standardized building
system. Factory-assembled panels serve as exterior surfaces
with integrated windows and a reflective aluminum finish.
Commissioned by the New York State Department of Mental
Hygiene, the center was planned as a total-care facility
for 750 children with special needs (physically disabled
and mentally handicapped) but was later scaled down
to accommodate 380 patients. In response to the industrial
site at the edge of a hospital campus, Meier designed
the building to turn inward. The structure, in effect,
creates its own context, with two large internal courtyards.
Although it received architectural accolades and was lauded
as a "place of refuge, a sanctuary," the center was later
controversial. Most problematic was that during the seven
years it was planned and built, the concept of large
institutions for the housing and care of the mentally
and physically disabled became obsolete. In addition,
the building's sleek, machine-made image was considered
by some to be antithetical to the notion of "home."
While the Bronx Developmental Center is not used
as it was originally intended, it is a compelling example
of how, already early in his work, Meier combined interests
in tectonics and abstraction.

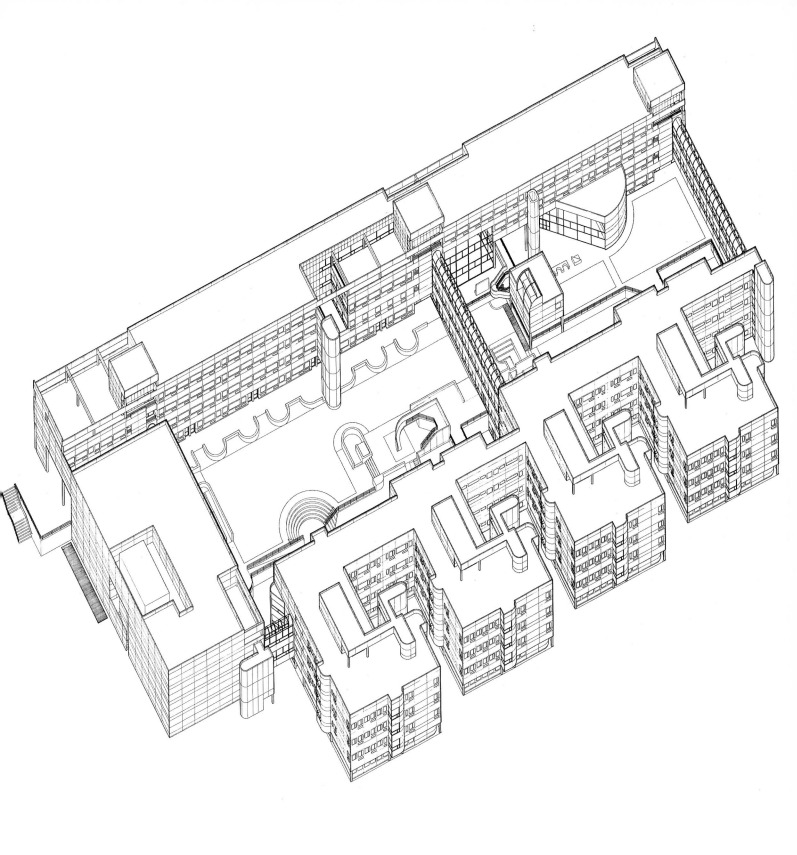

49

Elevation study of residential units

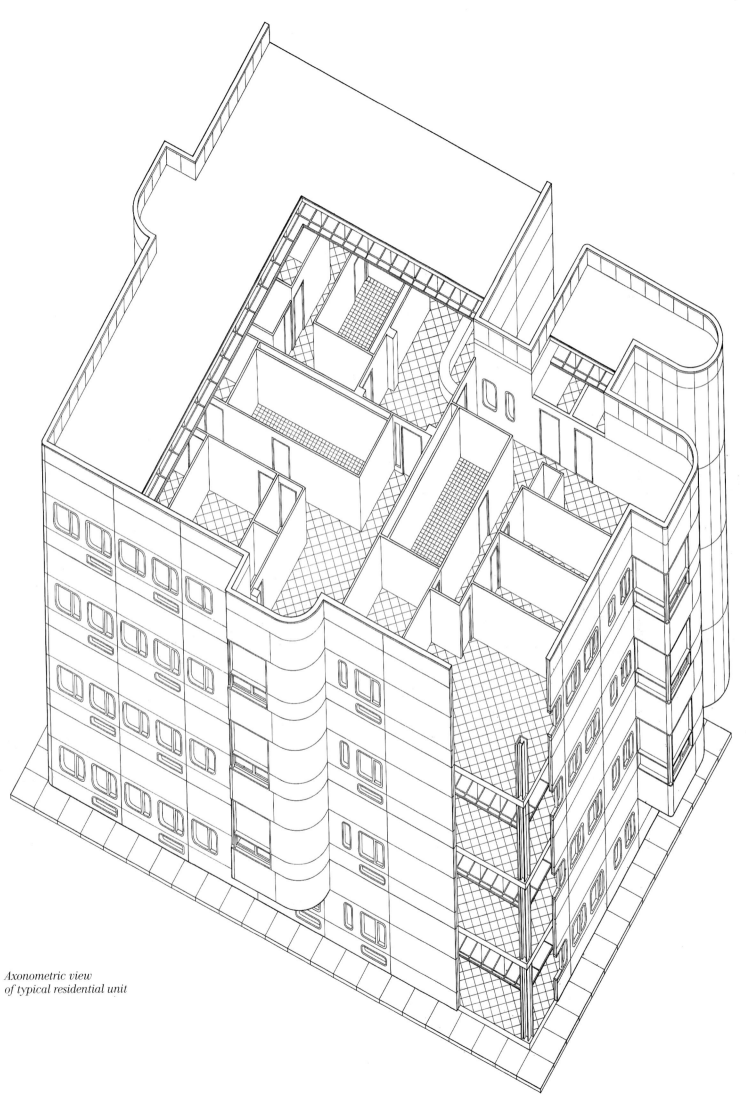

*Axonometric view
of typical residential unit*

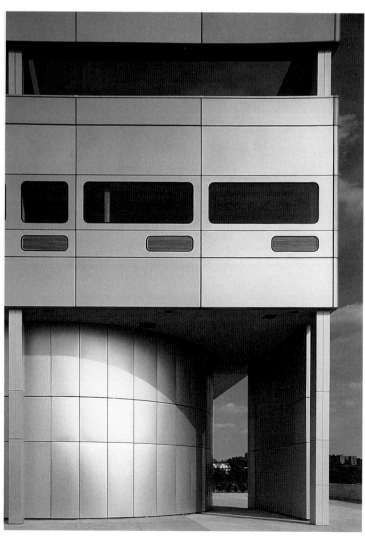

Douglas House

Harbor Springs, Michigan
1971–1973

The Douglas House largely established Meier's reputation
in the 1970s as the architect of luminous machinelike objects
set in nature. It also solidified his association with the
New York Five, a loosely knit group of American architects
including Peter Eisenman, Michael Graves, Charles Gwathmey,
and John Hejduk who were published together in
Five Architects (1972). The clients first approached Meier
to design a residence like the Smith House, which they had
seen published. In reaction to their request and the site—
a wooded hillside above Lake Michigan—Meier amplified
the plan of the earlier house to develop new spatial strategies
and heighten aspects of transparency, light, and abstraction.
He devised an ingenious four-story plan for the steep site
that explores visual continuity in plan and section. On the
house's topmost level is a ramp to the entrance and stairs
descending to living spaces. A central skylight projects light
through apertures that permit multiple views through the
building. Like the Smith House, the Douglas House separates
public and private functions and provides all the primary
shared spaces—living room, dining room, and library—
with dramatic waterfront vistas. And interestingly, like the
earlier house, the Douglas House projects a sharp-edged
machine aesthetic through a structure entirely composed
of a natural material—accented by a cantilevered steel stair,
metal pipe railings, and stainless-steel smokestacks.

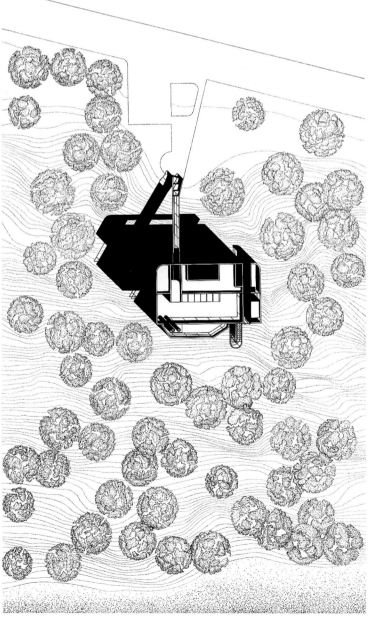

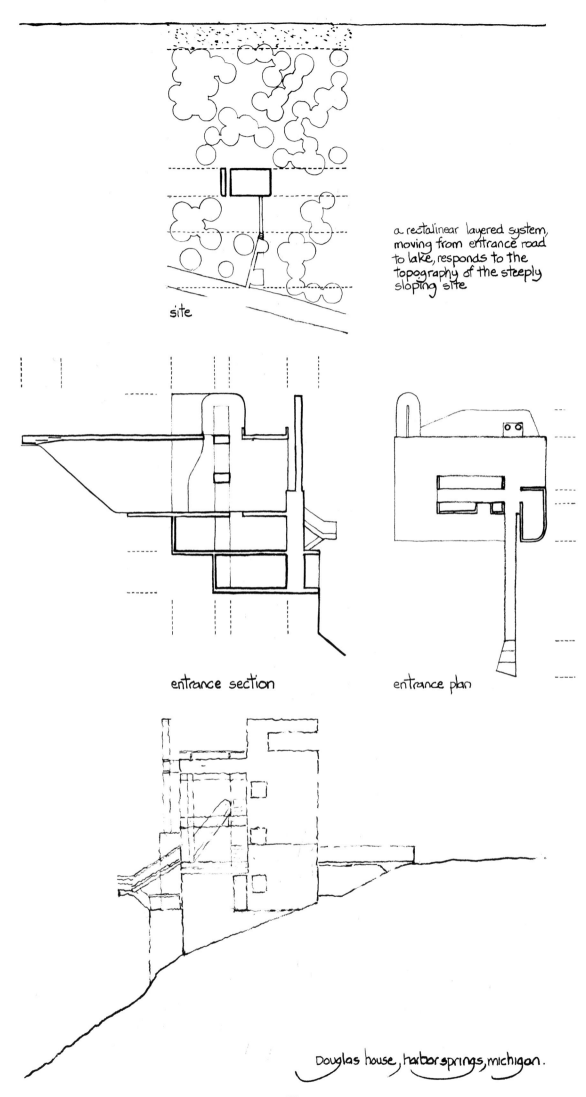

site

a rectalinear layered system, moving from entrance road to lake, responds to the topography of the steeply sloping site

entrance section

entrance plan

Douglas house, harborsprings, michigan.

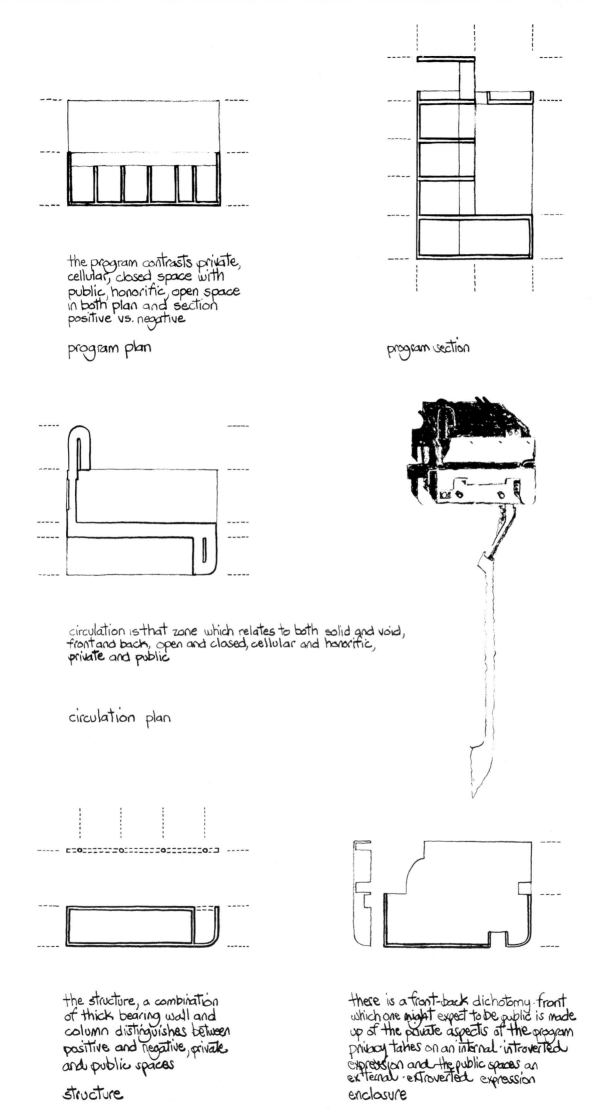

the program contrasts private,
cellular, closed space with
public, honorific, open space
in both plan and section
positive vs. negative

program plan

program section

circulation is that zone which relates to both solid and void,
front and back, open and closed, cellular and honorific,
private and public

circulation plan

the structure, a combination
of thick bearing wall and
column distinguishes between
positive and negative, private
and public spaces

structure

there is a front-back dichotomy. front
which one might expect to be public is made
up of the private aspects of the program
privacy takes on an internal introverted
expression and the public spaces an
external extroverted expression
enclosure

59

Middle floor plan

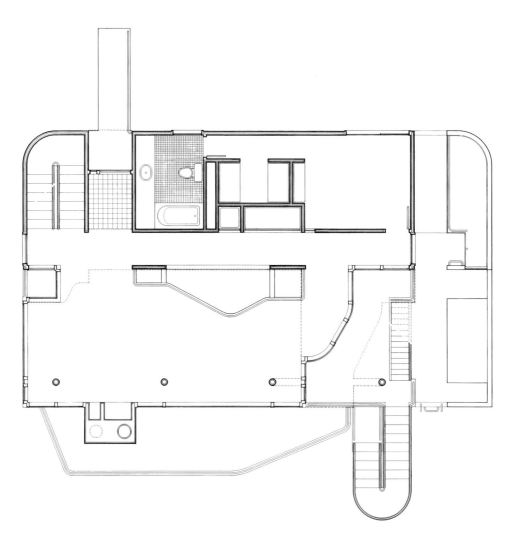

Upper floor plan

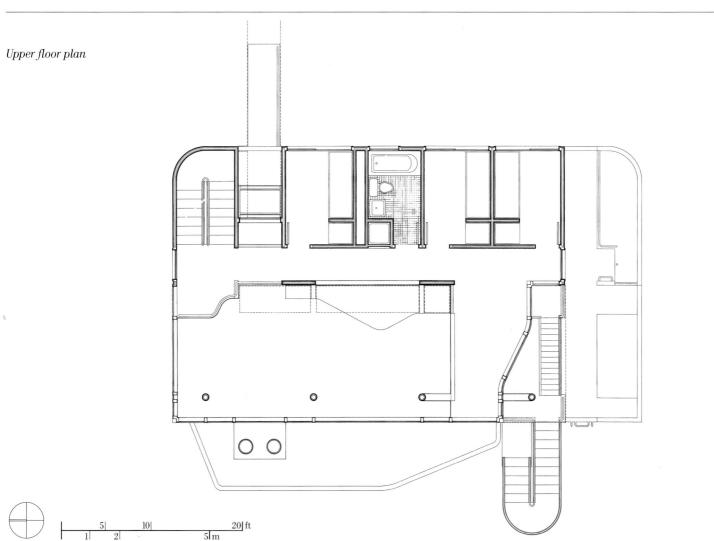

5| 10| 20| ft
1| 2| 5|m

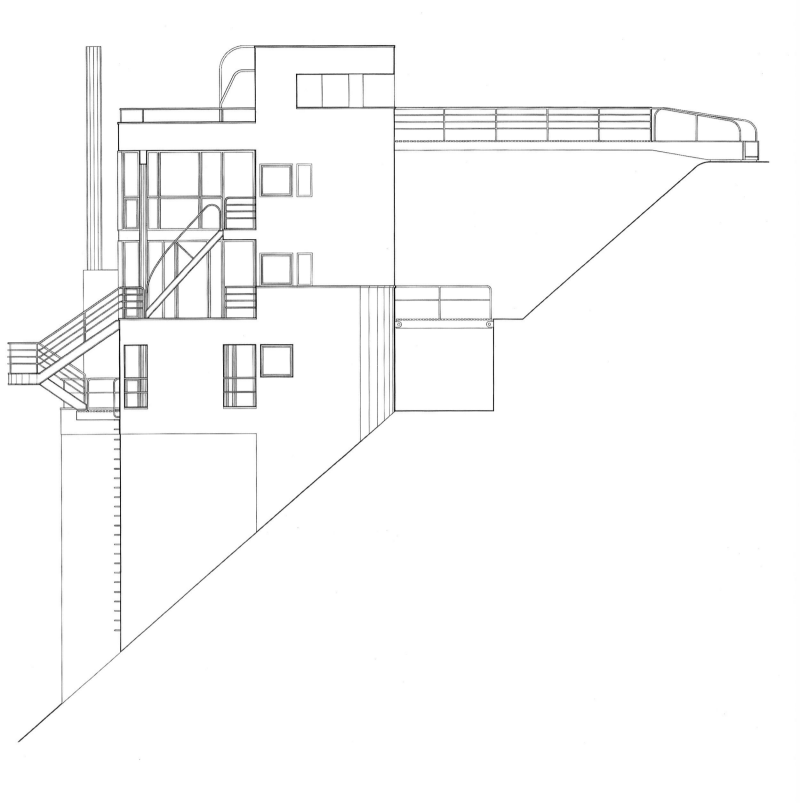

Olivetti Branch Office Prototype
1971

In 1971 the Olivetti Corporation asked Meier to design four buildings for its North American operations. The Italian business-machine manufacturer was one of the first companies to commission Meier to translate their aesthetic and culture into architecture. Fitting with Olivetti's modern designs, Meier produced a series of buildings that embody industrial process, prefabrication, mass production, and on-site assembly. It is with these projects (as well as the Fredonia Health and Physical Education Building and the Bronx Developmental Center) that Meier's work underwent a tectonic change—the development of a modular production— stimulated in part by the necessity for a systemic approach. Meier developed two prototypes for branch offices that were planned for thirteen cities in the United States. These designs concisely answer the commission's requirements: to have an identifiable image while being adaptable to various sites, flexible in size, capable of expansion, and self-contained. Demonstrations and sales took place in a curved glass room, while service and administrative functions were located in the enclosed half of the building. Meier expanded this vision for a headquarters building in Fairfax, Virginia. One writer compared Meier's Olivetti work with that of "an archeologist excavating and rebuilding [Le Corbusier's] Maison Stein." If Le Corbusier is an obvious influence, Meier also alludes to Alvar Aalto's Baker House in a fourth building he designed for Olivetti—a training-center dormitory in Tarrytown, New York, whose form echoes the curving topography of its sloping hill site above the Hudson River. While never built, these designs strongly informed Meier's subsequent work.

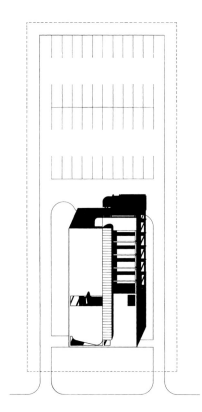

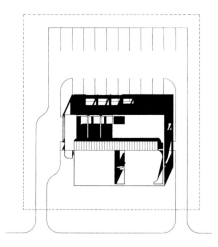

Prototypical site conditions

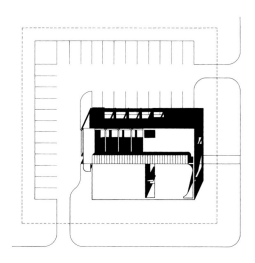

66

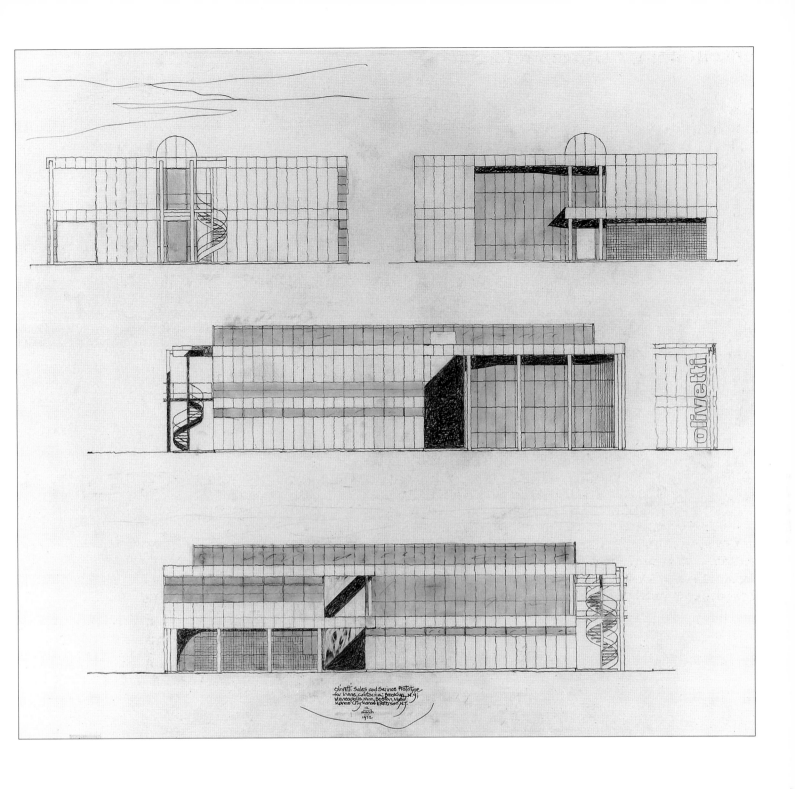

olivetti Sales and Service Prototype
for Irvine, California; Brooklyn, N.Y;
Minneapolis, Minn, Boston, Mass;
Kansas City, Kansas & Paterson, N.J.
12
March
1972

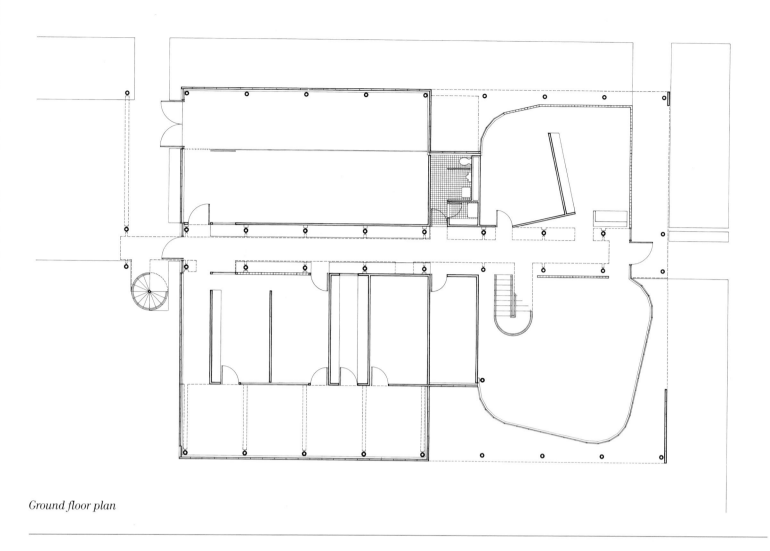

Ground floor plan

Upper floor plan

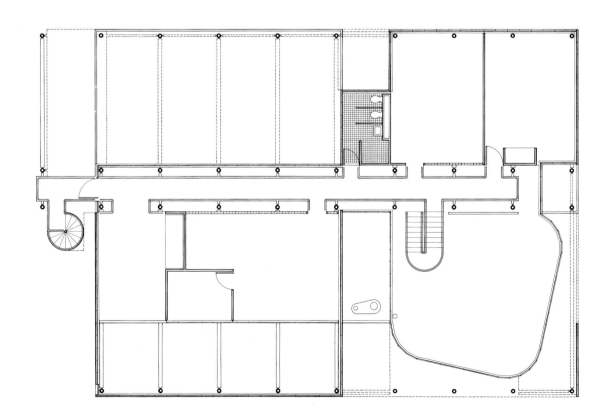

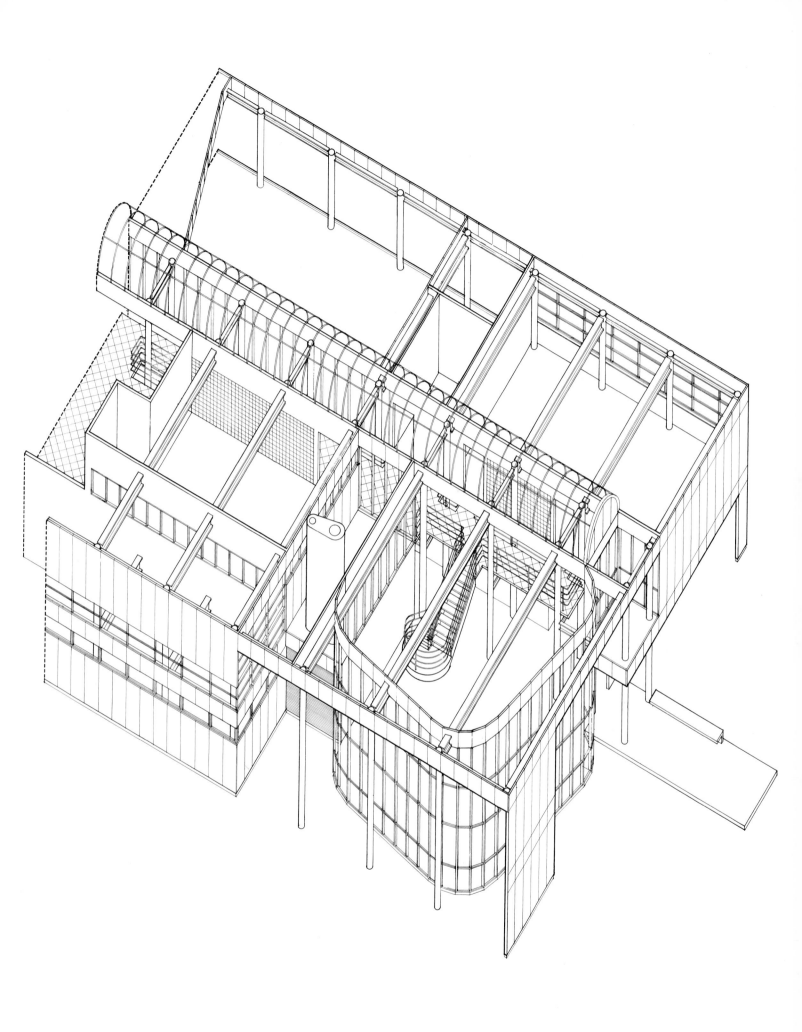

The Atheneum

New Harmony, Indiana
1975–1979

The Atheneum represents Meier's fullest expression
of architectural promenade as plan generator. The irregular
building form results from an internalized path as well as
shifted grids and abstracted references to the site and history
of New Harmony. The town was home to two utopian
communities: George Rapp's Harmony Society, founded
in 1815, and the Owenites, led by British social reformer
Robert Owen, in 1825. The tradition of enlightenment
continues in later buildings: Philip Johnson's Roofless Church
and the Atheneum, a center for visitor orientation and cultural
events. Here the ethereality inherent in Meier's architecture
of whiteness and light becomes palpable. Although the
program is not explicitly spiritual, the Atheneum embodies
the spirit of the place. Located on a plain near the banks of
the Wabash River, the building is situated on a raised podium;
during the flooding season, it suggests Rapp's "boatload
of knowledge," which brought settlers to New Harmony.
While contrasting with the town's rough-hewn fences and
clapboard houses, the radiant porcelain-paneled building
is woven into the community by design and use. Multiple
routes are incorporated into the building, including a long
pathway that extends through the Atheneum and connects
the riverbank to the town. Central to the concept is an
internal ramp that directs movement through the building.
Ascending the ramp, visitors travel through exhibition spaces,
up and around the building, up to rooftop observation decks,
and then down to enter the town itself.

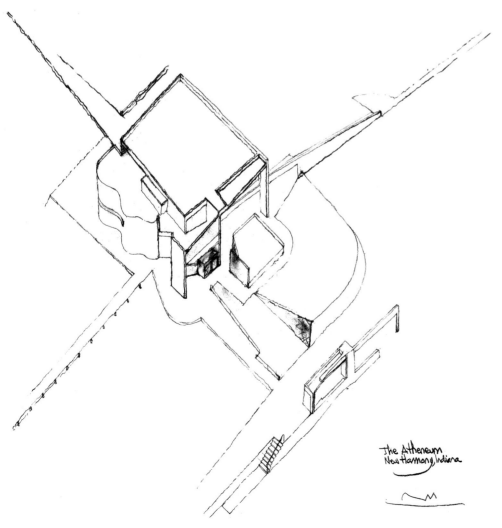

The Atheneum
New Harmony, Indiana

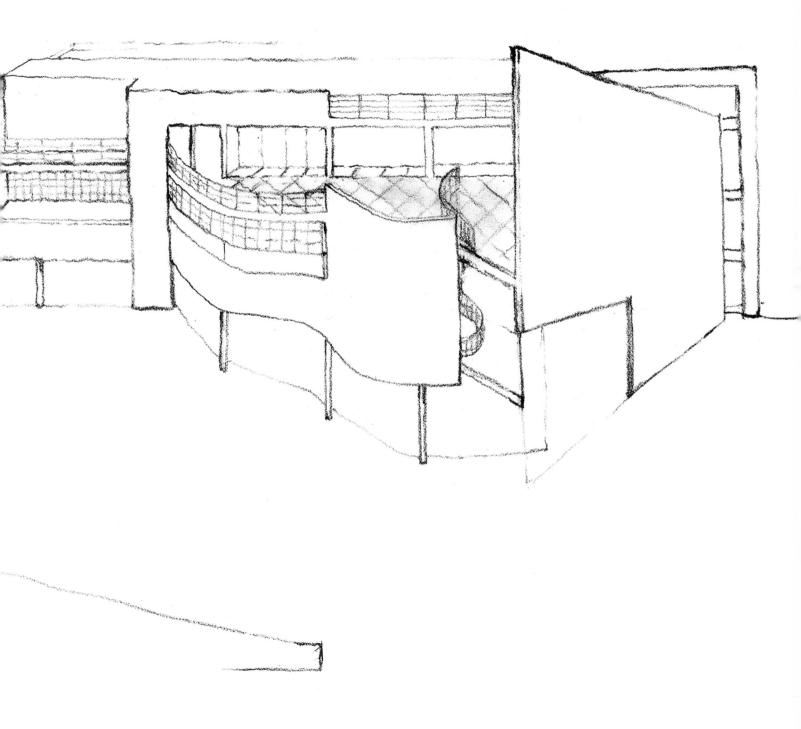

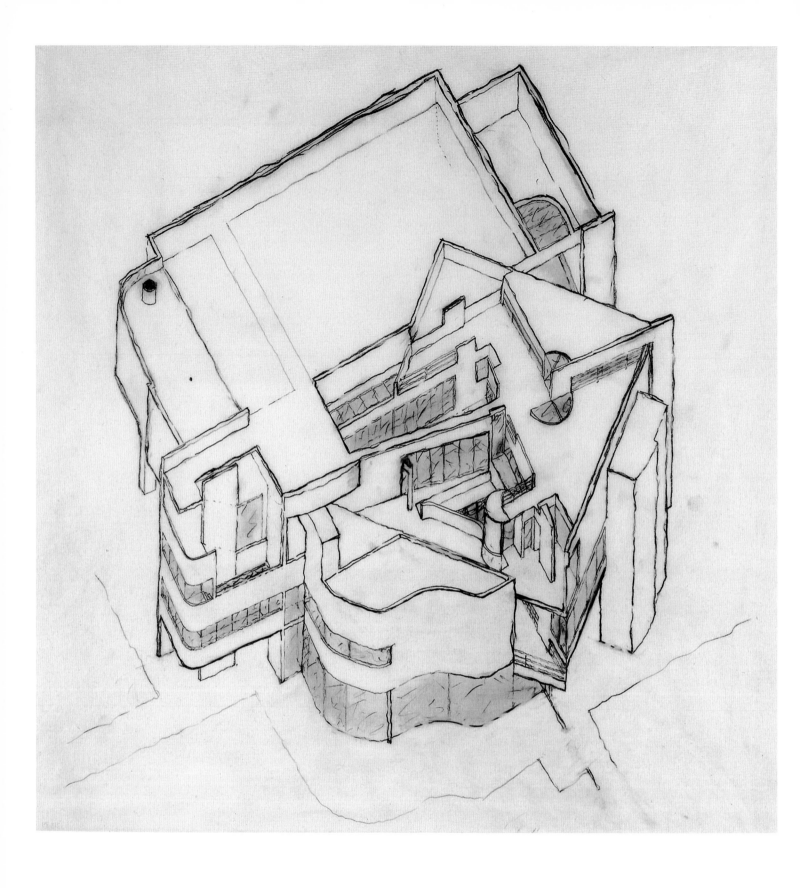

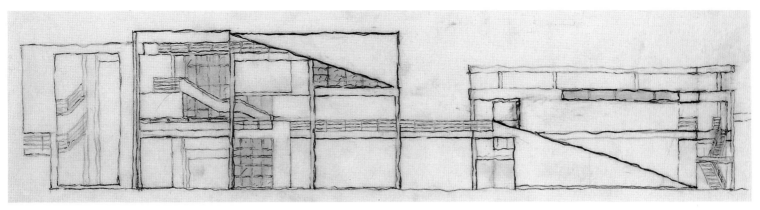

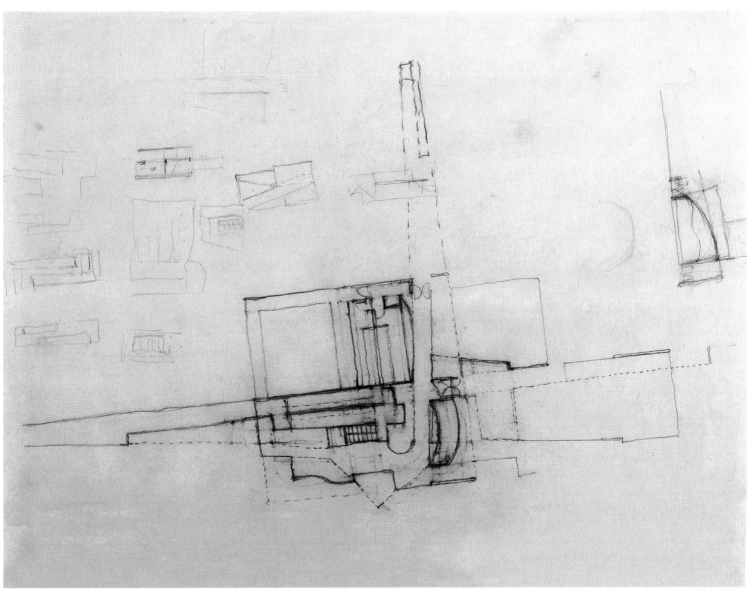

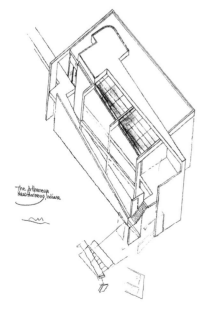

The Atheneum
New Harmony, Indiana

75

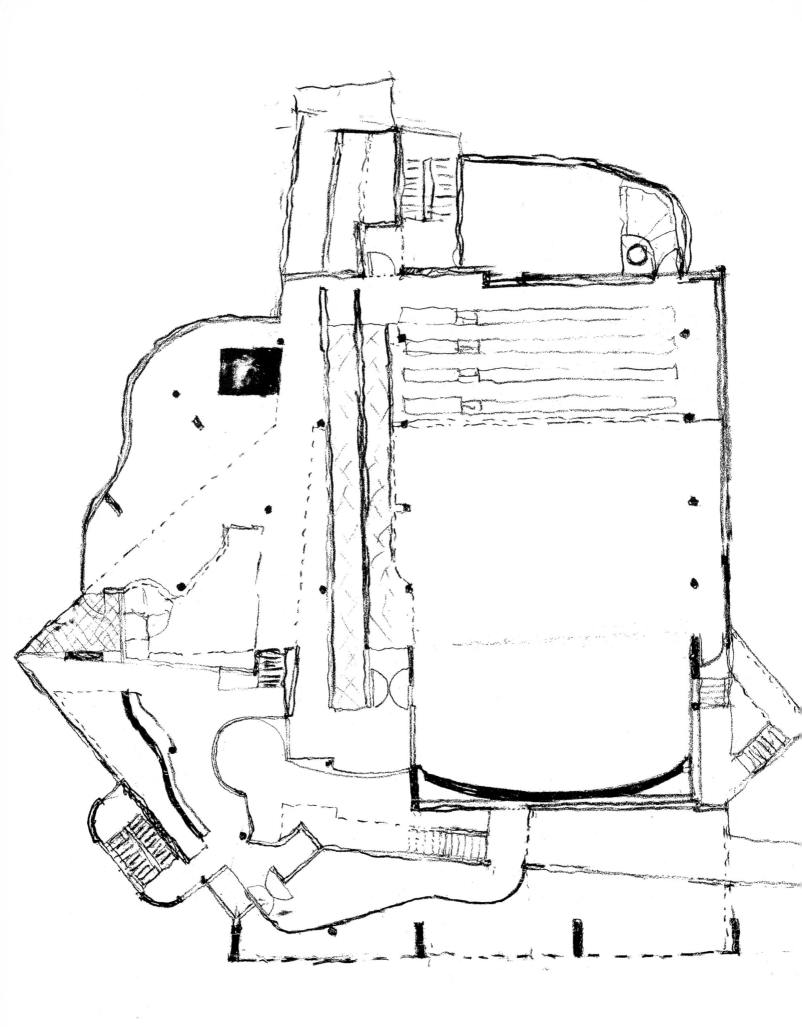

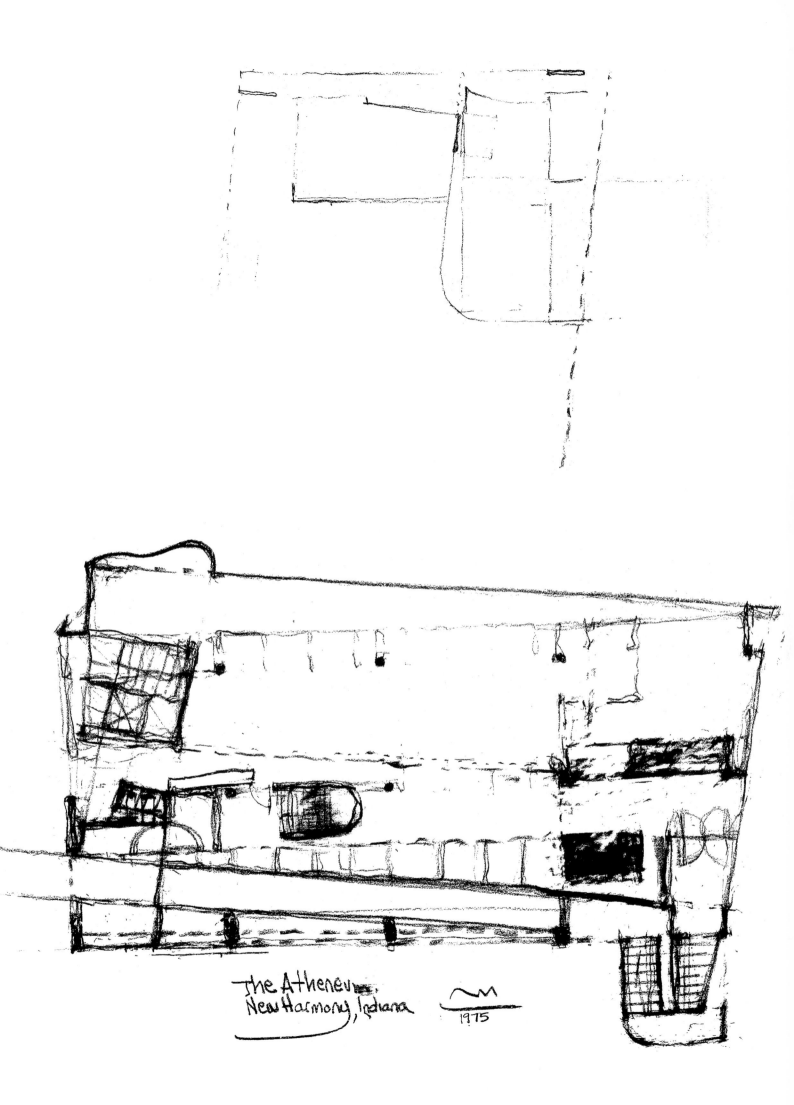

The Atheneum,
New Harmony, Indiana
1975

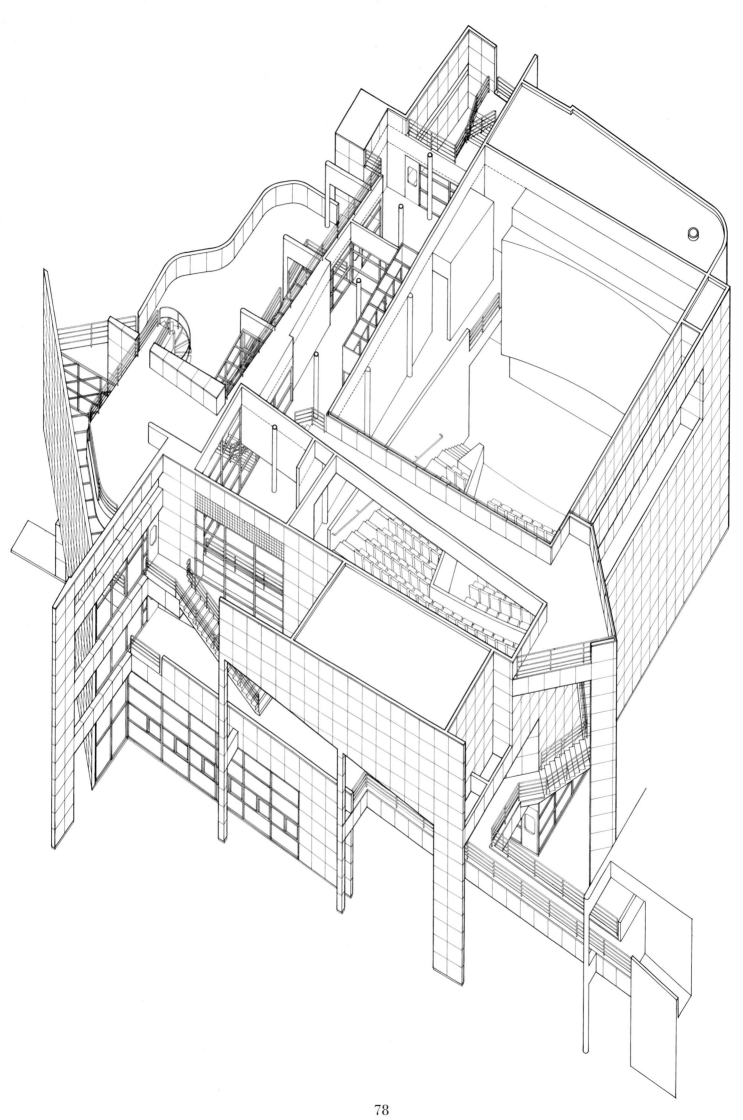

Ground floor plan

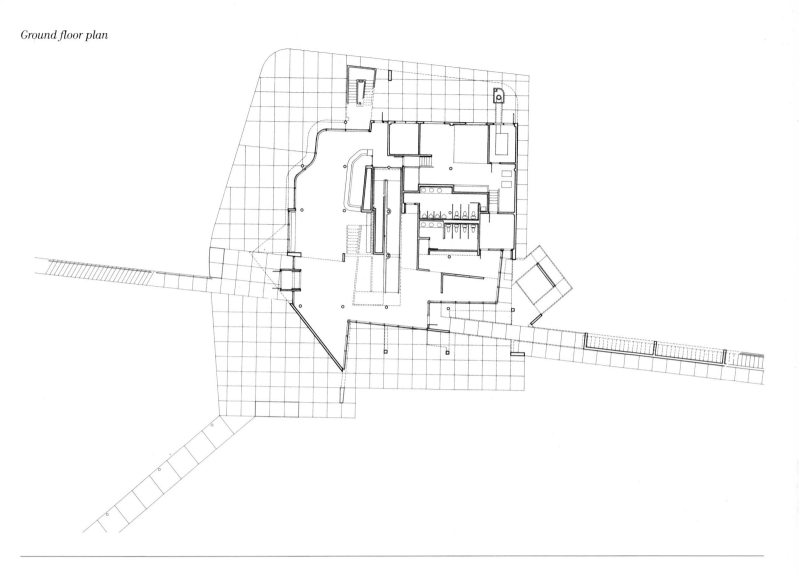

Second floor plan

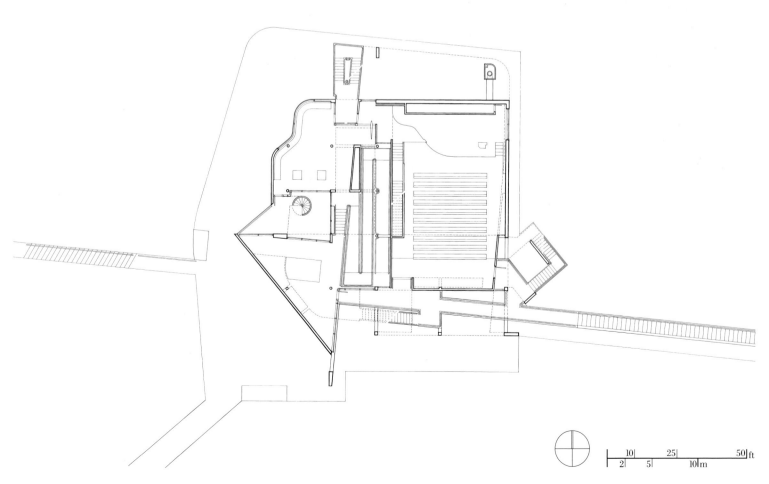

The Hartford Seminary

Hartford, Connecticut
1978–1981

Meier rigorously applied his evolving formal language
to signify the program of the Hartford Seminary. Avoiding
conventional religious imagery, the gleaming white building
celebrates clarity and light. Set back from the residential
street by a great lawn, the interdenominational theological
center comprises classrooms, workrooms, a large meeting
room, library, chapel, and offices. As conceived by Meier,
the seminary is arranged according to its dual roles
of scholarship and contemplation and of public outreach
and service. The L-shaped plan separates public spaces
from more cloistered areas intended for quiet study.
Throughout the building are the architect's characteristic
white porcelain-enamel panels. These metal panels
and the building's windows are based on a three-foot-square
module, and both are incrementally sized according to
the horizontal and vertical proportions of individual spaces.
The resulting composition of multiple grids includes
large planes of glass block, also scaled appropriately
to the module. The building integrates many signature
Meier details: glass-block screen walls enclosing interior
staircases, a main entrance encased in a cubelike receptacle,
and a freestanding wall plane that abuts an outdoor stair.
For the chapel, he created a minimal, abstract space as the
background for a small cross. Light filters through a hidden
skylight fitted with a panel of blue glass and casts a hint
of color over the otherwise unadorned back wall.

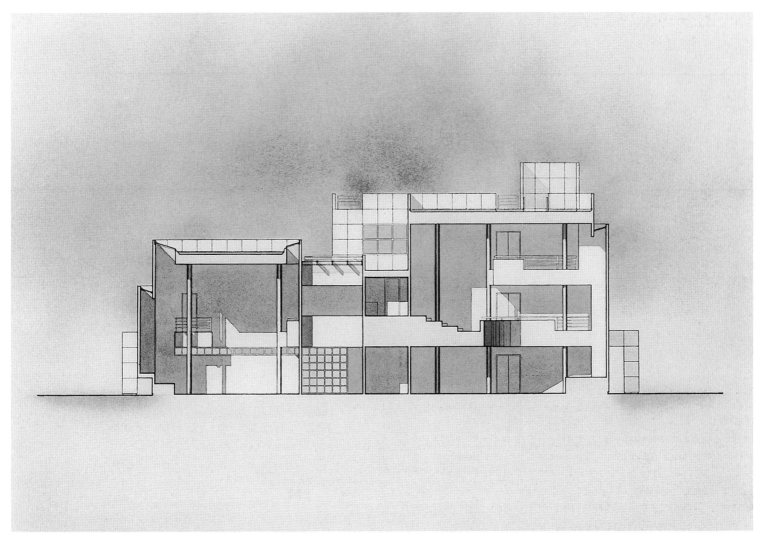

Cross section through chapel and meeting room facing south

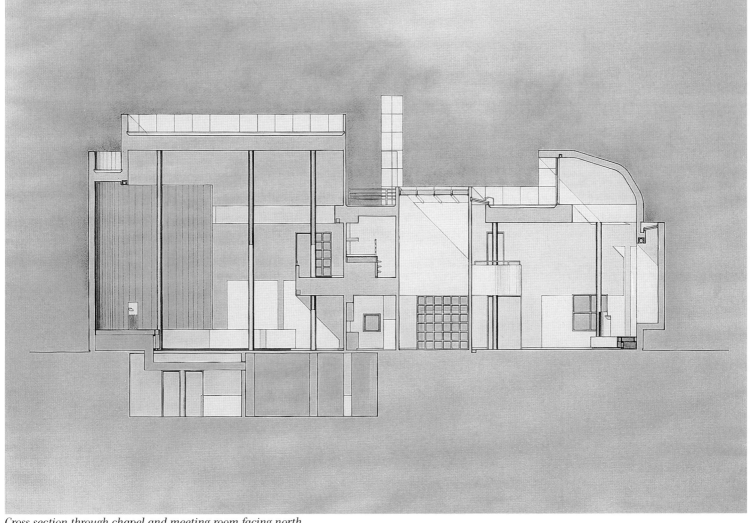

Cross section through chapel and meeting room facing north

East elevation

West elevation

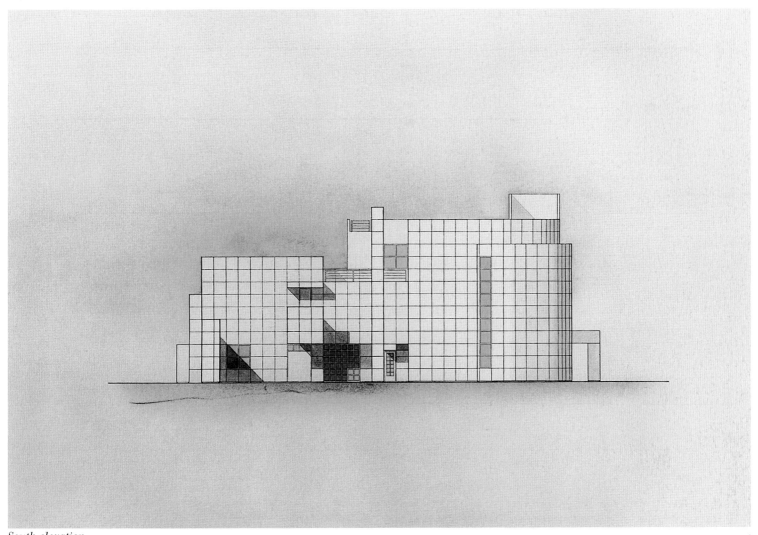

South elevation

North elevation

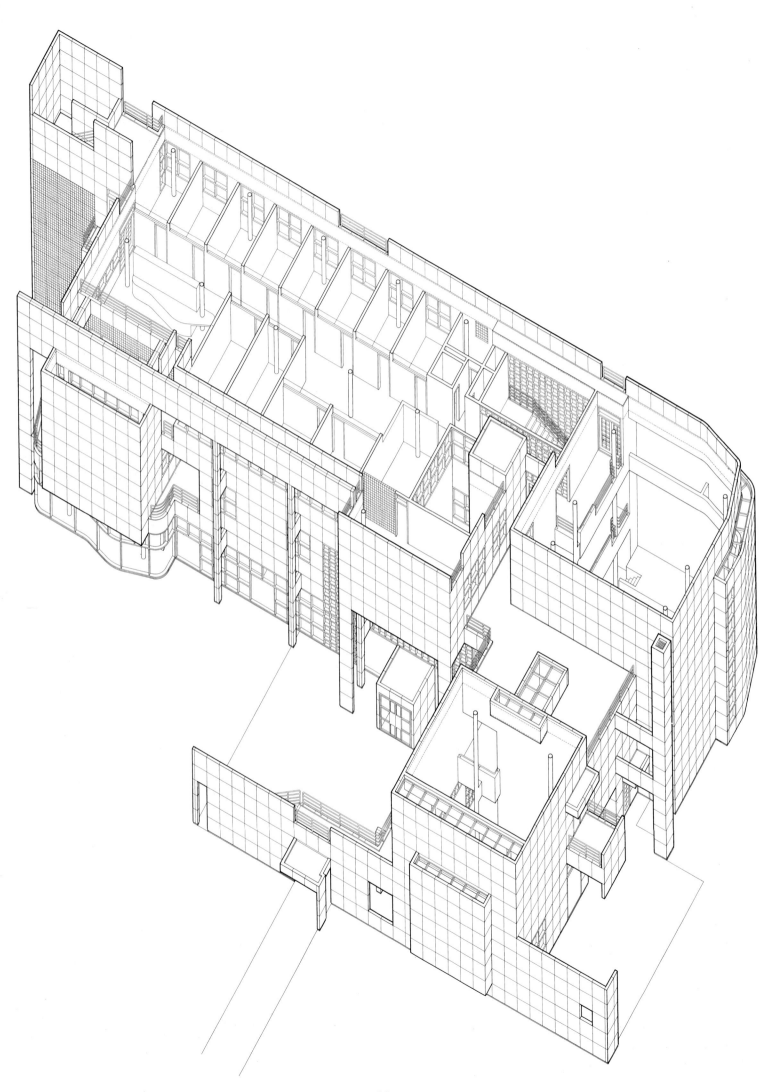

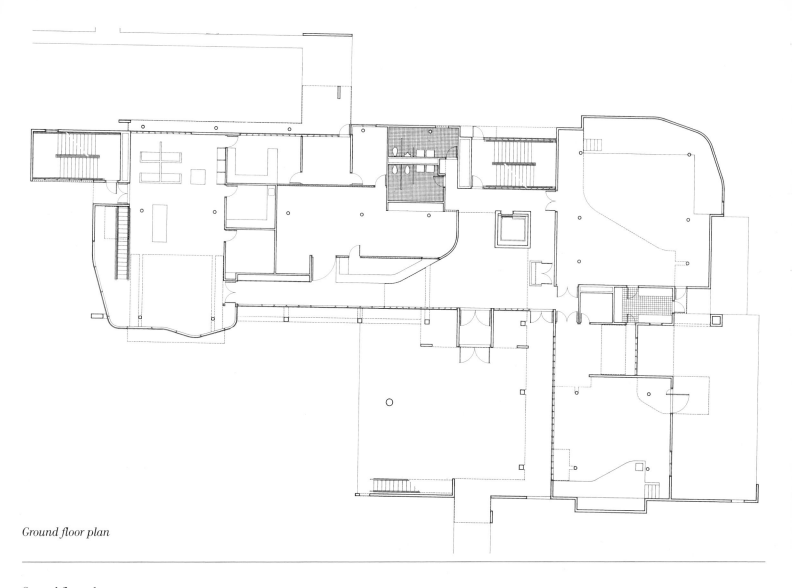

Ground floor plan

Second floor plan

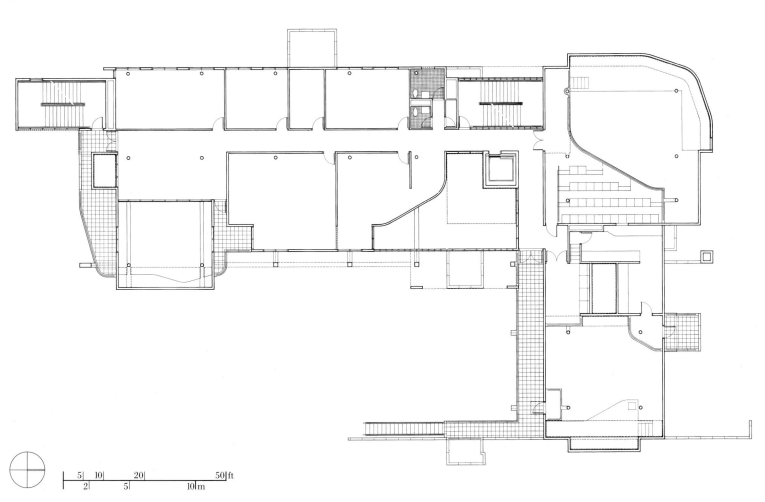

5| 10| 20| 50|ft
2| 5| 10|m

Museum for the Decorative Arts

Frankfurt am Main, Germany
1979–1985

The Museum for the Decorative Arts marks an important
turning point for Meier. Significant as both the first of his
high-profile European projects and the first of his major art
museums, it presaged a new compositional complexity
and contextual richness in his oeuvre. Crucial to the project
is how Meier works the new decorative-arts museum into
the fabric of Frankfurt's Museumsufer and nearby residential
neighborhood. Pathways pass crosswise through the plan,
bringing pedestrians and cyclists through the building
and adjacent park. Architectural elements—suggesting
fragments of classical ruins, gated archways, and follies—
are threaded into the park, and greenery transforms
the open screens on the west facade into a trellis.
The new building is also meticulously integrated into
its immediate site, which includes the museum's previous
venue, the Villa Metzler. Meier based the organization grid
and module on the cubelike dimensions of the nineteenth-
century neoclassical palazzo and linked it by a second-story
bridge to the new building. A secondary grid parallels
the angle of the nearby riverbank. The dynamic of these
overlapping grids, rotated 3.5 degrees, creates a visceral
sensation as the perspectives unfold. The museum in essence
becomes a machine of the promenade. Ramps figure
prominently in the plan, initiating a fixed procession
that takes the visitor alternately through galleries and
around green courtyards as the history of decorative arts is
traversed—a circulation strategy that Meier returned to
for the Getty Museum.

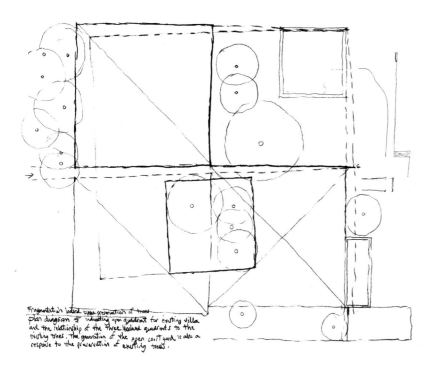

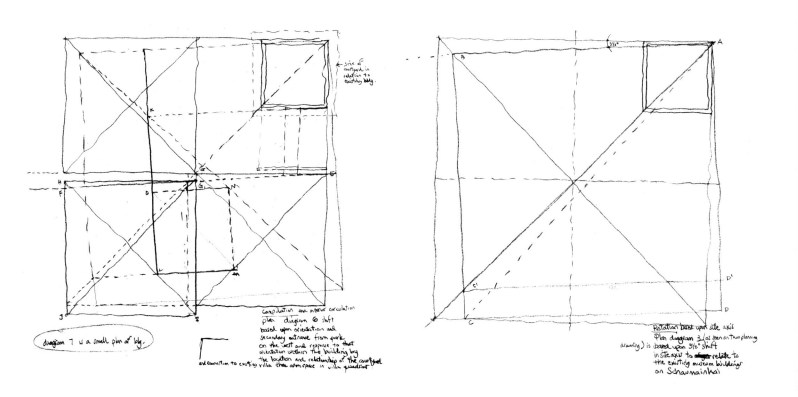

site of
courtyard in
relation to
existing bldg.

Compilation and interior circulation
plan diagram 6 shift
based upon orientation and
secondary entrance from park
on the west and respone to that
orientation within the building by
the location and relationship of the courtyard
and connection to existing villa thru open space in villa quadrant

diagram 7 is a small plan of bldg.

Rotation based upon site axis
Plan diagram 3 (as seen on template drawing
drawing) is based upon 3½° shift
in site axis to relate to
the existing museum building
on Schaumainkai

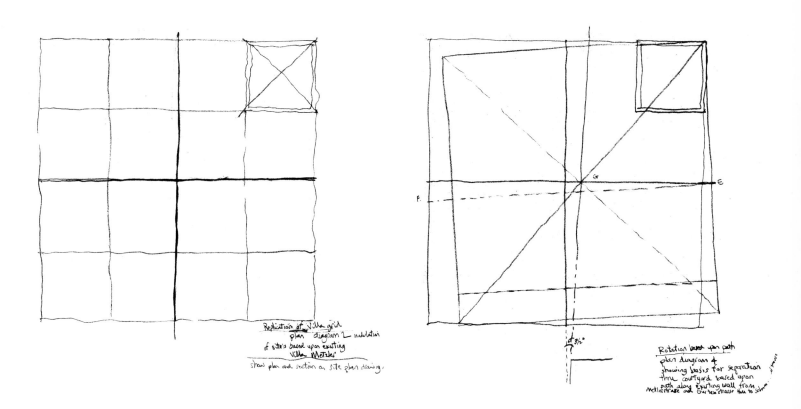

Replication of Villa grid
plan diagram 2 modulation
of site's based upon existing
Villa Metzler
show plan and section on site plan drawing.

Rotation based upon path
plan diagram 4
showing basis for separation
thru courtyard based upon
path along existing wall from
Metlerstrasse and Garten strasse thru to Schau...

at 3½°

Facade study of Villa Metzler

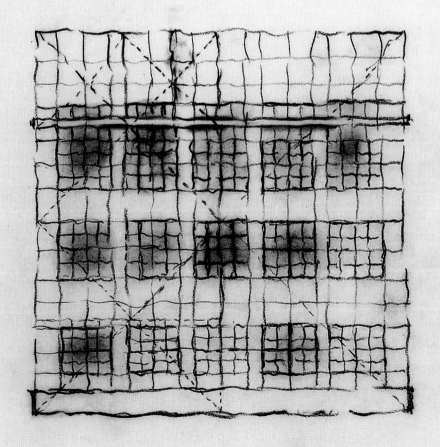

Facade study of new building

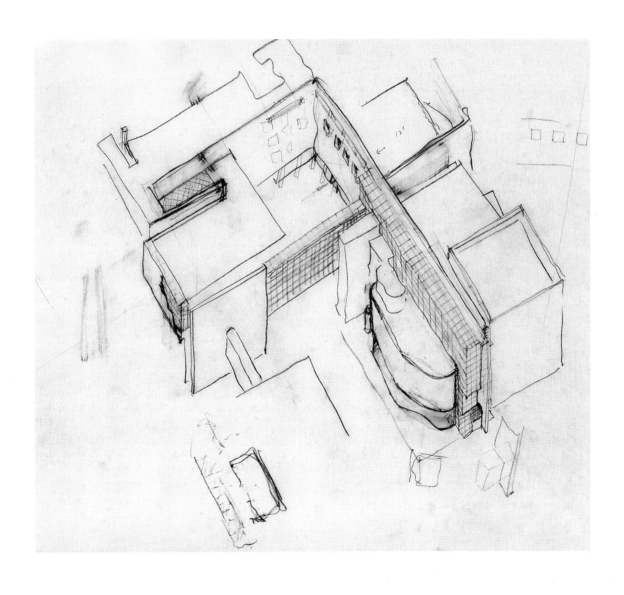

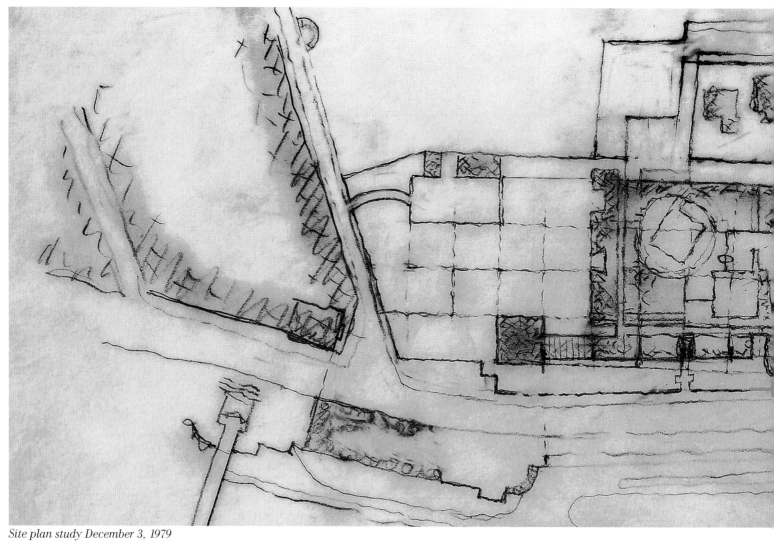

Site plan study December 3, 1979

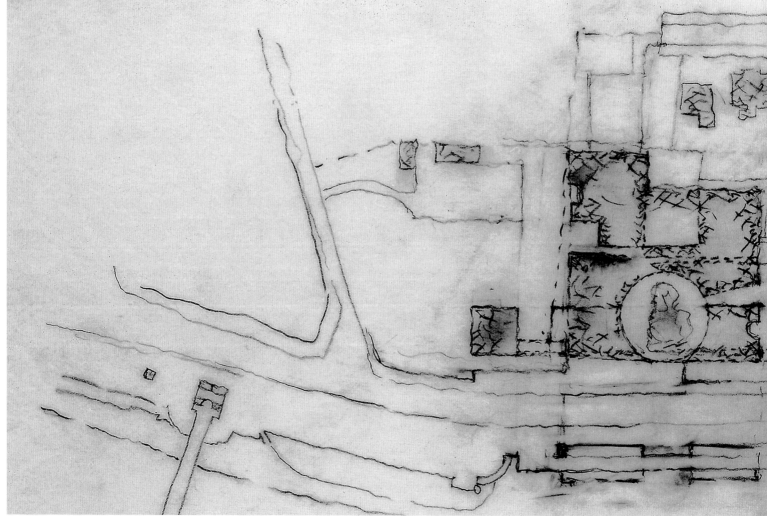

Site plan study December 4, 1979

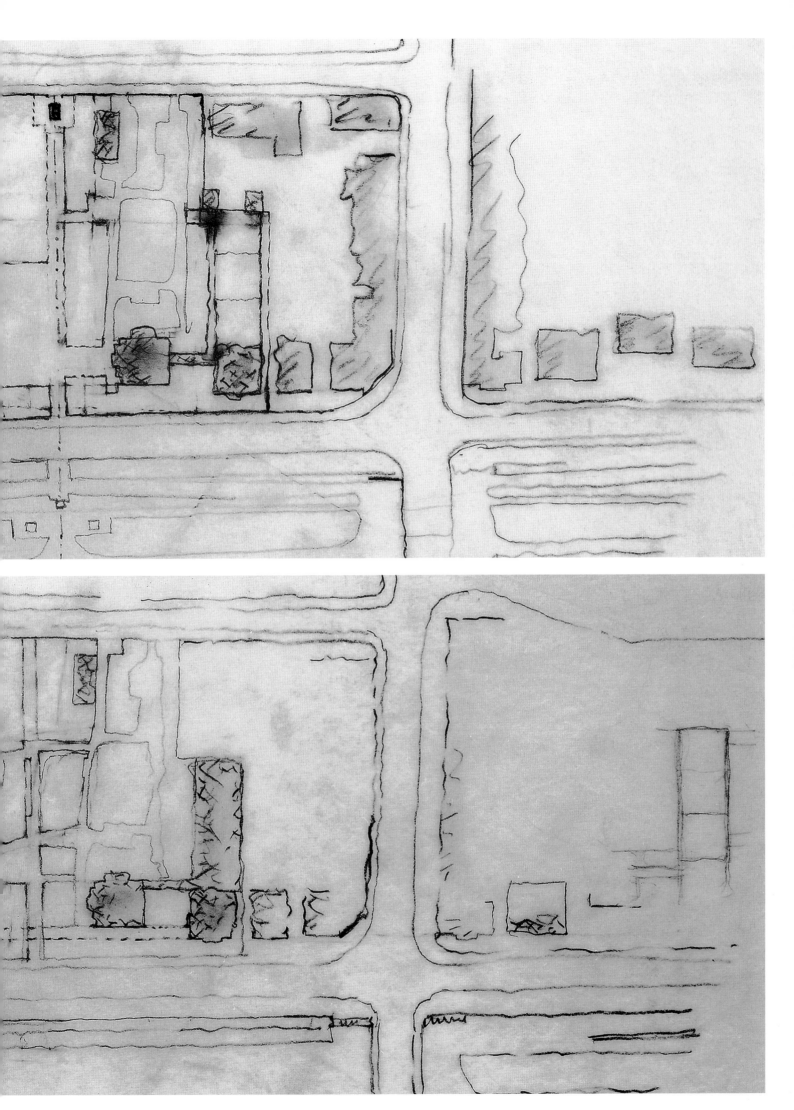

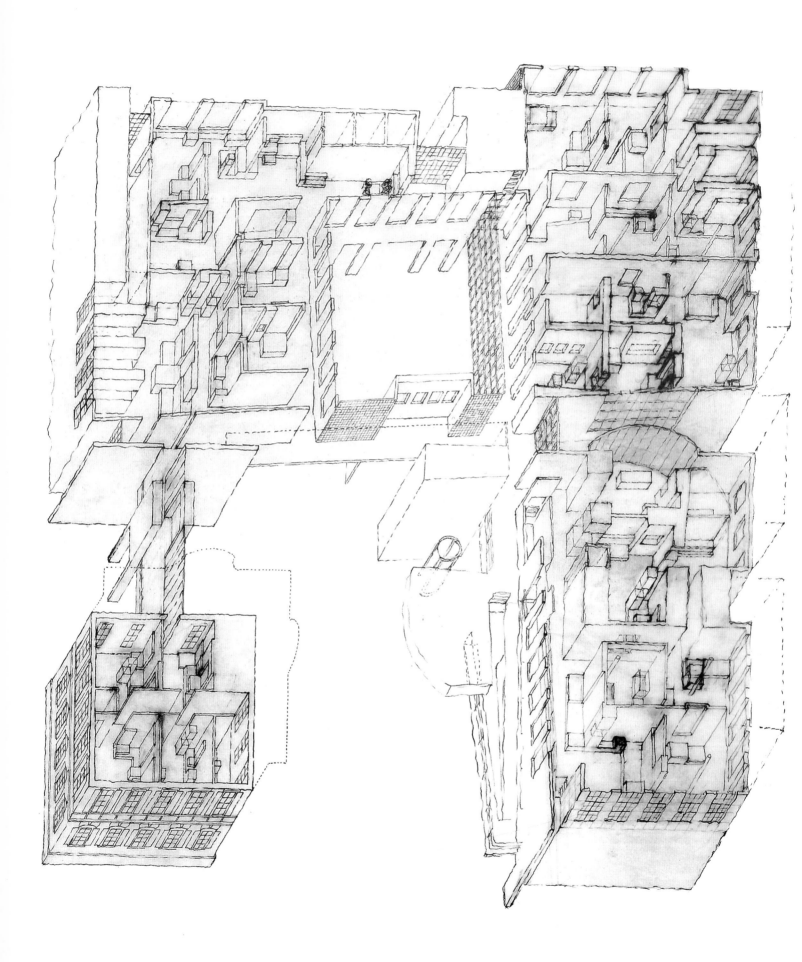

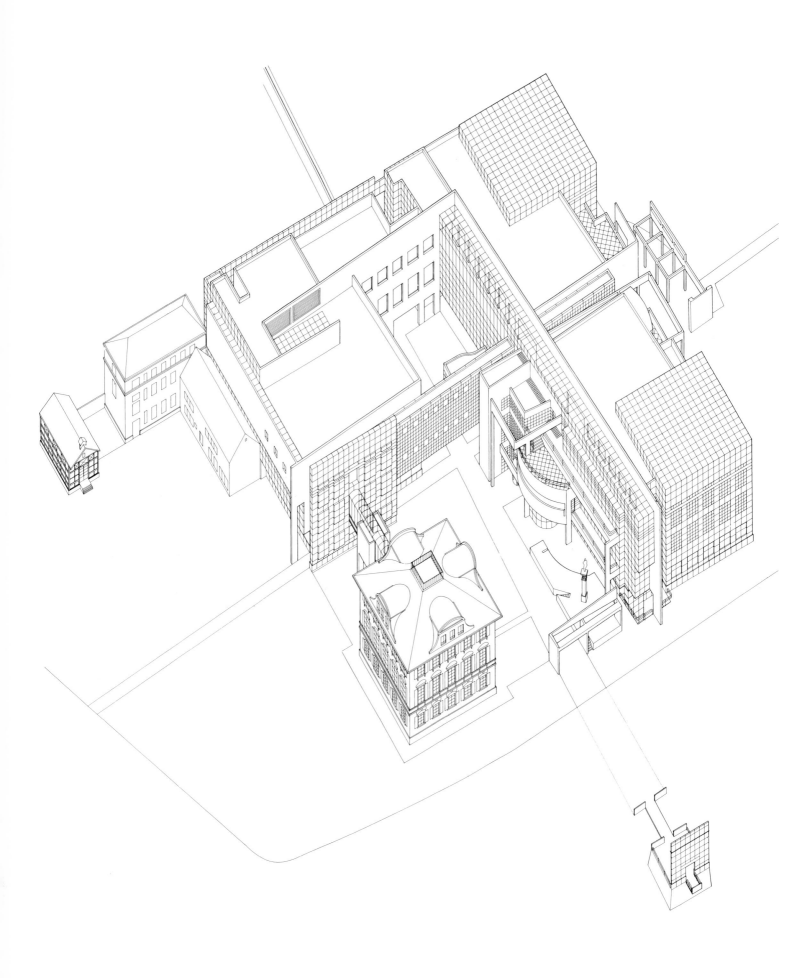

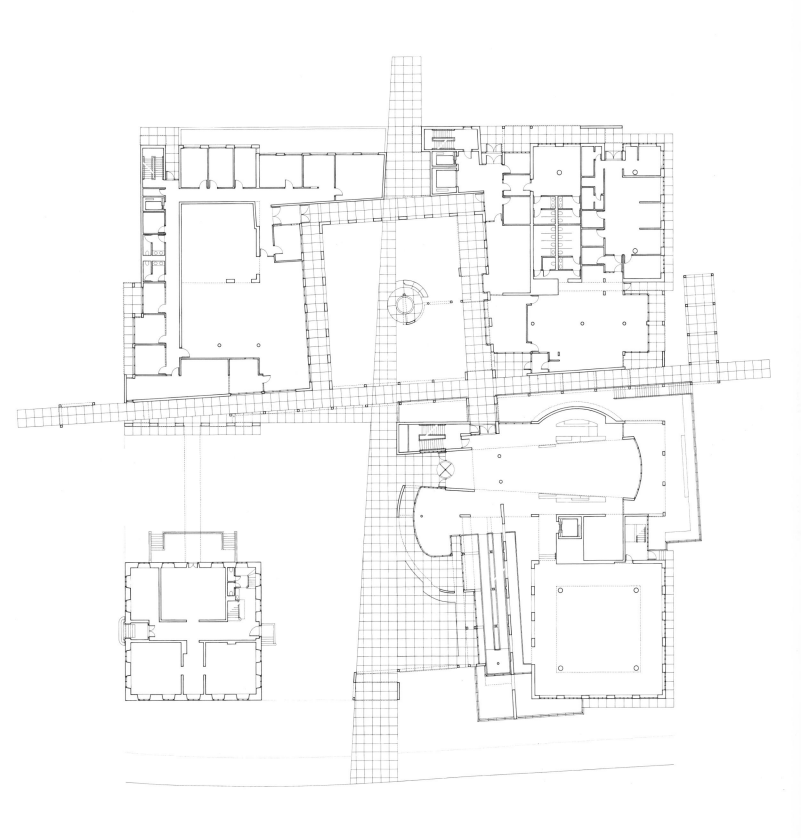

High Museum of Art

Atlanta, Georgia
1980–1983

The High Museum of Art solidified Meier's reputation
as a leading museum architect. Although he received the
commission largely on the basis of the design for the
Frankfurt Museum for the Decorative Arts, construction of
the High Museum was completed first. Its design continues
the examination of circulation and compositional systems
evident in Frankfurt, this time focused around a main atrium.
The High Museum, unlike the Frankfurt museum, makes
minimal contextual reference to its site; instead it stands
apart from its surroundings as a fantastical object. Its real
subject is what constitutes an ideal museum for art. The result
is Meier's homage to and critique of Frank Lloyd Wright's
Guggenheim Museum in New York. Both museums feature
an atrium with a circulation ramp. At the High Museum, the
ramp connects floors by looping around a convex wall that
follows the curve of the exterior wall. Here, however,
Meier extracted the exhibition component from the ramp;
circulation and gallery spaces are distinct. The wedge-shaped
atrium is inscribed into one quadrant of the building's parti,
while galleries comprise the three remaining quadrants.
Without art and its attendant requirements, the atrium space
is a grand mechanism of light and shadow. The spokes of the
skylight produce a play of light on all surfaces, spreading down
over multiple panels on the walls of the atrium. Windows
along the curved wall create a perforated rhythm of color
from outside and provide visitors with framed city views.

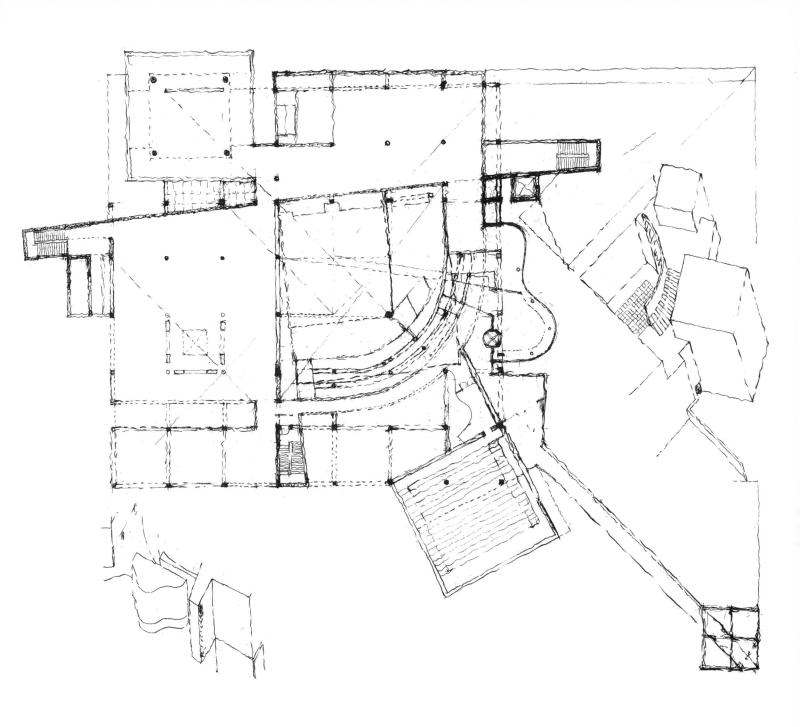

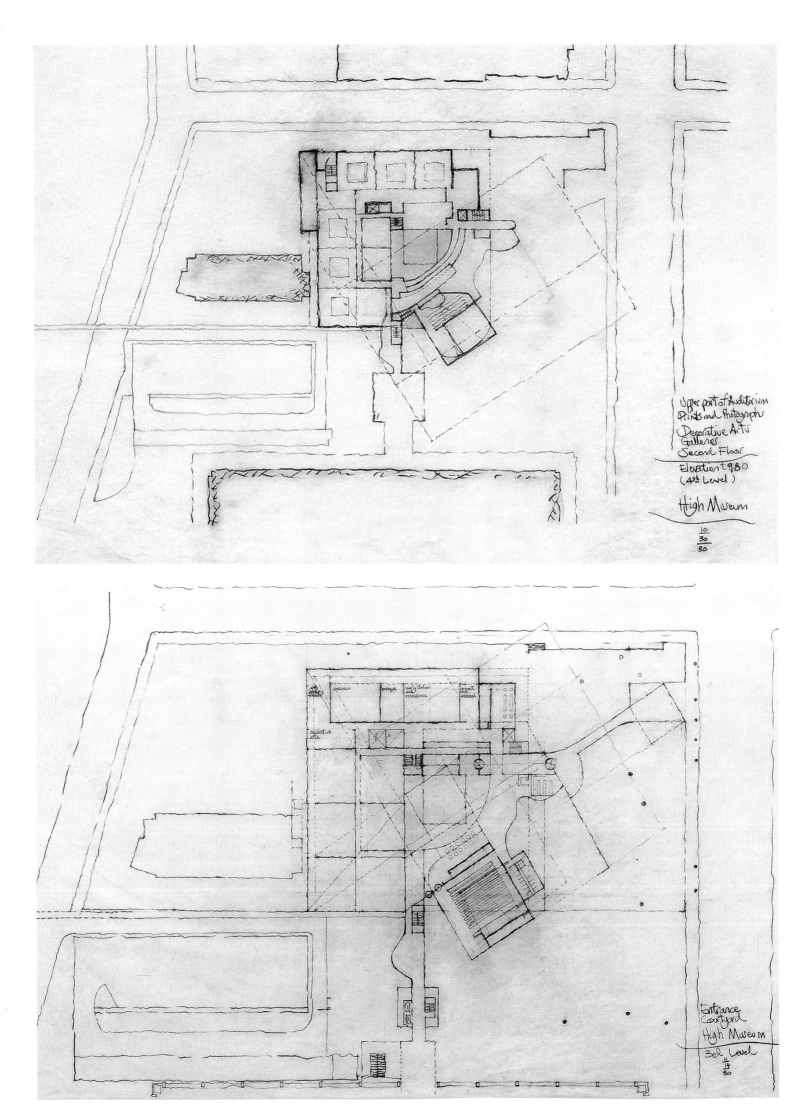

Upper part of Auditorium
Prints and Photographs
Decorative Arts
Galleries
Second Floor
Elevation ± 980
(4th Level)

High Museum

10
30
80

Entrance
Courtyard
High Museum
3rd Level
11
14
80

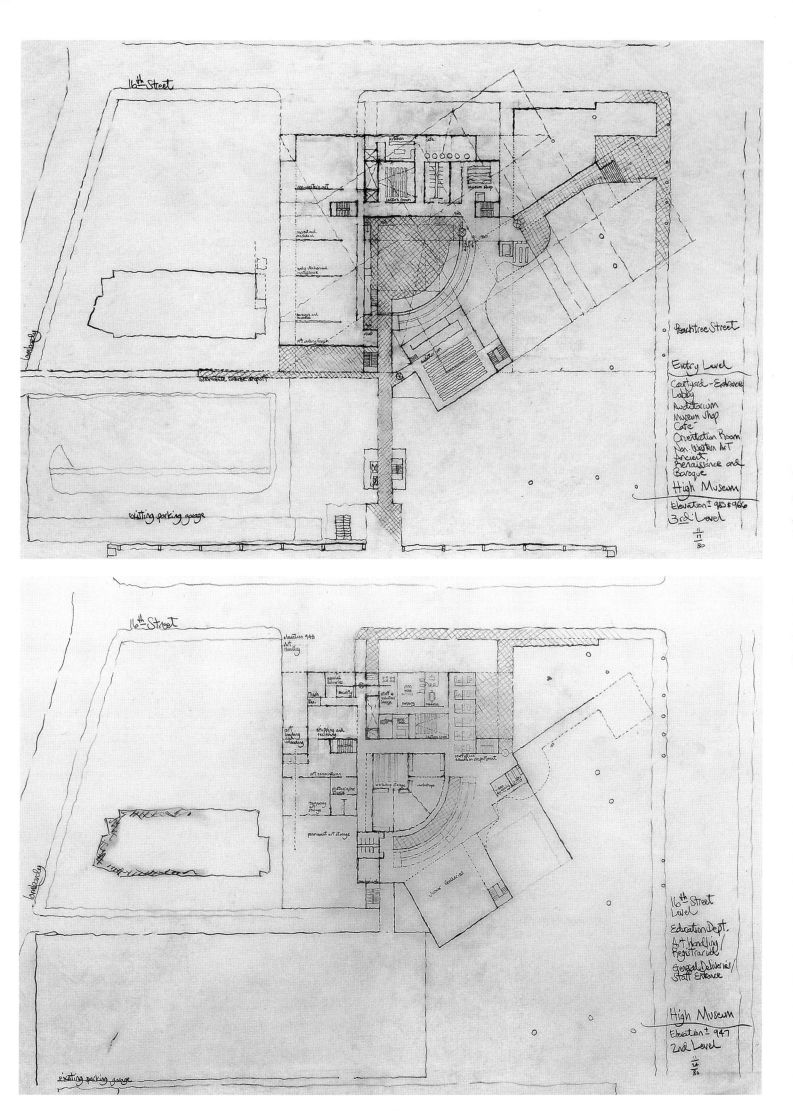

16th Street

Peachtree Street

Entry Level
Courtyard - Entrance
Lobby
Auditorium
Museum Shop
Café
Orientation Room
Non-Western Art
Ancient
Renaissance and
Baroque
High Museum
Elevation ± 960 ± 966
3rd Level
11/17/80

existing parking garage

16th Street

16th Street
Level

Education Dept.

Art Handling/
Registrarial

General Deliveries/
Staff Entrance

High Museum
Elevation ± 947
2nd Level
11/14/80

existing parking garage

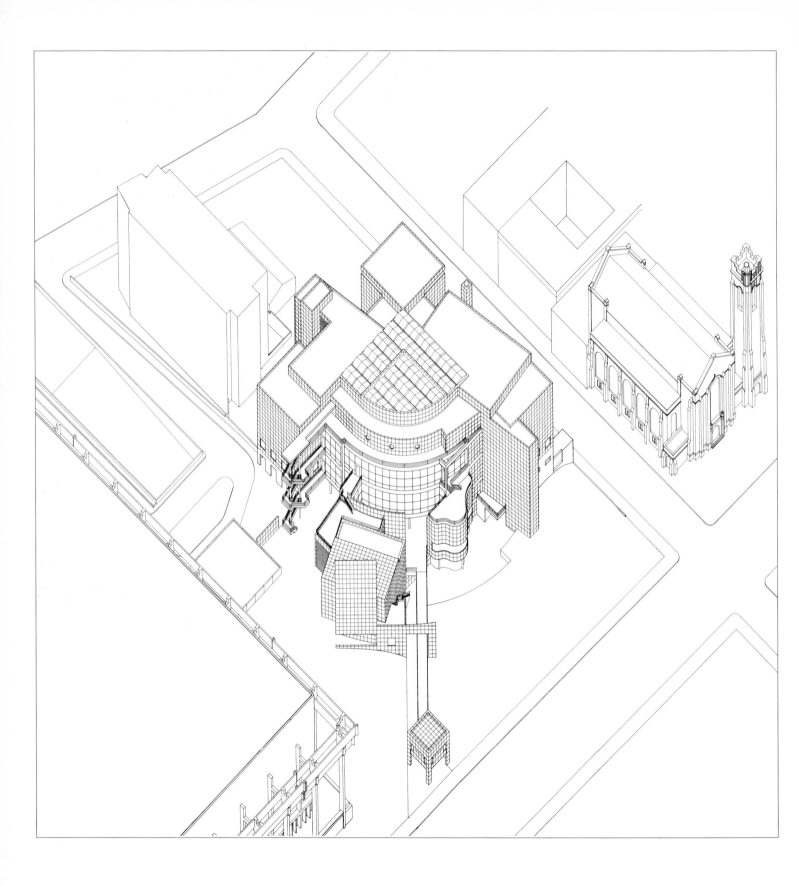

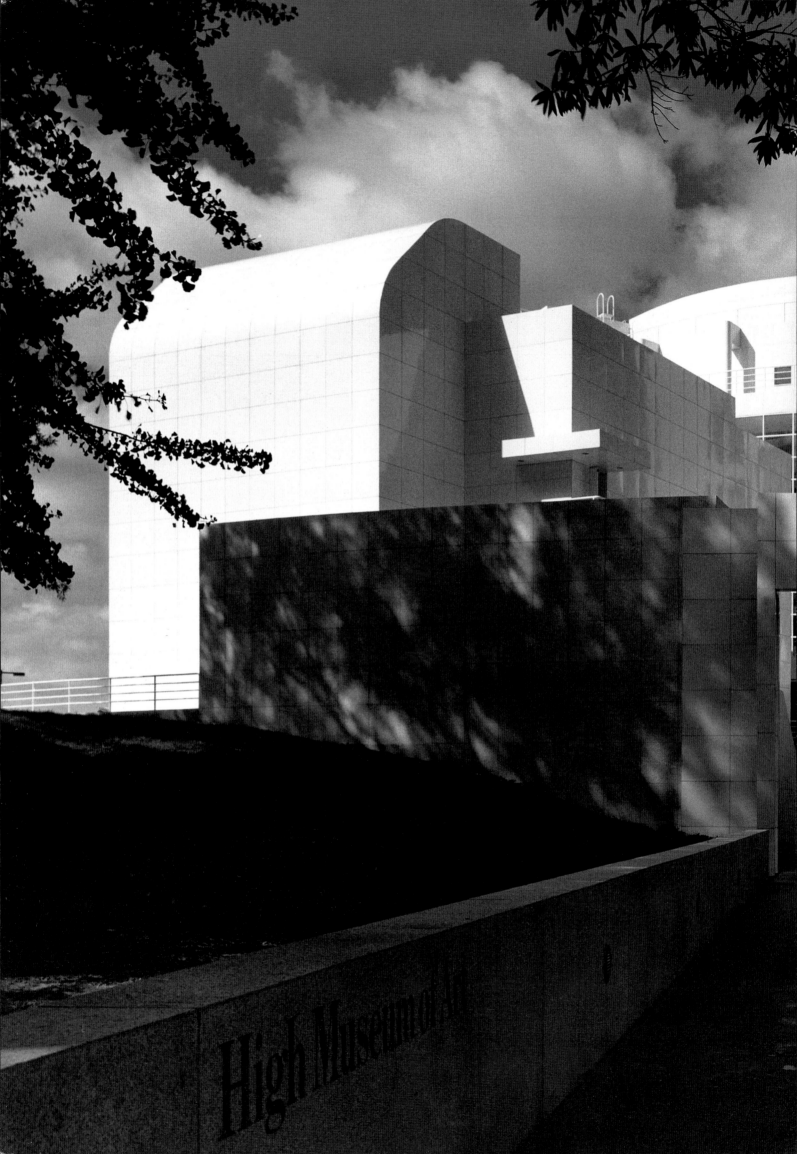

High Museum of Art

Siemens Corporate Headquarters

Munich, Germany
1983–1999

This project for a new corporate office building in the
historic center of Munich exemplifies the challenges central
to much of Meier's work in Europe since the 1980s:
how to confront issues of historical context, existing urban
fabric, and intervention of the new. For this commission
Meier designed a new centerpiece for a large office complex
that would link to the existing Siemens headquarters.
The focus of the design was grounded in planning issues
for both this project and the larger urban context. Meier's
formal strategies included integrating freestanding buildings
into a unified whole, forming a continuous street wall along
the Oskar-von-Miller Ring, creating four open courtyards,
and enhancing north-south pedestrian circulation through
the site with a new entry plaza. The diagrams for the
Siemens project reveal key elements of Meier's compositional
method—analysis of the geometries inherent in the urban
plan, the main components of the parti, the relationship
between project massing and existing context, and the
definition of the edge for the entire ensemble. Consistent with
Meier's later European work, the Siemens project (revised in
1990) both differs from and blends with the existing
architectural context. Here, his signification of the modern—
his particular palette of glass, steel, and aluminum panels—is
inflected through a building scale sympathetic to the urban
fabric; forms that allude to but do not imitate neighboring
architecture; and the use of stone.

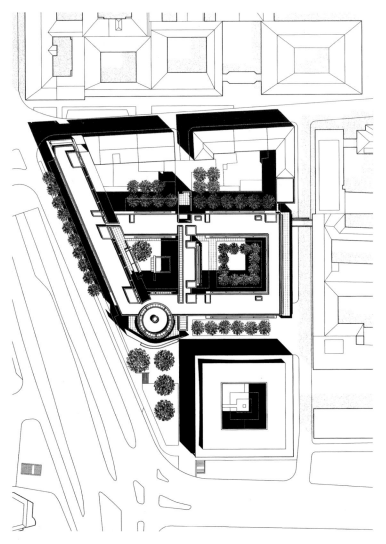

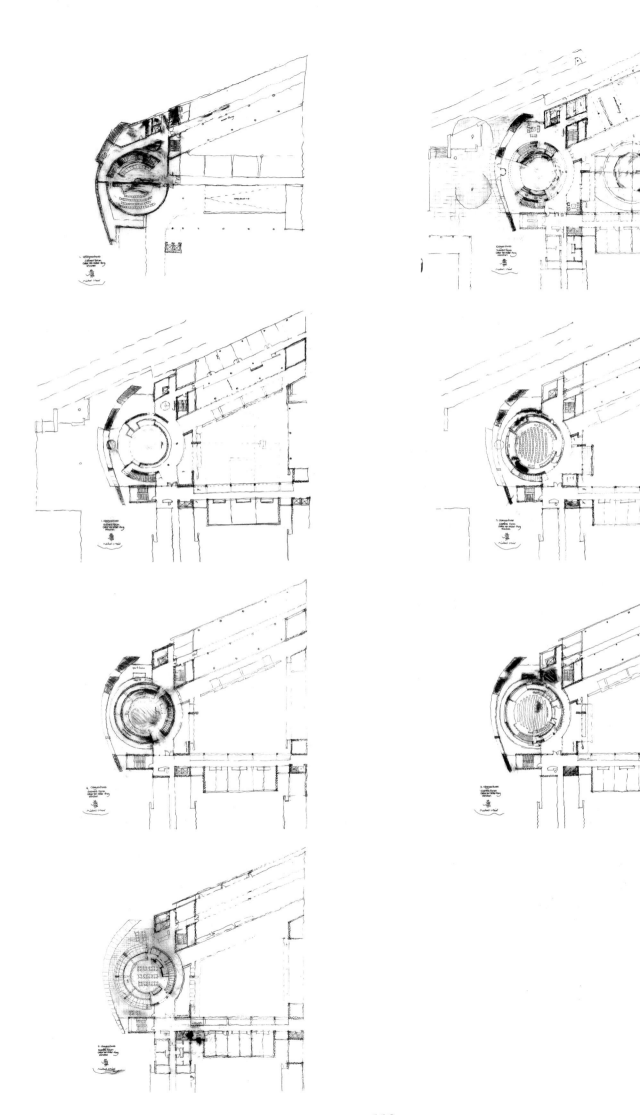

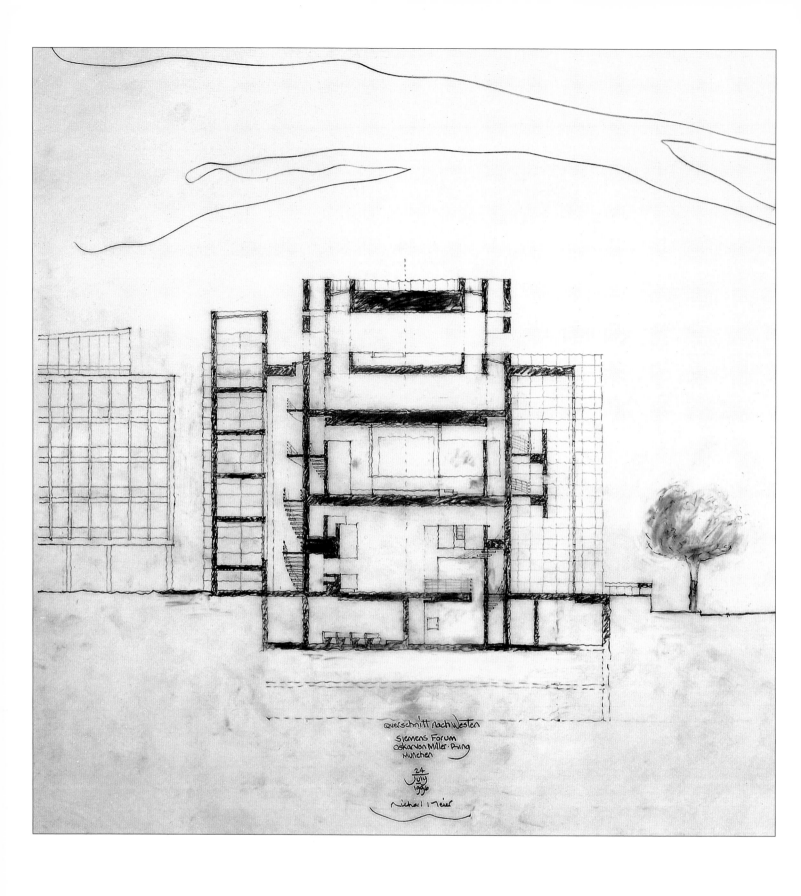

Querschnitt nach Westen

Siemens Forum
Oskar von Miller-Ring
München

24
July
1996

Michael Meier

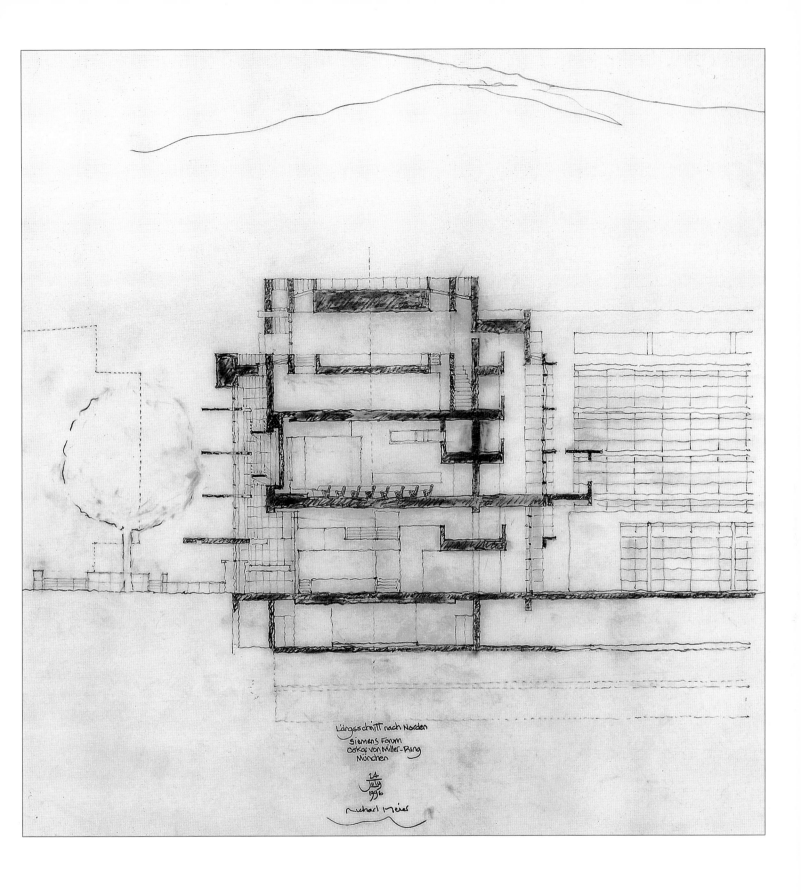

Längsschnitt nach Norden

Siemens Forum
Oskar von Miller-Ring
München

24
July
1996

Richard Meier

121

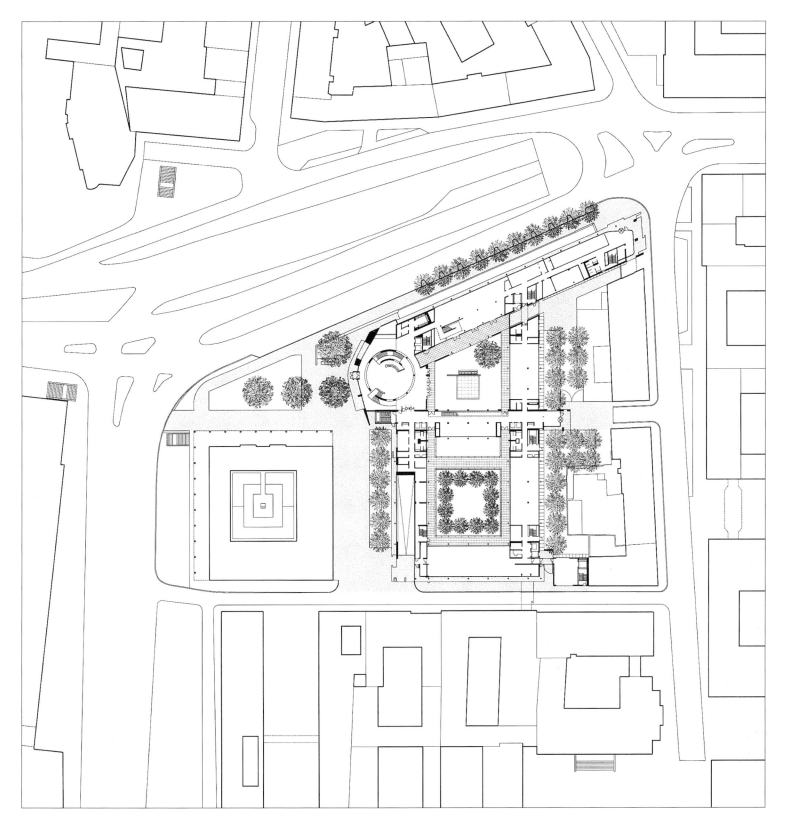

Ground floor plan

The Getty Center

Los Angeles, California
1984–1997

Called the "commission of the century," the Getty Center is
the largest, most complicated project of Meier's career: a
six-building "acropolis" on a spectacular 110-acre hillside in
Los Angeles for the internationally renowned visual-arts and
cultural institution. The center includes the J. Paul Getty
Museum, two buildings for Getty Trust offices and institutes,
the Research Institute for the History of Art and the
Humanities, a 450-seat auditorium, and a restaurant/café.
Only after the Getty Trust selected Meier in 1984 did the
complexities emerge. Among them were a conditional use
permit that imposed myriad limitations; the selection of
others to design gallery interiors and the central garden;
and the Getty's initial mandate not to build an all-white
building. Meier's response was a palette defined by a warm
sand-colored Italian travertine. Stone, he stated, would
establish an "image of solidity and permanent presence
in the landscape." Although primarily clad in what was
for the architect a new material, the Getty Center is
the culmination of Meier's architectural ideas over three
decades. The site plan derives from the 22.5-degree angle
between the axes of the topography and those of the urban
grid and adjacent freeway, with circulation based on the
notion of the architectural promenade. Meier subtly inflected
the buildings and outdoor areas with references to the city's
architectural traditions: long uninterrupted walls; continuity
between interior and exterior spaces; openness and access to
nature; multiple shading strategies; and materials related
to the site in tone and texture.

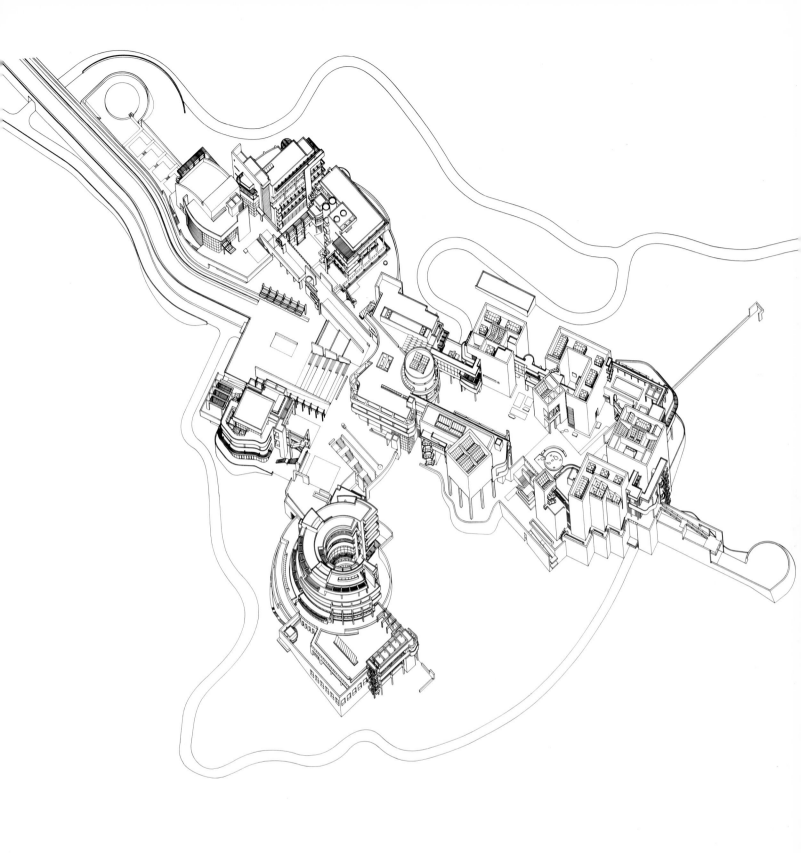

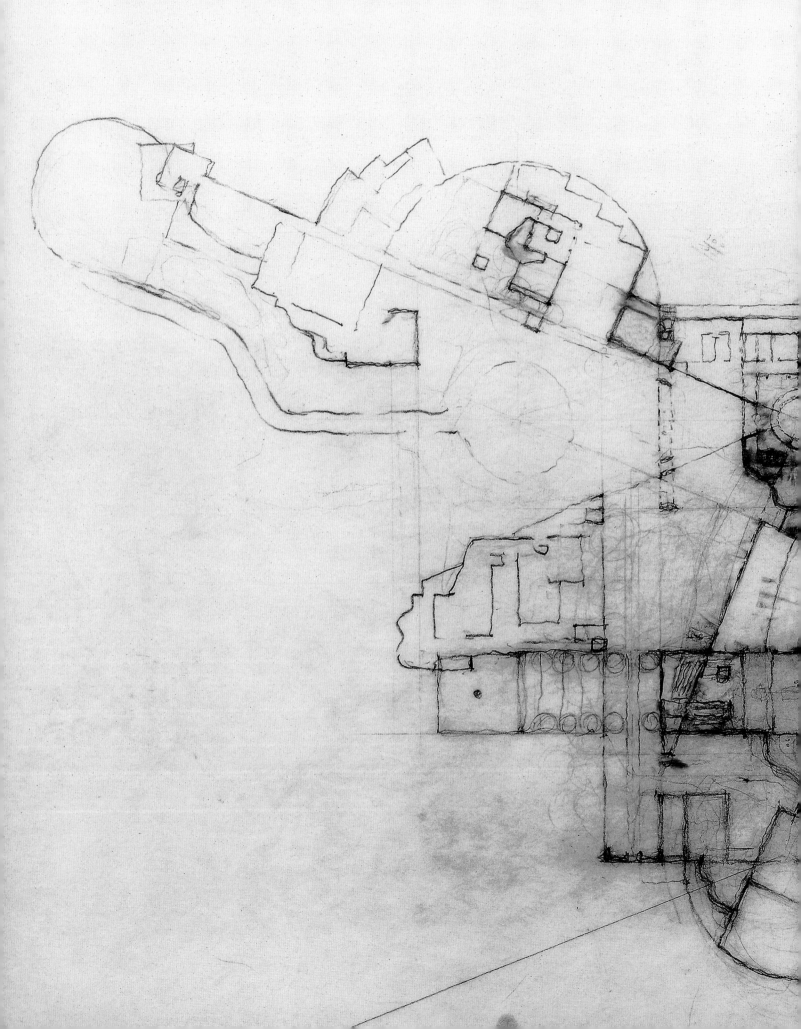

2.4.87

Museum entrance area

August
1991

museum courtyard

May
1991

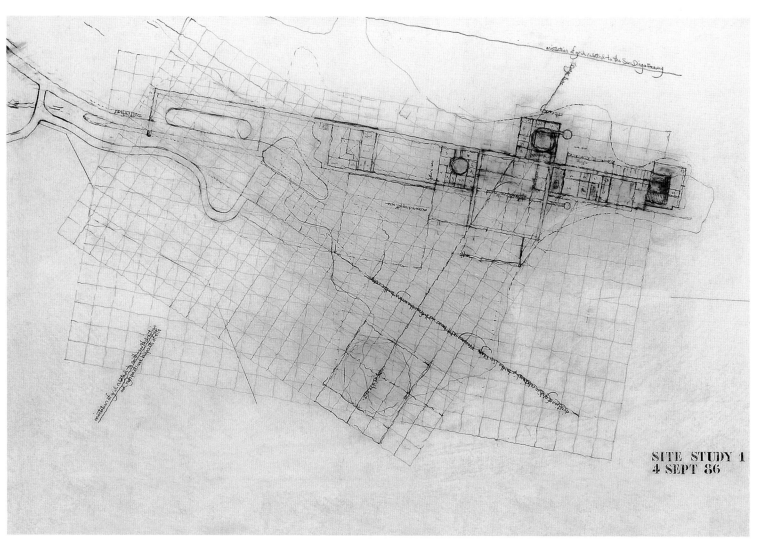

SITE STUDY 1
4 SEPT 86

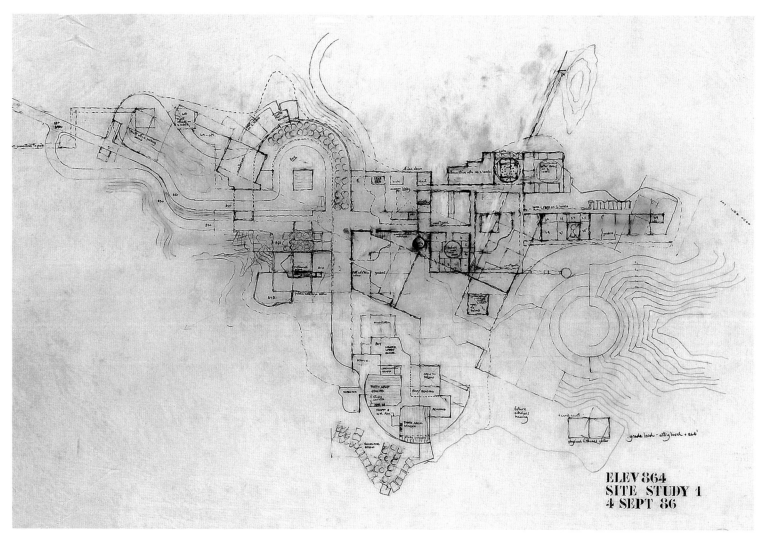

ELEV 864
SITE STUDY 1
4 SEPT 86

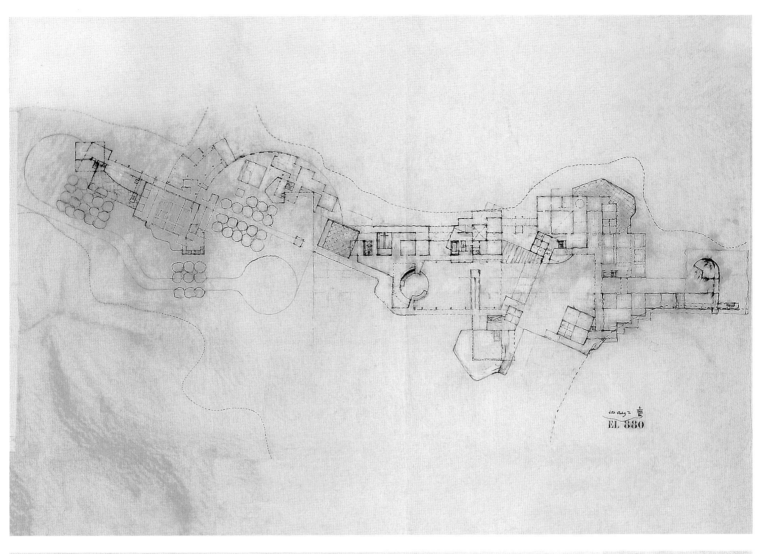

EL 880

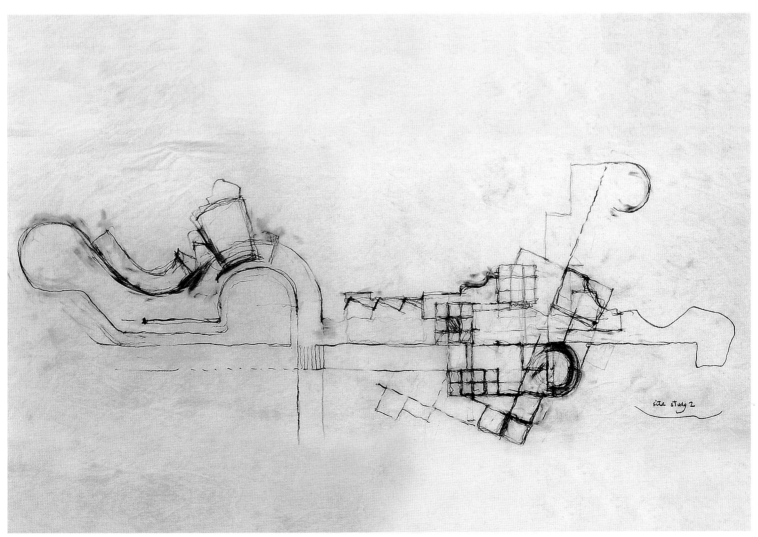

site study 2

135

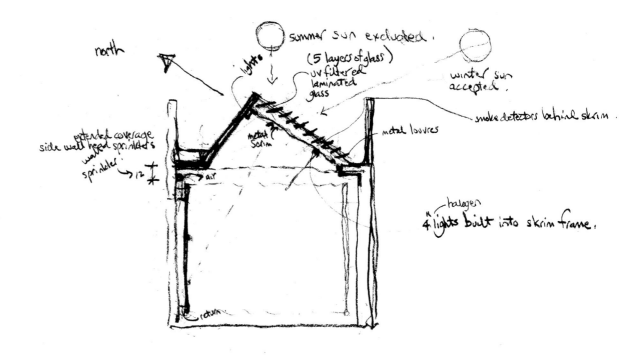

north

summer sun excluded.

(5 layers of glass)
uv filtered
laminated
glass

winter sun
accepted.

lights

metal
scrim

smoke detectors behind scrim

metal louvres

extended coverage
side wall head sprinklers
water
sprinkler →12

air

return

halogen
4" lights built into skrim frame.

Assemetrical prism skylight scheme

North skylight with movable louvres.
· mechanically operated.
½" scale drawings
of sections both ways thru galleries

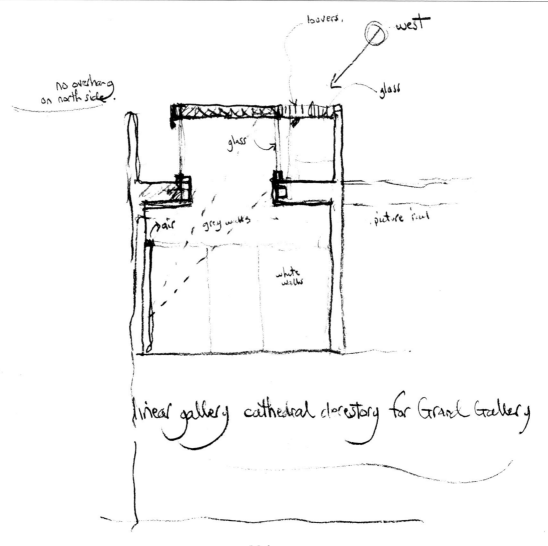

no overhang
on north side.

louvers.

west

glass

glass

air

grey walls

picture rail

white
walls

linear gallery cathedral clerestory for Grand Gallery

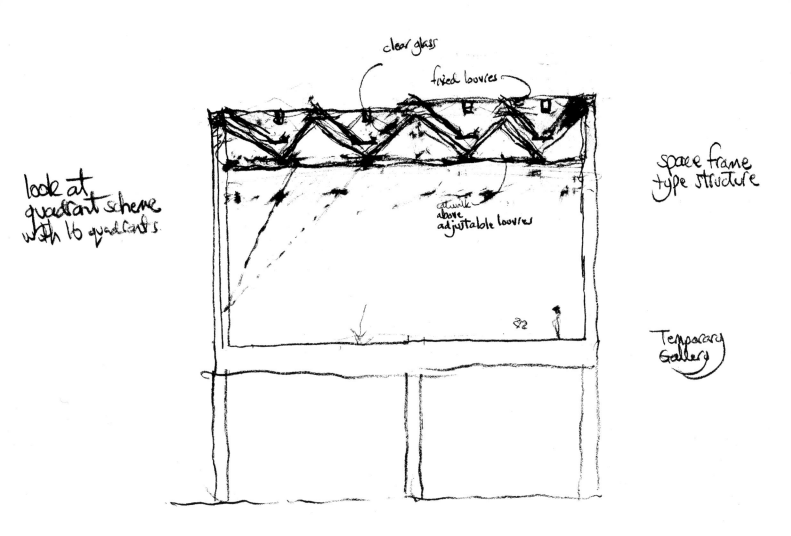

clear glass

fixed louvres

space frame
type structure

look at
quadrant scheme
with 16 quadrants.

catwalk
above
adjustable louvres

Temporary
Gallery

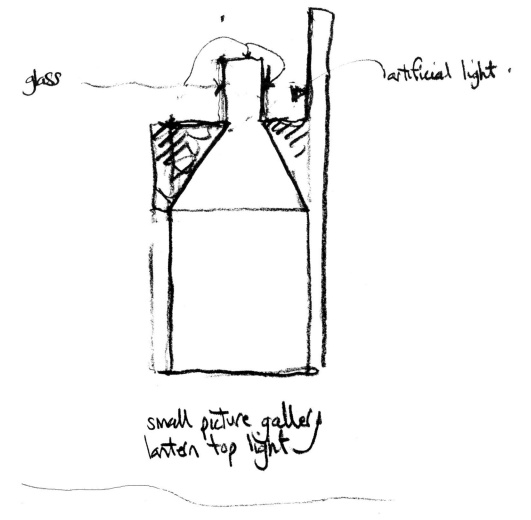

glass

artificial light.

small picture gallery
lantern top light

137

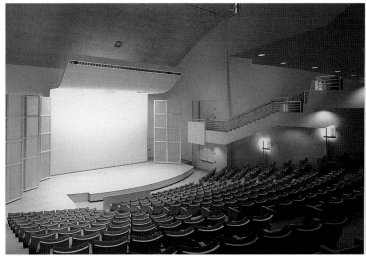

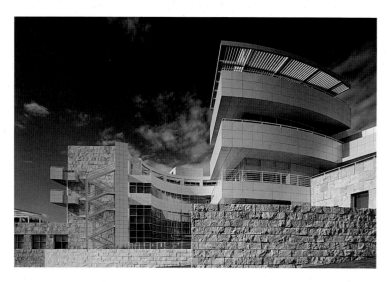

Westchester House

Westchester County, New York
1984–1986

One of a quintet of residential commissions in the mid-1980s, the Westchester House exhibits many of Meier's design tendencies at the time. As with his cultural buildings of the early 1980s—Atlanta's High Museum and the Des Moines Art Center Addition, in particular—the house combines rectilinear and curvilinear forms, a restricted yet multichromatic palette, and multiple grids. The house displays Meier's abiding interest in collage through abrupt juxtapositions: varying scales of white metal panels demarcate different components of the house; an angular piano curve at one end plays off the planar qualities. The integration of fieldstone-toned masonry into the white composition makes reference to the color of existing stone walls in the area. Like the Smith and Douglas houses, this three-level house is vertically oriented, with double- and triple-height spaces, but with a new connection to its site in the hilly terrain of Westchester County. The plan is organized by access routes: a top-lit circulation spine, which divides public from private spaces, becomes a path to the pool outside. Unlike the earlier houses, the Westchester House does not face any one direction and its main entry is on the ground floor. A further departure for Meier is the use of art-glass windows in the living-room clerestory, a request of the clients. Of the little square panes of red and blue glass, he writes "A small amount of color goes a long way."

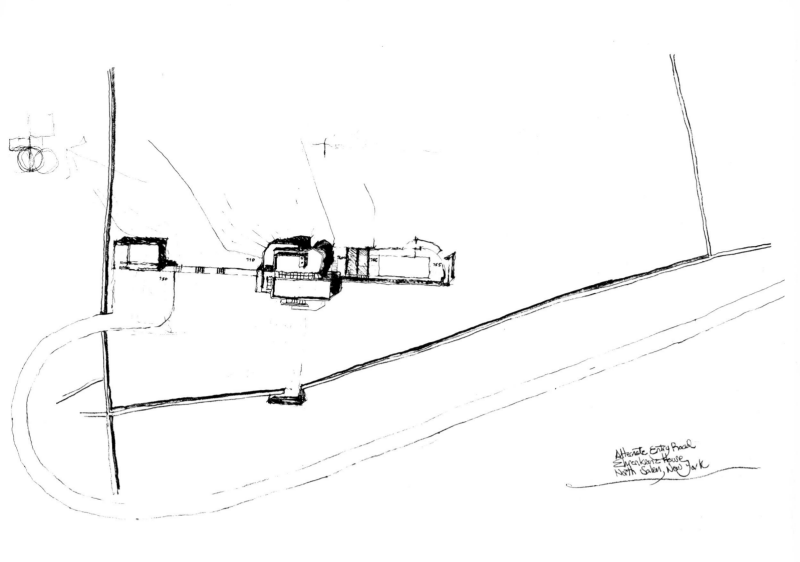

Alternate Entry Road
Shenkertz House
North Salem, New York

Ehrenkranz House   North Salem, NY
Ground Floor Plan   10 Aug 1983

154

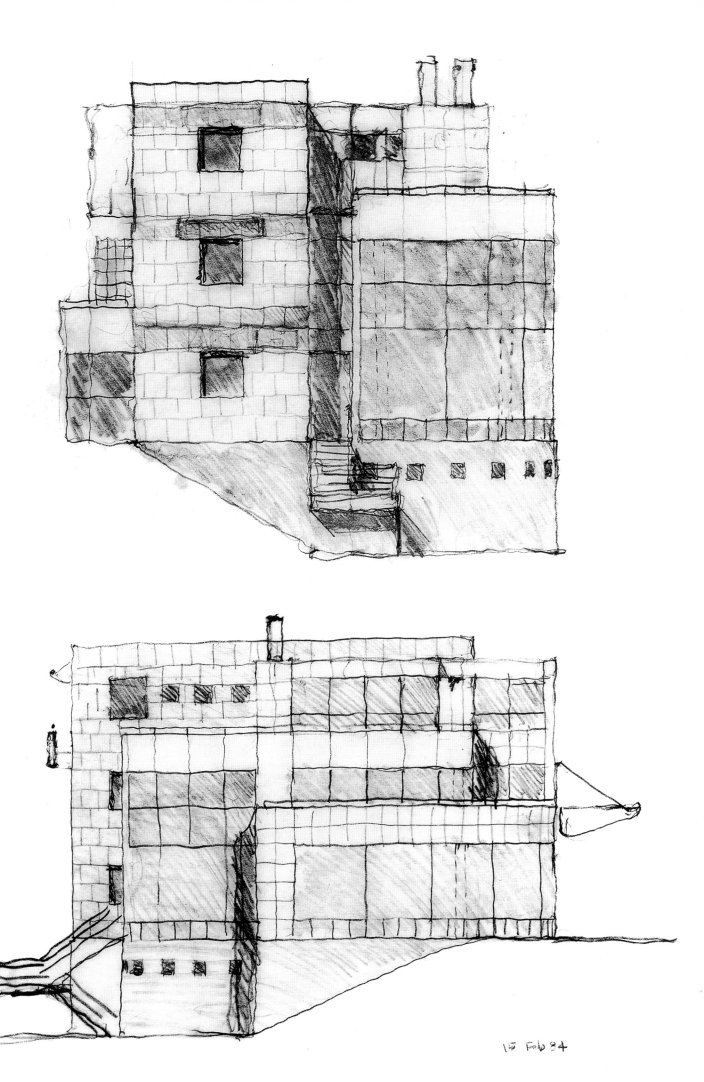

15 Feb 94

155

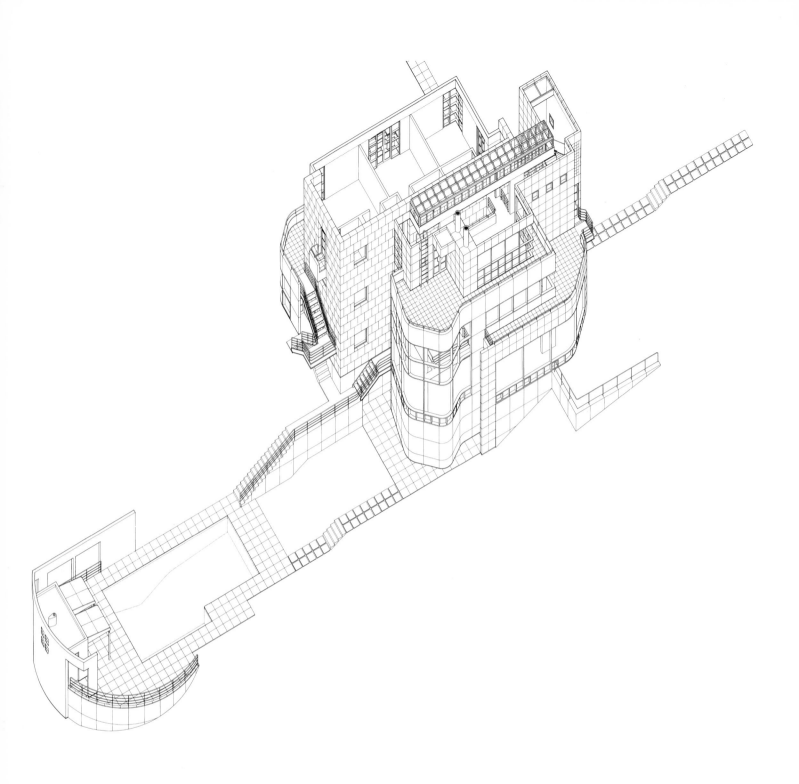

Ground floor plan

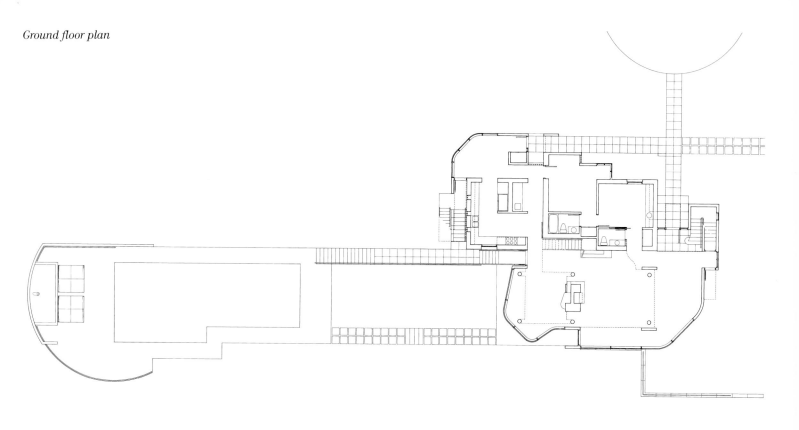

Second floor plan

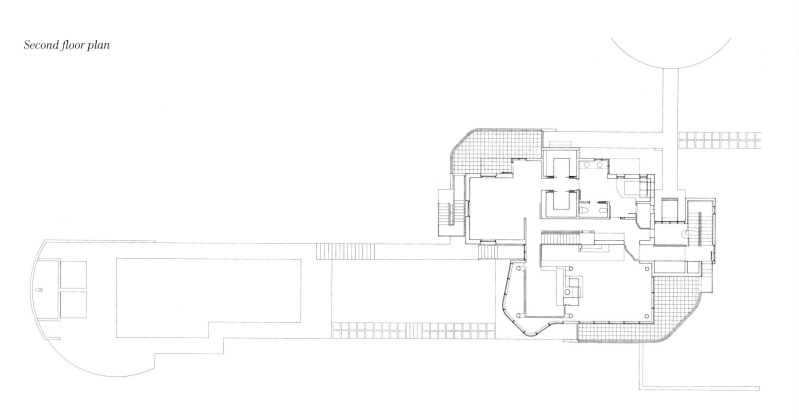

5| 10| 20| 40| 80| ft
2| 5| 10| 20| m

Ackerberg House
Malibu, California
1984–1986, Addition 1992–1994

For his first residential commission in Los Angeles, Meier
drew upon the notion of an abstract Mediterranean villa.
Like his earlier houses, the Ackerberg House capitalizes
on waterfront views, in this case of the Pacific Ocean.
Its precedent, the house Meier designed in Palm Beach,
Florida in 1977–78, clearly anticipated the design concept:
a horizontally oriented plan, ample glazing along the
water-facing facade, and myriad modes of egress to
the outdoors. The windows along the ocean facade of the
Ackerberg House are more extensive, the interpenetration
between indoor and outdoor spaces more fluid than those
of its Florida cousin. Visitors enter through the nearly solid
street facade into a sequence of alternating interior
and exterior spaces. In the heart of the U-shaped plan is a
courtyard, which alludes to the tradition of Spanish colonial
revival architecture in southern California. Two forms of
glazing bring the ocean view into the double-height living
room: small square clerestories and square sliding doors,
which open onto terraces and the front loggia. A simple form
of brise-soleil frames ocean views and adds another layer of
light and shadow to the architectural collage. With pipe
railing along balconies and loggia, use of glass block, and
an open composition of white planes and grids, the house
defines one archetype of contemporary California
architecture in the 1980s. According to Meier, this house
provided an important laboratory for ideas he would use
at the Getty Center.

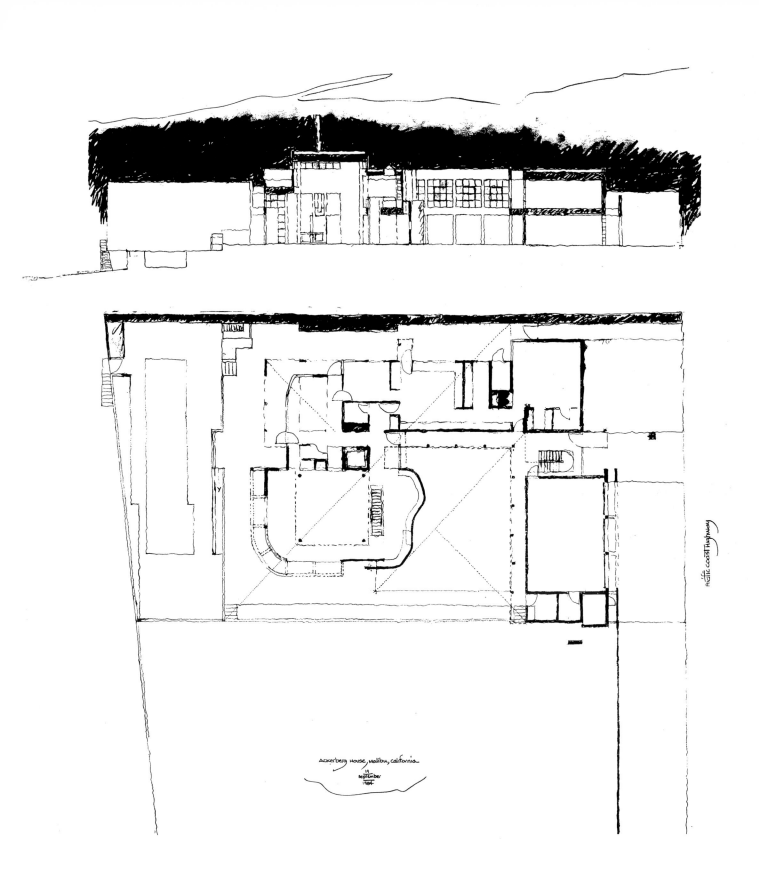

ackerberg house, malibu, california
19
september
1984

pacific coast highway

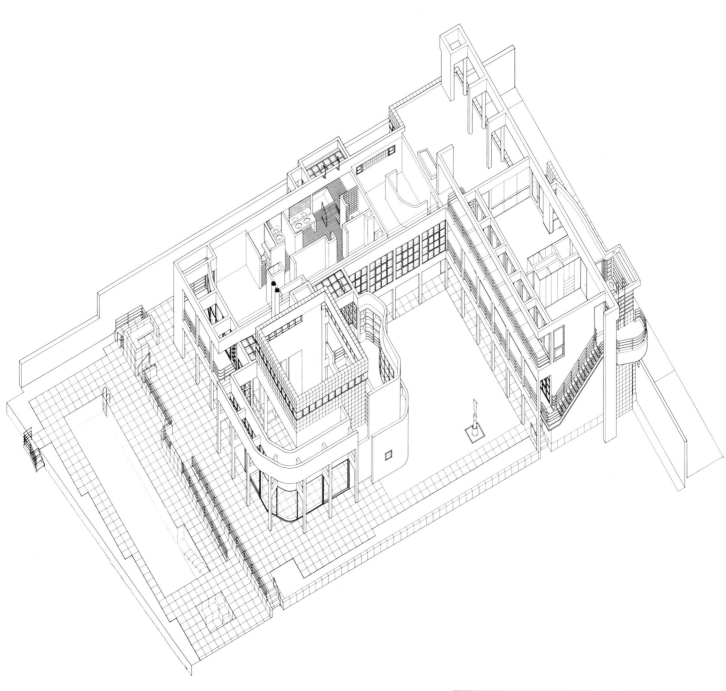

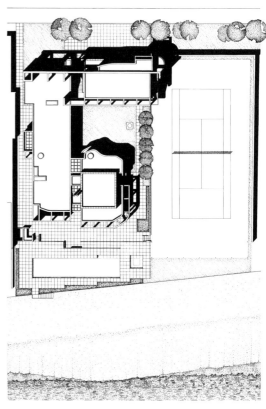

164

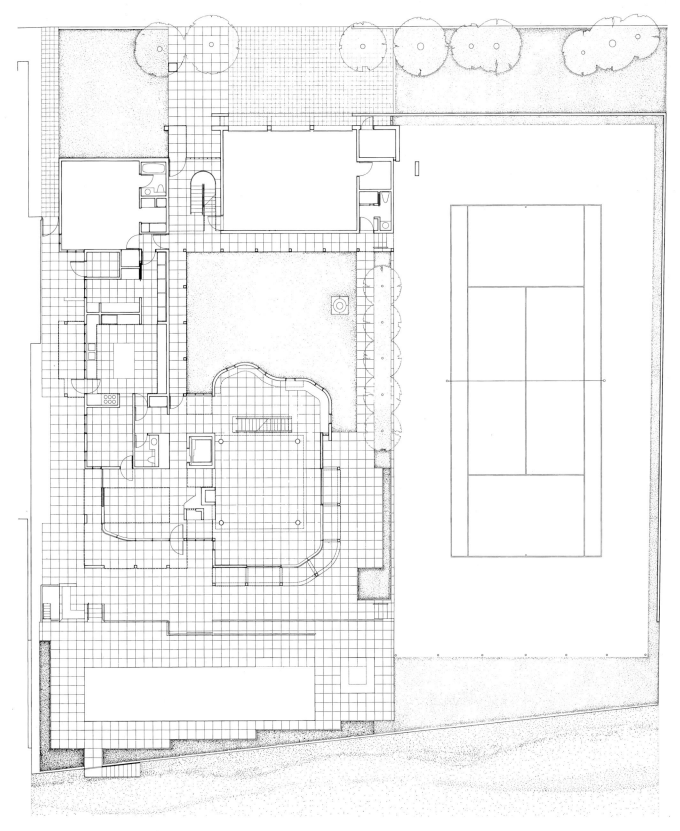

Ground floor plan

Grotta House

Harding Township, New Jersey
1985–1989

In the mid-1980s, Meier increasingly began to use circular
elements in plans, often as rotundas and entry pieces, and
also as focal points and fulcrums in the plans for cultural
and civic institutions and corporate headquarters. For the
Grotta House, the circular room serves as a double-height
living space, its area intersected by the circulation routes
of the plan. Unlike many of Meier's residential designs,
the Grotta House takes the form of a low-slung pavilion,
its arcade and walkway on opposite ends reaching out into
the sloping rural site in northwestern New Jersey. Meier
placed the house onto a plateau just below the highest point
of the site, and the house's second-floor living area and roof
deck provide key vantage points from which to survey the
surrounding woods and valley. Given the precision necessary
to construct Meier buildings, the clients hired a contractor
with commercial experience to build the house. Although
primarily of wood construction, the house is a hybrid,
integrating an array of materials that permit and articulate
the close tolerances the architect demands: porcelain-enamel
exterior panels, curved glazing, concrete block, and slate
for terraces and flooring. Both the Grotta House and the
Westchester House were commissioned by long-time friends
of the architect who are major art collectors. The Grotta
House was therefore also designed to provide an optimal
setting for the owners' collection of crafts.

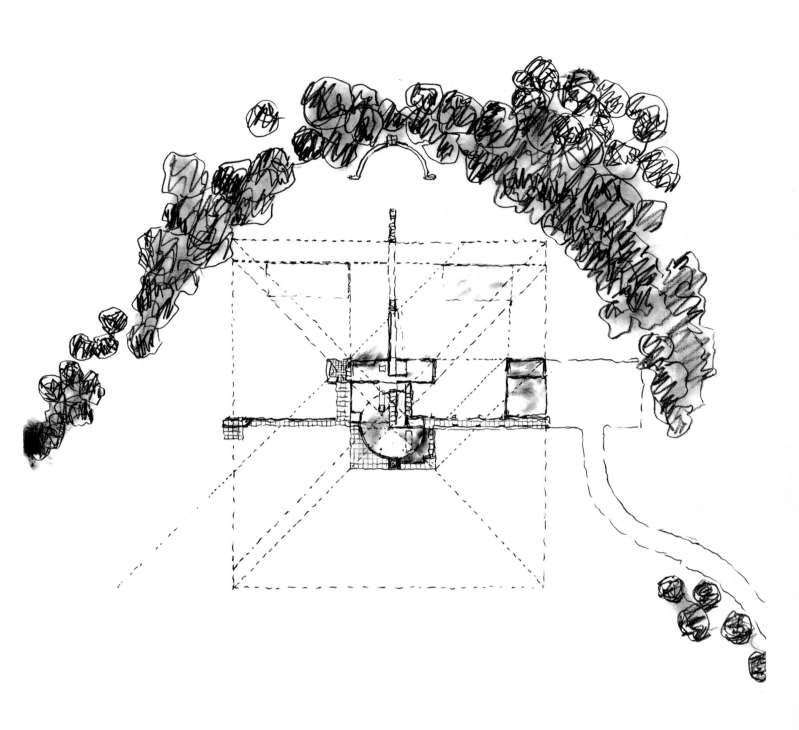

Grotta Residence
Harding Township, N.J.

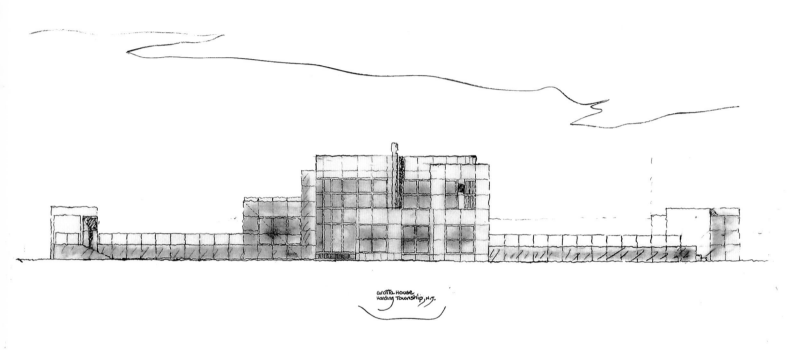

Grotta House
Harding Township, N.J.

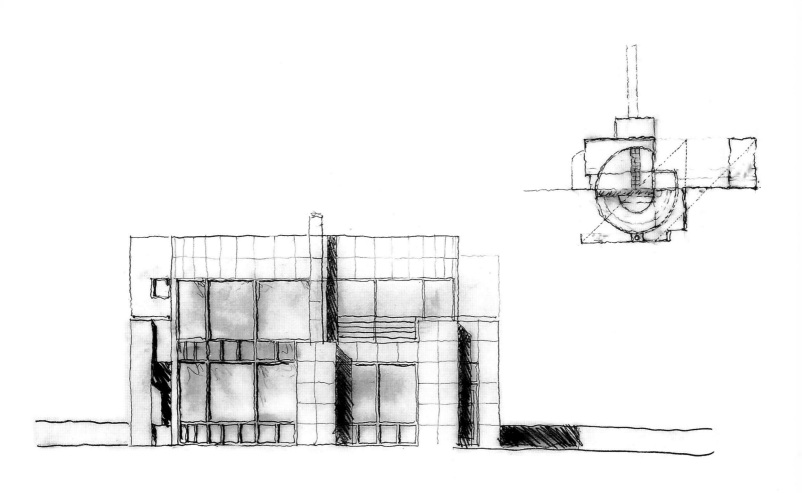

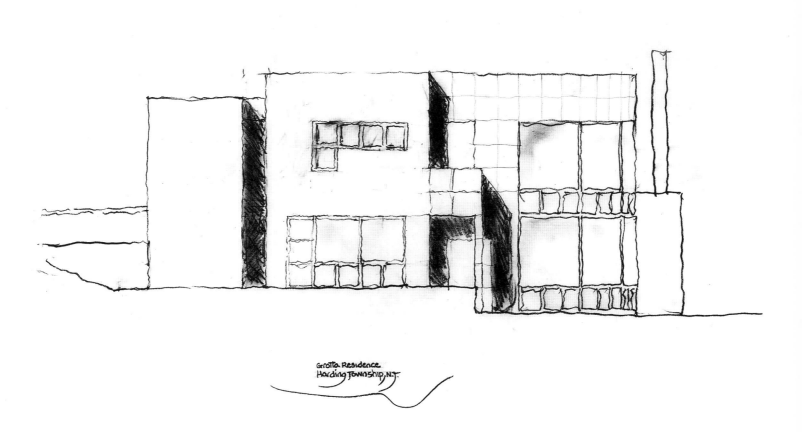

Grotta Residence
Harding Township, N.J.

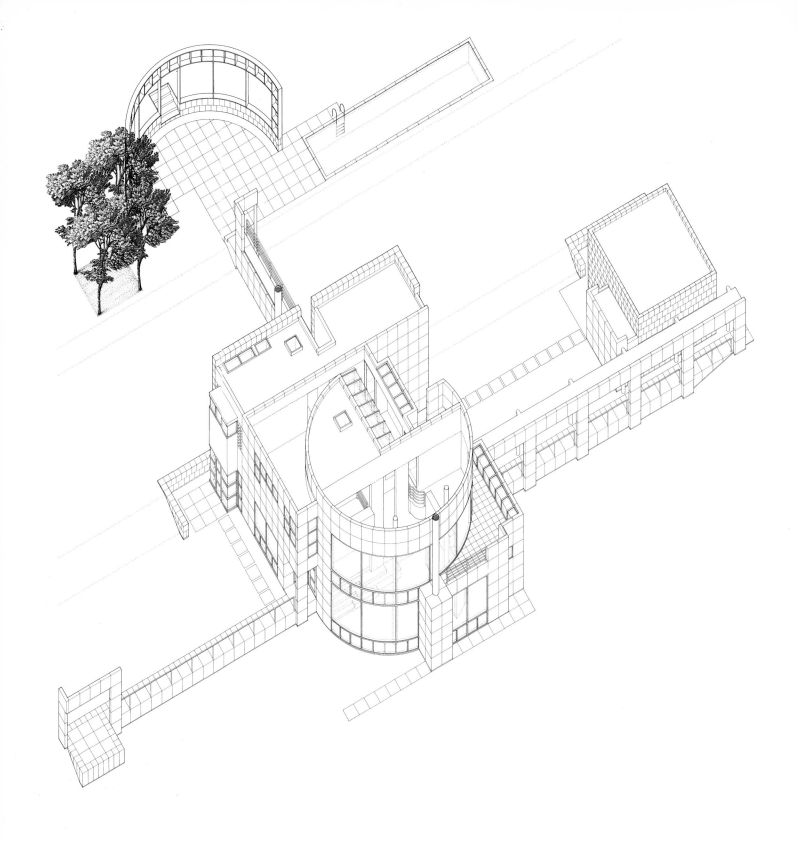

174

Ground floor plan

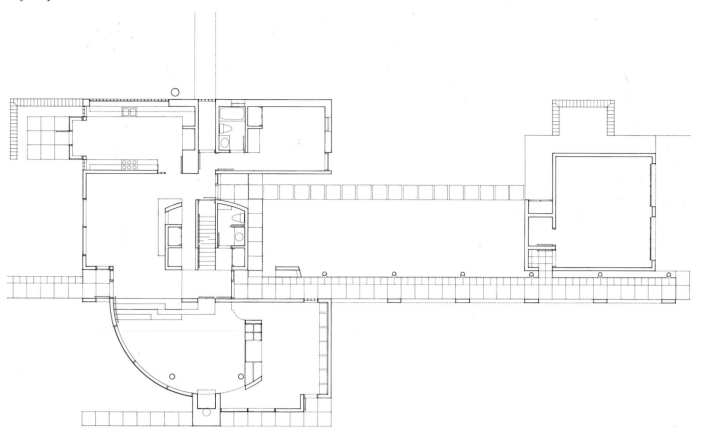

Second floor plan

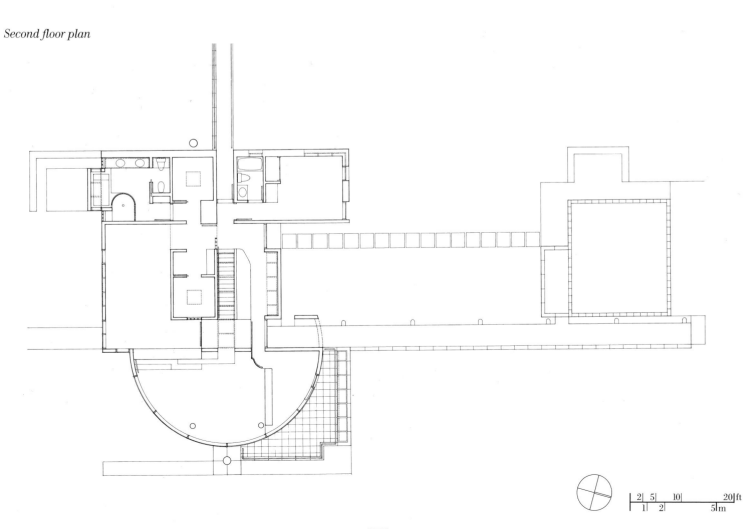

City Hall and Central Library

The Hague, The Netherlands
1986–1995

Meier expanded his exploration of collage as an organizing device with the design for the City Hall and Central Library in The Hague. Instead of single monolithic blocks, the complex's components become a microcosm of the city or, in Kenneth Frampton's phrase, a "city in miniature"— but in this case, it is hardly Lilliputian. Recognized as the largest covered plaza in Europe, the city hall is a vast, fantastic set piece of white surfaces, rows of catwalks, and enormous walls of grids. It is Meier's most extreme manifestation of light and space, layering, transparency, and use of white. However phenomenal its effects, the building represents a synthesis of Meier's rational site analysis and efforts to embody the civic values that town halls play in Dutch democratic tradition. Indeed, the city council

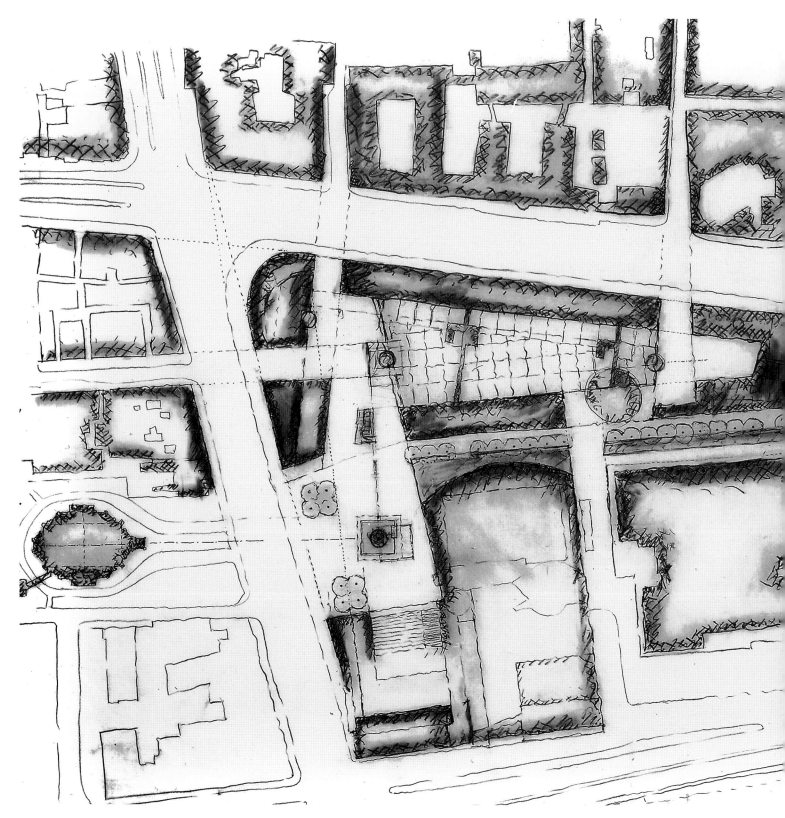

awarded the commission according to public preference, and a public survey and various city-council debates deemed Meier's proposal most popular. Symbolic of these democratic impulses is the design's central atrium enclosed by long office wings—a huge open public space in the city center. The luminous room with expansive glass windows extends outdoors to a square along the Spui. While firmly rooted in Meier's formal and compositional vocabulary, the building complex—which includes the central library and commercial office spaces—makes references to Dutch modern architecture, in particular the nearby De Bijenkorf Department Store and, in Rotterdam, Brinkman, van der Vlugt, and Stam's Van Nelle Factory.

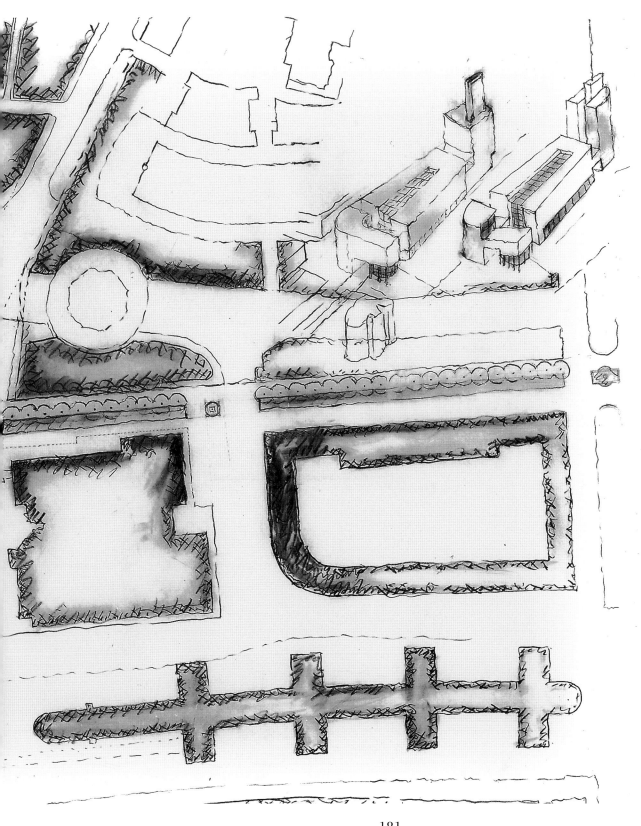

Atrium van het Stadhuis in Den Haag
kijkend naar de trouwzaal

15
nov
1991

zicht van de trap naar de trouwzaal in het stadhuis atrium
view of the city hall atrium looking towards the wedding stairway

Ground floor plan

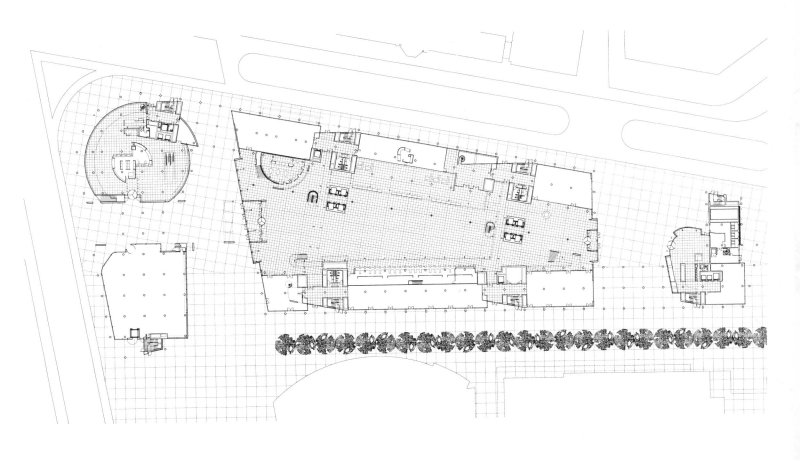

Southeast elevation

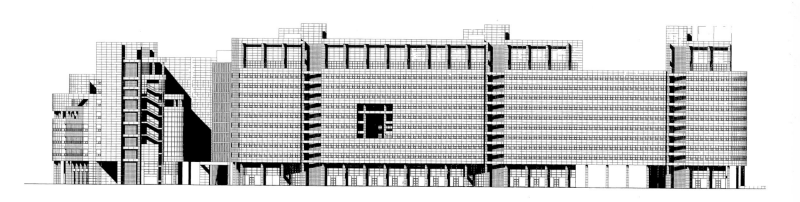

185

Exhibition and Assembly Building
Ulm, Germany
1986–1993

The Exhibition and Assembly Building represents
a mature response to the challenge of historic context,
posed in the form of the majestic Ulm Cathedral, or Münster,
which dates from the fourteenth century. The architectural
competition called for the completion of the cathedral square.
Meier's scheme enhanced vistas of the cathedral and
maintained the openness of the civic space. He organized
the Münsterplatz with new paving (whose module derives
from the cathedral), as well as an arcade of sycamores,
a fountain, and the Exhibition and Assembly Building, a
curved structure of white plaster and light beige stone,
all placed respectfully along the edge of the square.
As a multipurpose center for the community, the building
houses the city's tourist office and ticket agency, exhibition

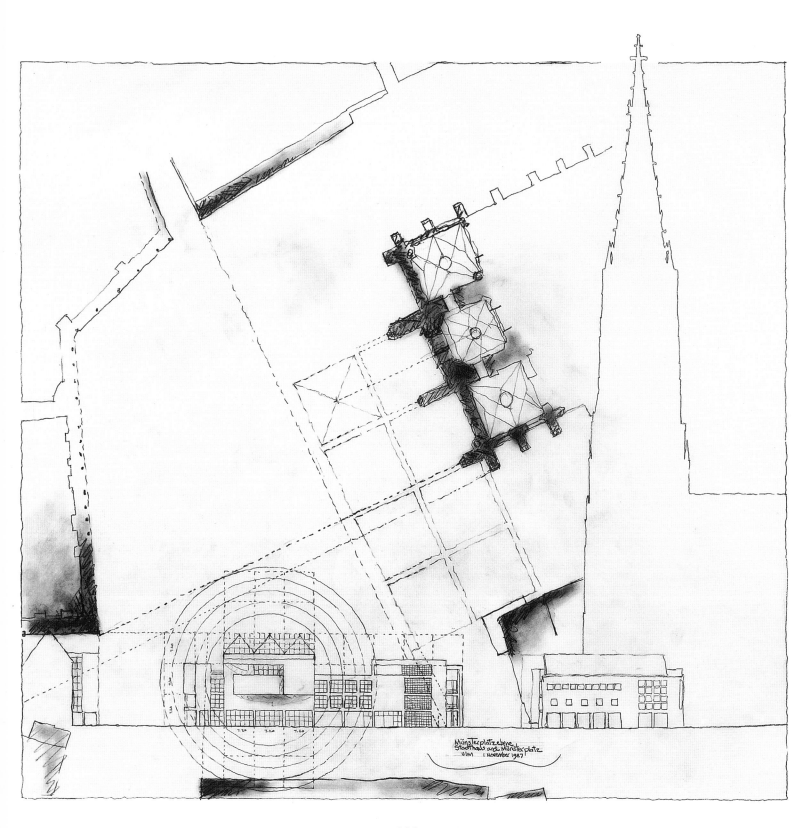

space, an assembly room and lecture hall, and a restaurant and café. In an unusual move for Meier, the shape of the building's skylights echoes the gabled rooftops of neighboring buildings. What is particularly notable about this project is how the building becomes a neutral backdrop and a viewing platform for the cathedral. The cathedral's magnificent spires can be seen through skylights in the galleries. A large window in the second-story assembly room looks out to the square and the base of the cathedral. Like the New Harmony Atheneum, the building draws visitors up to the observation deck on the roof and then back to the ground level, where the restaurant and café are also placed for optimal views of the cathedral.

stadthaus and Münsterplatz
Ulm 1 November 1987

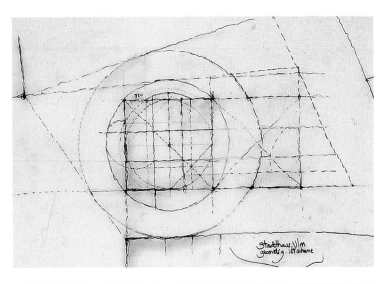

Stadthaus, Ulm
geometry: 1st scheme

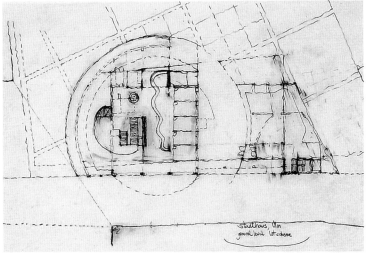

Stadthaus, Ulm
ground level: 1st scheme

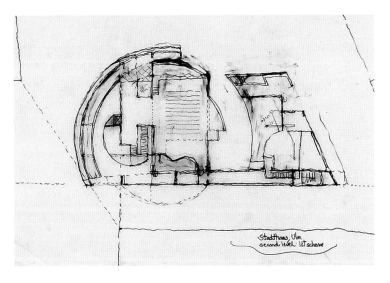

Stadthaus, Ulm
second level: 1st scheme

192

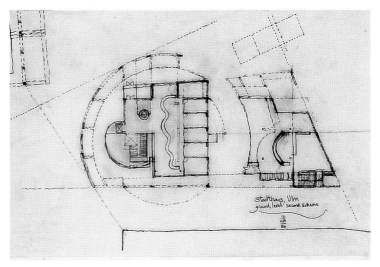

Stadthaus, Ulm
ground level · second scheme

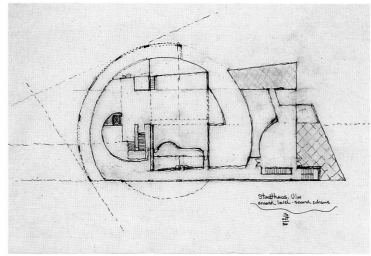

Stadthaus, Ulm
second level · second scheme

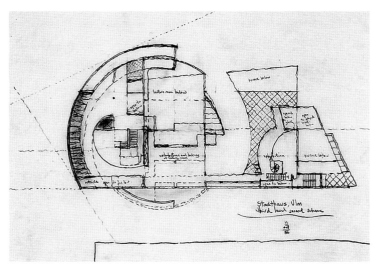

Stadthaus, Ulm
third level · second scheme

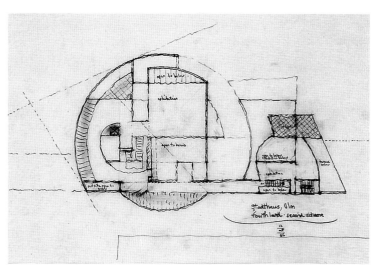

Stadthaus, Ulm
fourth level · second scheme

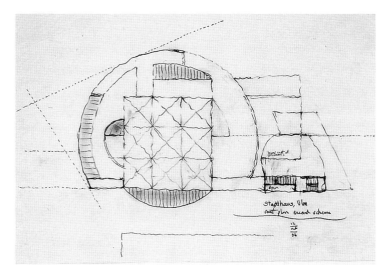

Stadthaus, Ulm
roof plan · second scheme

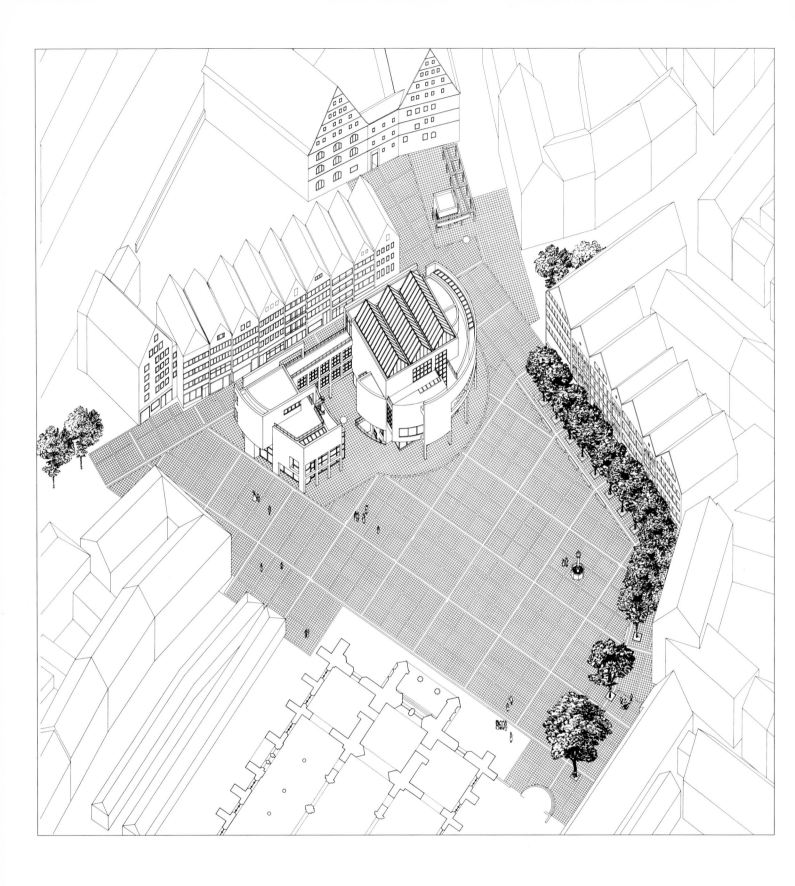

194

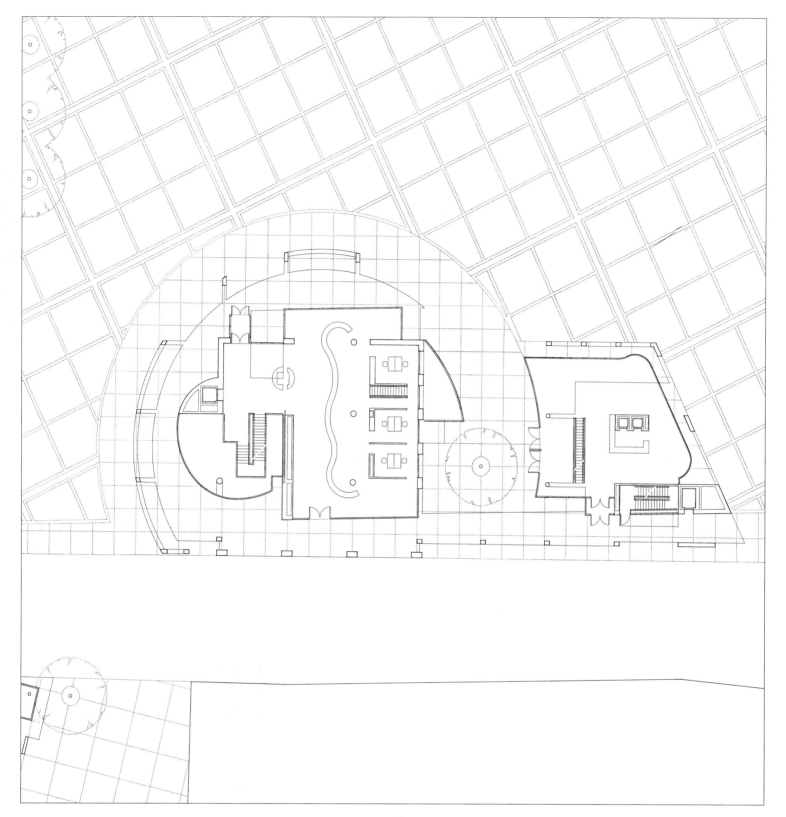

Ground floor plan

| 5| 10| | 20| | 40|ft |
| 1| 2| | 5| | 10|m |

Weishaupt Forum

Schwendi, Germany
1987–1992

After the Museum for the Decorative Arts in Frankfurt
am Main, Meier built a series of projects in southern Germany.
In 1986, he won the competition for the Exhibition and
Assembly Building in Ulm, and two nearby commissions
followed: the Daimler-Benz Research Center in Ulm and
the Weishaupt Forum. In 1987, Max Weishaupt GmbH, a
heating-systems manufacturer, asked Meier to design
a new building for their headquarters that would provide an
"orientation to the future." The Forum indeed presents
a scintillating image as the new entry piece —an aluminum
paneled "gateway"—to the company's industrial complex in
the Upper Swabian countryside. The U-shaped plan of the
Forum opens up to and embraces the surrounding landscape,
with a single oak tree as the courtyard's focal point.
The two-story building serves several functions as a training
center, exhibition space, and dining hall. Meier fulfilled
the complex program by juxtaposing a number of disparate
typologies developed in previous projects: art gallery,
auditorium, demonstration area and classrooms, and dining
rooms for staff and guests. One striking aspect of the project
is the gallery, which combines an installation of late
twentieth-century art with a product display of combustion
engines and equipment. The craftsmanship and precision
of construction details throughout the buildings are
immaculate, providing a testament to the excellence of
German craftsmanship as well as a benchmark for the
perfection possible and required in a Meier work.

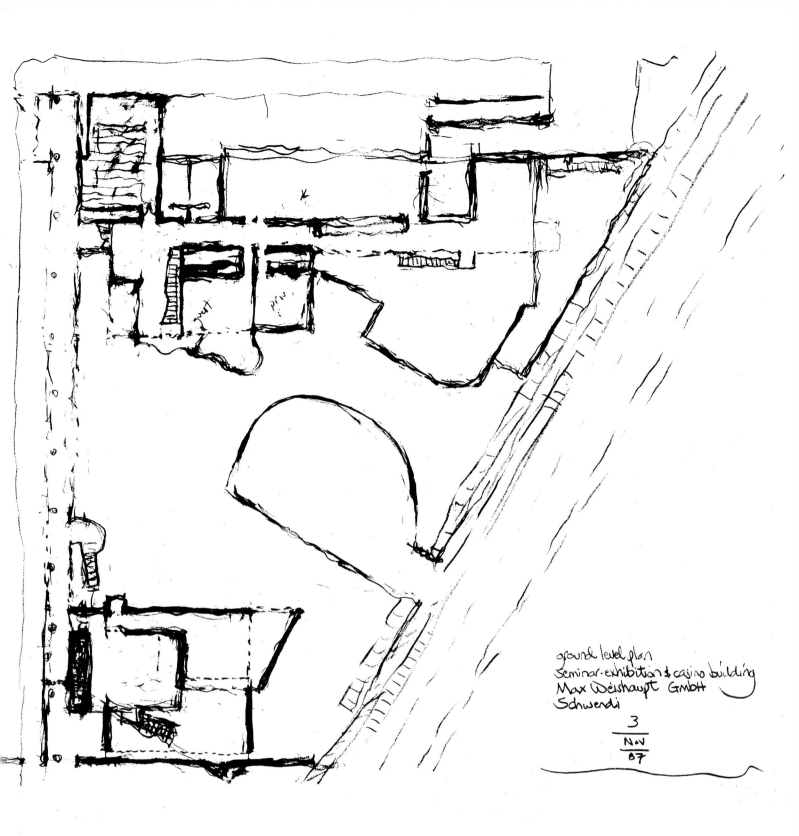

ground level plan
Seminar-exhibition & casino building
Max Weishaupt GmbH
Schwendi

$$\frac{3}{\frac{Nov}{87}}$$

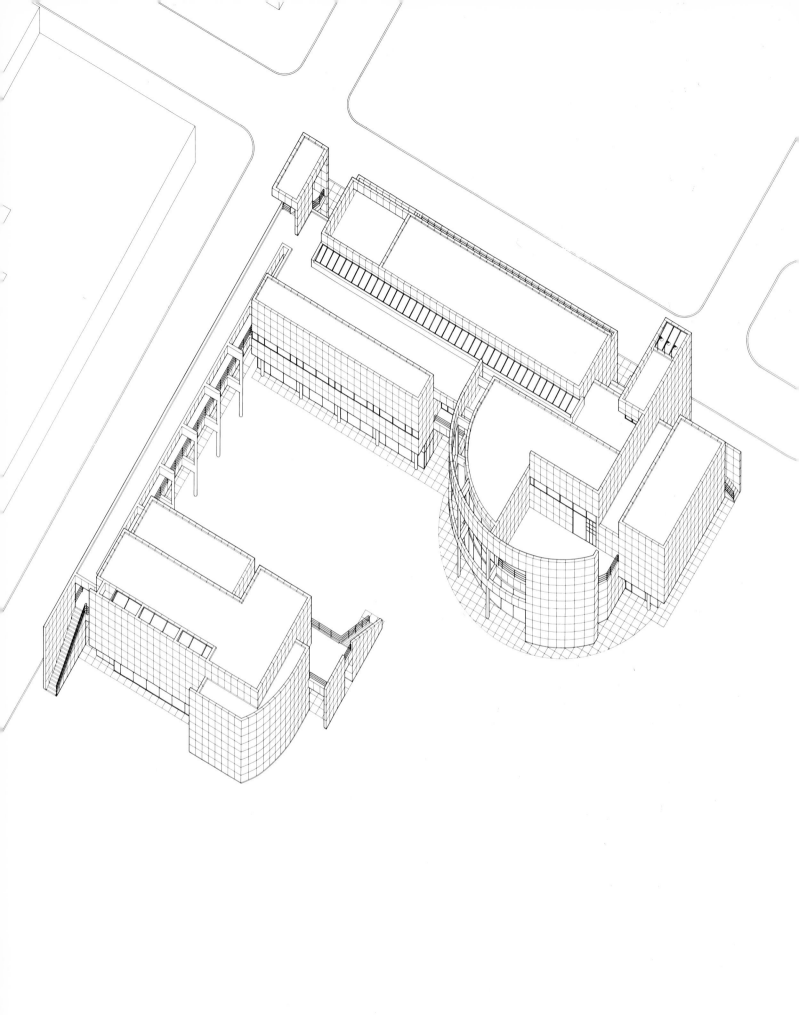

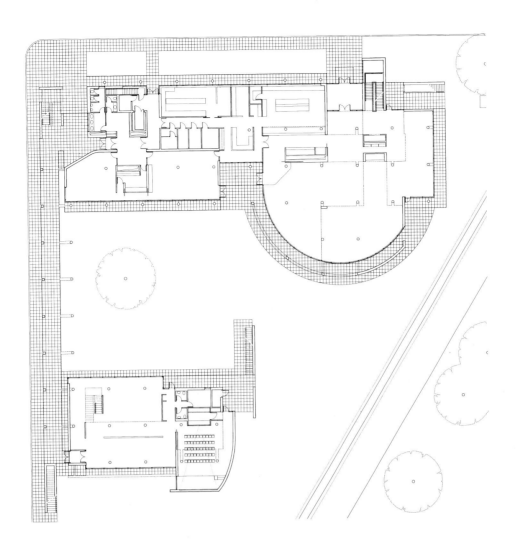

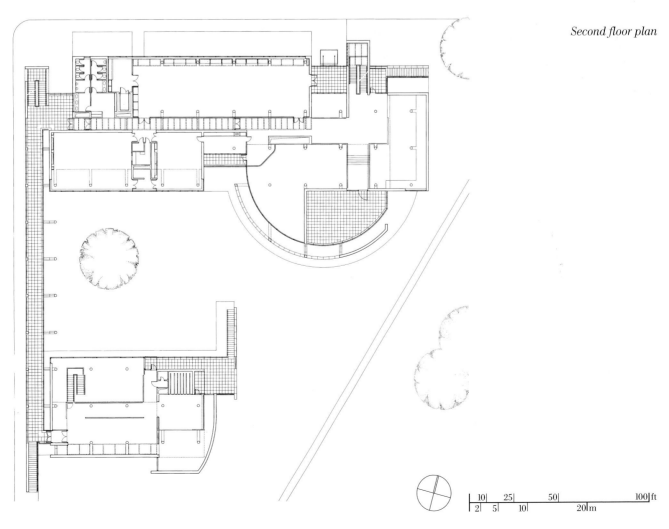

| 10 | 25 | 50 | 100 ft |
| 2 | 5 | 10 | 20 m |

Museum of Contemporary Art

Barcelona, Spain
1987–1995

In 1987, the mayor of Barcelona asked Meier what kind of building he would like to design for the city, which was then preparing for the 1992 Summer Olympics. Not surprisingly, Meier's choice was an art museum. The city had yet to develop a contemporary art museum as part of its large-scale urban renewal; the Museum of Contemporary Art was soon begun. With no museum staff in place or specific artworks to accommodate, Meier was able to design a building to his idealized specifications. With Mayor Pasqual Maragall, he selected the site in the city's medieval quarter, El Raval, and placed the museum so as to create a large public plaza, the Plaça dels Angels. As in the Frankfurt Museum for the Decorative Arts, a passageway cuts through the building, connecting the front plaza to a square adjacent to the new Center of Contemporary Culture. The museum otherwise is set in contrast to the bleached earth tones and narrow streets of the historic neighborhood. The large-scaled white rectilinear building looms atop a gray granite podium, its main, south-facing facade of horizontal brise-soleils framed by a projecting plane at the entrance and a sculptural protuberance to the east. As in Atlanta's High Museum, circulation spaces are separated from exhibition areas, which are large, open, flexible galleries with discrete curvilinear spaces for special exhibitions. The main attraction, however, is the museum's three-story atrium, a ramped circulation space that is Meier's most lavish expression of light.

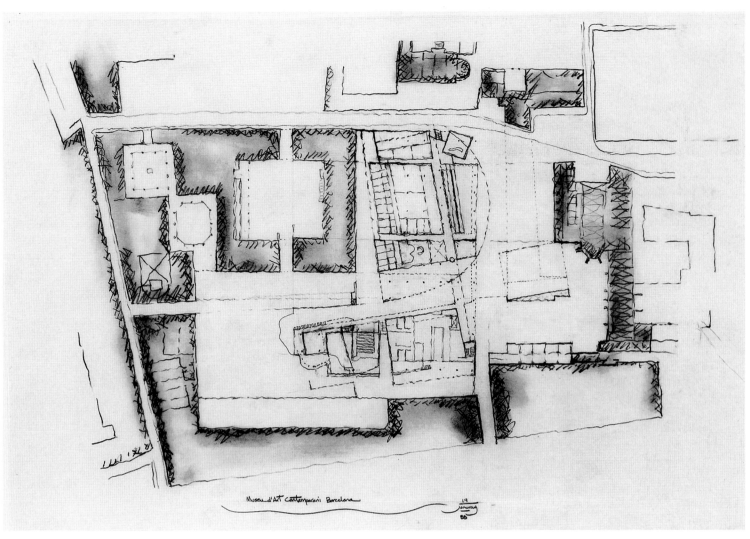

Museu d'Art Contemporani Barcelona 19 January 88

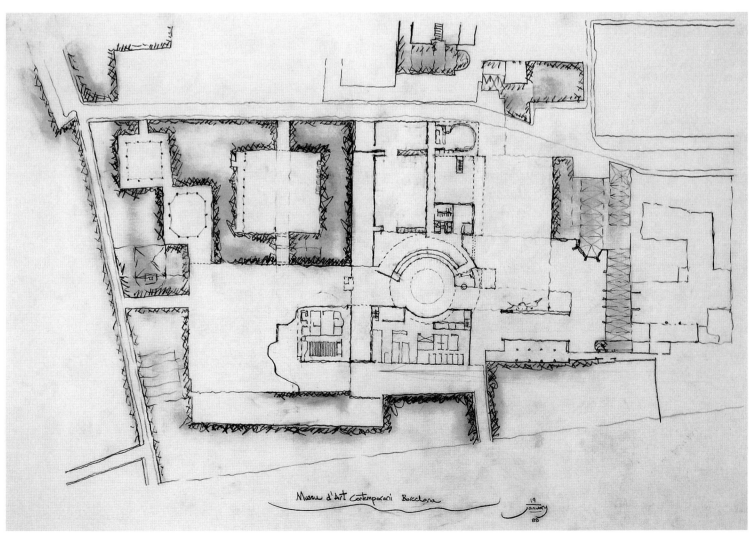

Museu d'Art Contemporani Barcelona 19 January 88

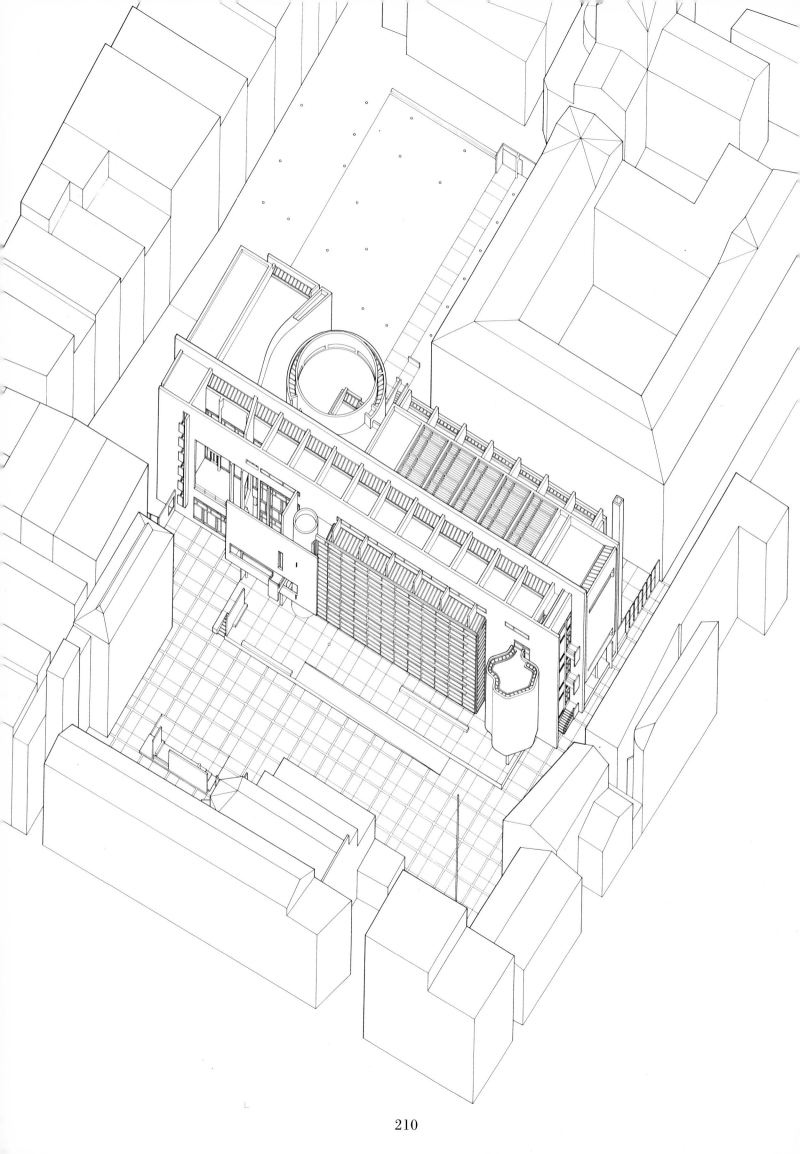

Ground floor plan

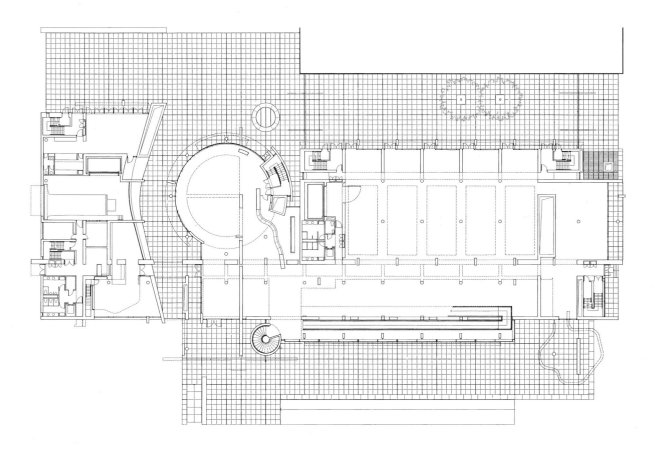

South elevation

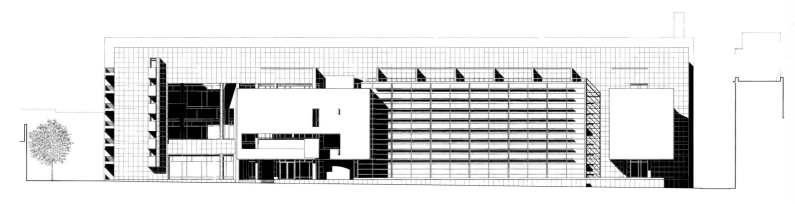

| 10 | 25 | 50 | | 100 ft |
| 2 | 5 | 10 | 20 m | |

Royal Dutch Paper Mills Headquarters

Hilversum, The Netherlands
1987–1992

The Royal Dutch Paper Mills Headquarters building
masterfully incorporates Meier's late-1980s compositional
approach and formal vocabulary. Originally designed
for a paper company and now occupied by a television-and
theatrical-production company, the building is located
in the residential area of a burgeoning entertainment center
in Hilversum. The corporate headquarters comprises two
residentially scaled buildings: a four-story cubic reception
pavilion—containing dining facilities, meeting rooms,
a conference room, and lecture hall—and a two-story
office slab. The reception building makes use of many
characteristic Meier features: a cantilevered front canopy,
a freestanding entry cube, a three-story reception area
scaled like a living room, multiple sources of indirect light,
and a white interior accented by light-colored stone.
A two-level enclosed glass bridge leads to the administrative
office slab. Sitting upon pilotis, this portion of the building
integrates parking on the ground level and two floors
of offices above. Sunlight streams into the office area
through a winglike roof, and light wells bring sunlight
to the lower floor. Of particular interest is how the curved
concrete roof, projecting balconies, and window and wall
details filter the forms of Le Corbusier through Meier's
own sensibility. Relative to earlier works, however,
the building's aluminum-plate exterior skin has deeper
reveals and sharper edges. Meier cites W. M. Dudok's
nearby Hilversum Town Hall and the work of J. J. P. Oud
and Gerrit Rietveld as key influences.

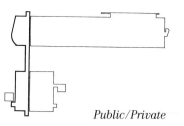

Public/Private

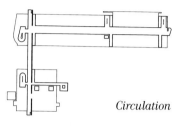

Circulation

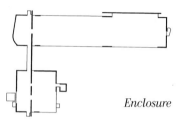

Enclosure

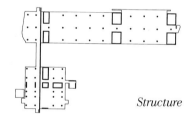

Structure

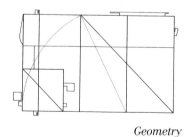

Geometry

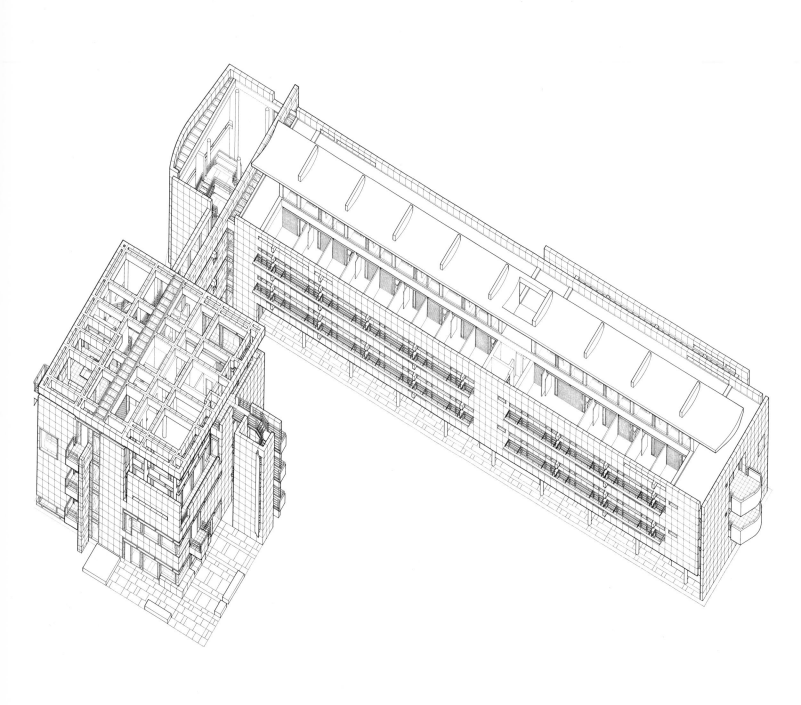

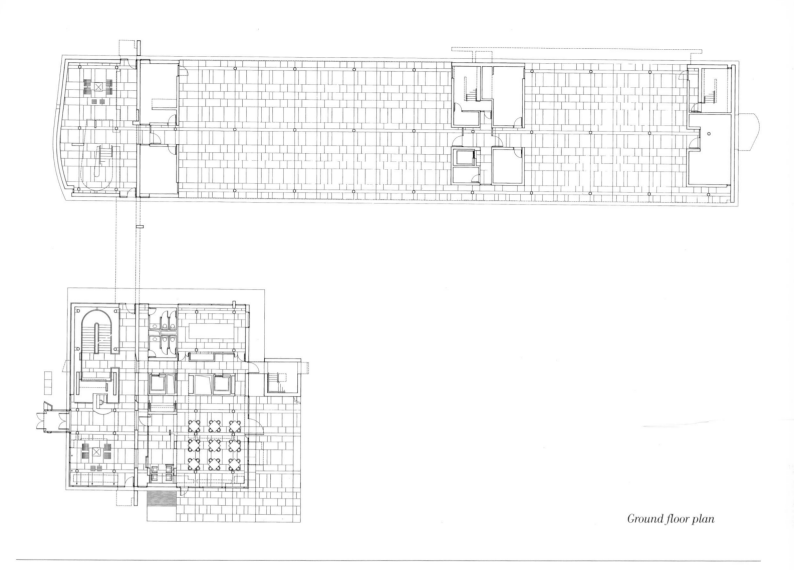

Ground floor plan

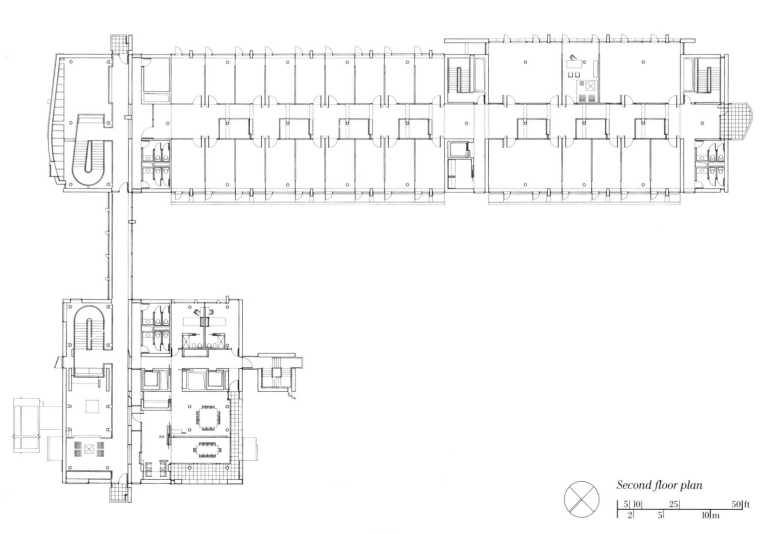

Second floor plan

| 5| 10| | 25| | 50| ft |
| 2| | 5| | 10| m |

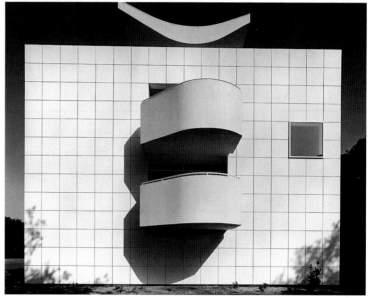

221

Madison Square Garden
Site Redevelopment

New York, New York
1987

For a prominent New York architect with many corporate
clients, the small number of skyscrapers in Meier's portfolio
is surprising—especially since the towers proposed for the
Madison Square Garden site in New York City are among
the architect's most elegant designs. The main precedent for
this project is Bridgeport Center in Bridgeport, Connecticut.
An anomaly in his oeuvre, Bridgeport Center is an ensemble
of low- and medium-rise towers whose collage of massing
and materials (red granite, gray and white metal panels)
reflects Meier's strategies to reduce the scale of the project
and connect it to the context of nearby commercial buildings.
In contrast, the Madison Square project features unrelentingly
white, sleek, highly articulated towers. These forms appear
coolly self-contained, the skin freely and asymmetrically
interrupted by various apertures, projecting balconies, and
brise-soleils. The proposed development of approximately
4.4 million square feet includes two seventy-two-story
skyscrapers and a thirty-eight-story office building and
conference center, all of which sit on a podium that slopes
down to Eighth Avenue. Ultimately, the commission
was jointly awarded to Skidmore, Owings & Merrill and
Frank Gehry, but it was later shelved. Meier has since
designed a midrise office building in Frankfurt and built
a medical-center tower in Singapore.

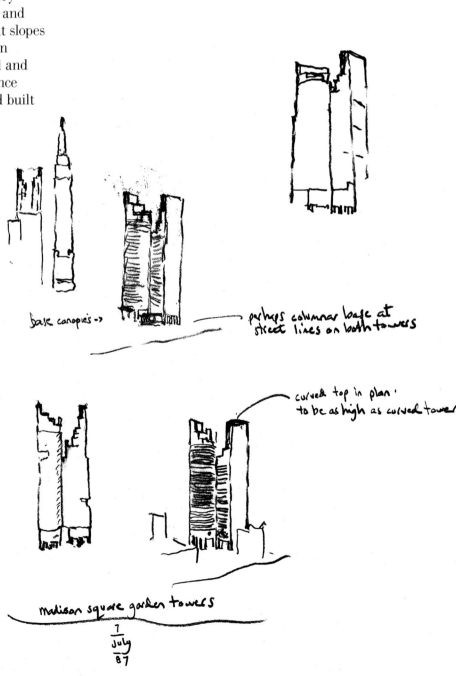

224

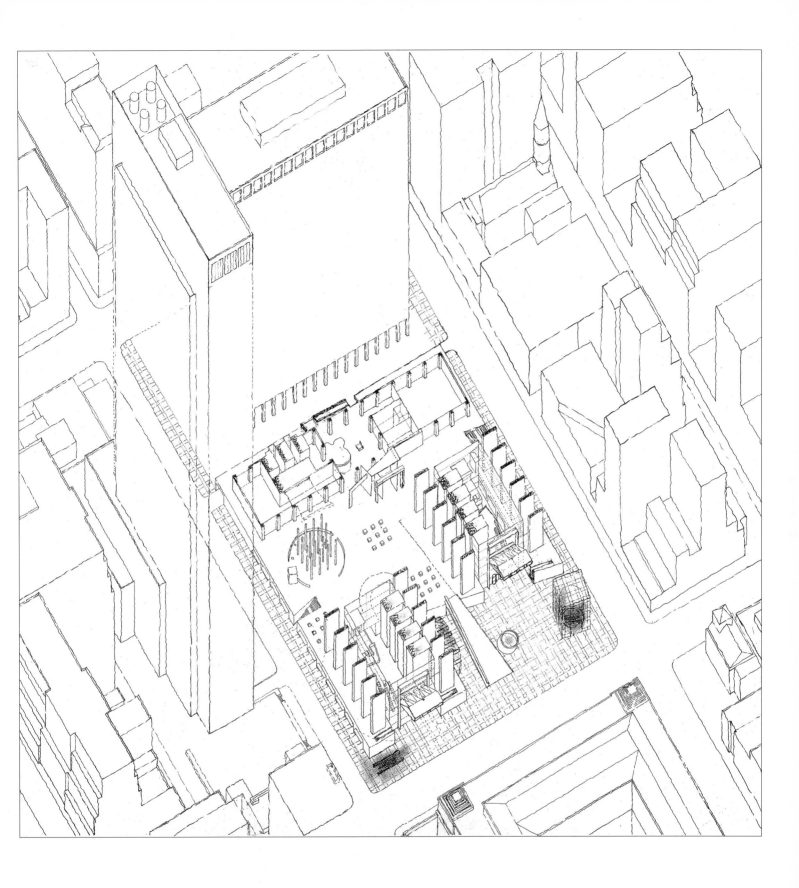

225

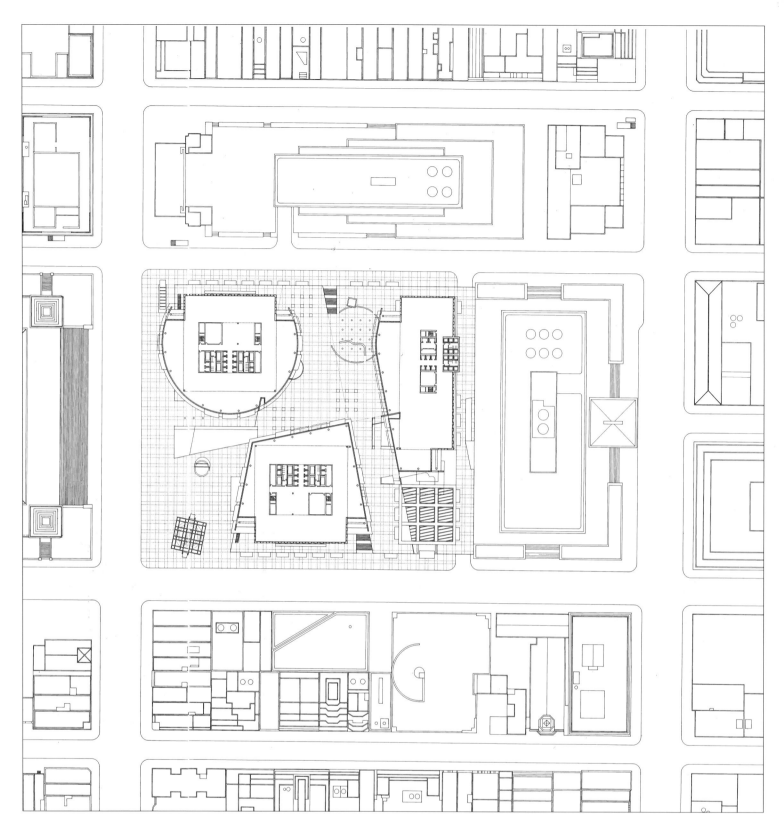

Typical floor plan

| 25| 50| 100| 200|ft
| 5|10| 20| 40|m

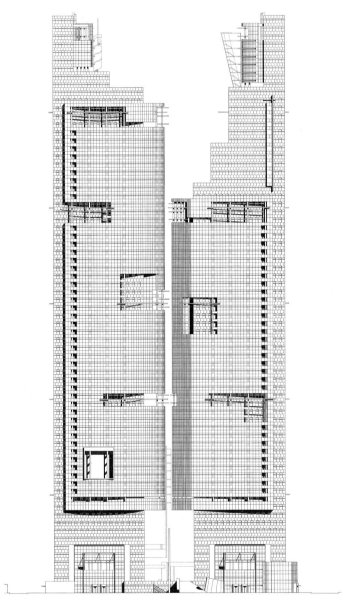

West elevation

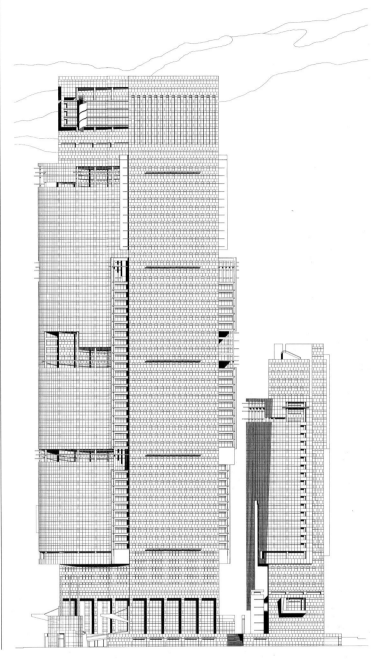

South elevation

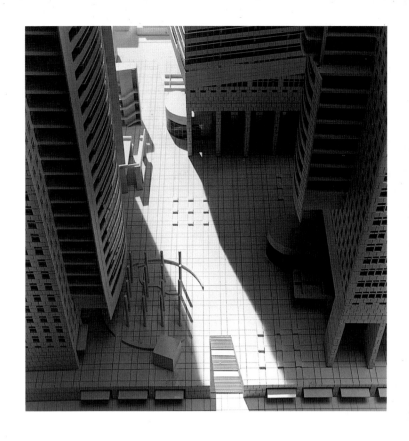

Canal+ Headquarters

Paris, France
1988–1992

Like much of Meier's European work, the commission for the Canal+ Headquarters came to him through a design competition. The European pay-television company sought a new building to house its headquarters and production facilities on a site along the left bank of the Seine, just east of the Parc Citroën and west of Pont Mirabeau. The resulting L-shaped plan adheres closely to the restrictions of the site and programmatic requirements. The administrative office wing, whose curve mirrors the nearby riverbanks, is situated alongside the Seine, with audiovisual production and recording facilities, including three four-story studios, to the east. The building's sleek white forms provide an aura of technology and sophistication appropriate to Canal+'s corporate identity and dramatically set it apart from the

Canal+
Rue des Cevennes Elevation
19
Nov
1988

context of Paris's fifteenth arrondissement. To create the prominent "urban" window on the Seine facade, Meier successfully negotiated city building codes. Among the details of his late-1980s building vocabulary present here are the cantilevered metal canopy at the front entrance, a three-story atrium reception area, projecting brise-soleils, and a conical roof form that corresponds to the circular plan of the theater below. Unique to the building is an aerodynamic motif that unifies the design. Meier recasts the motif throughout, from the thin, tapering plan of the administrative wing to the curved, cantilevered roof over the studios to the streamlined lighting fixtures.

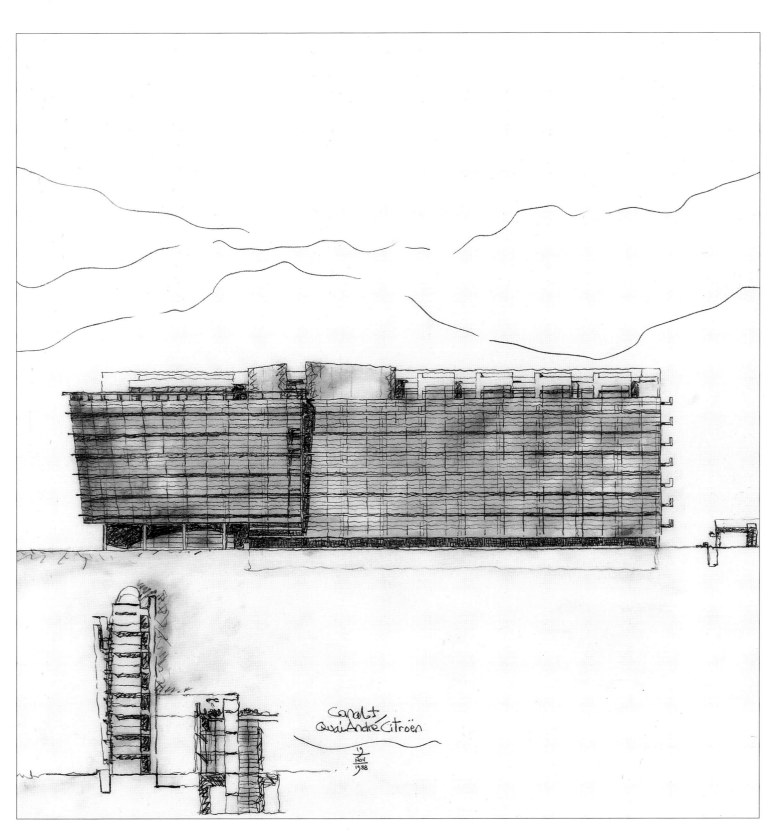

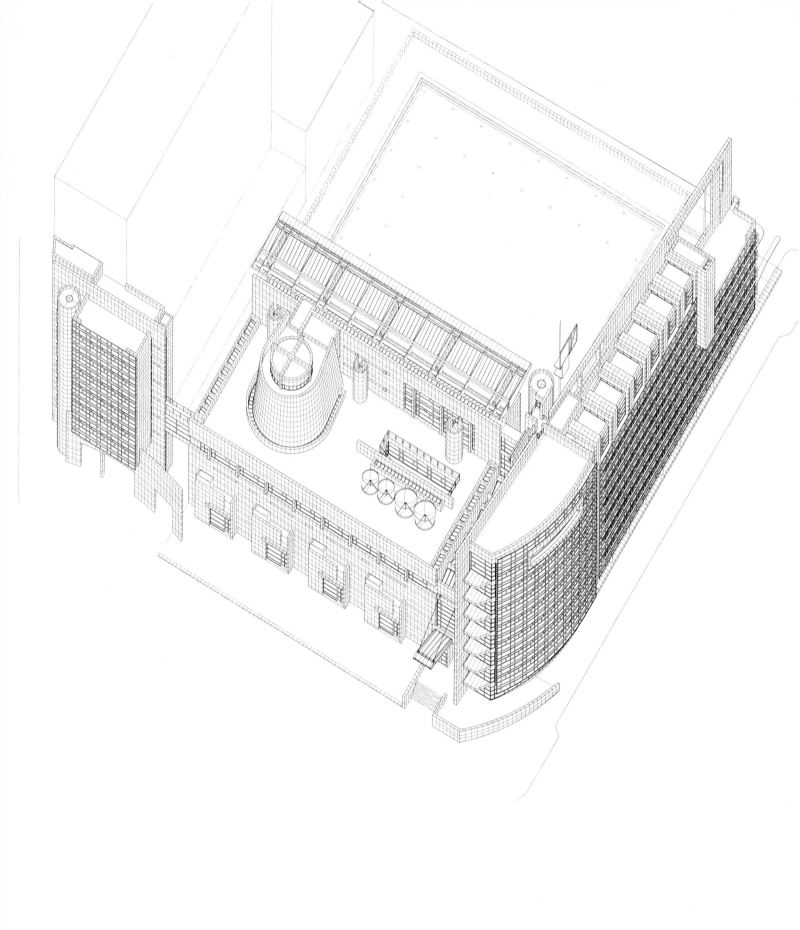

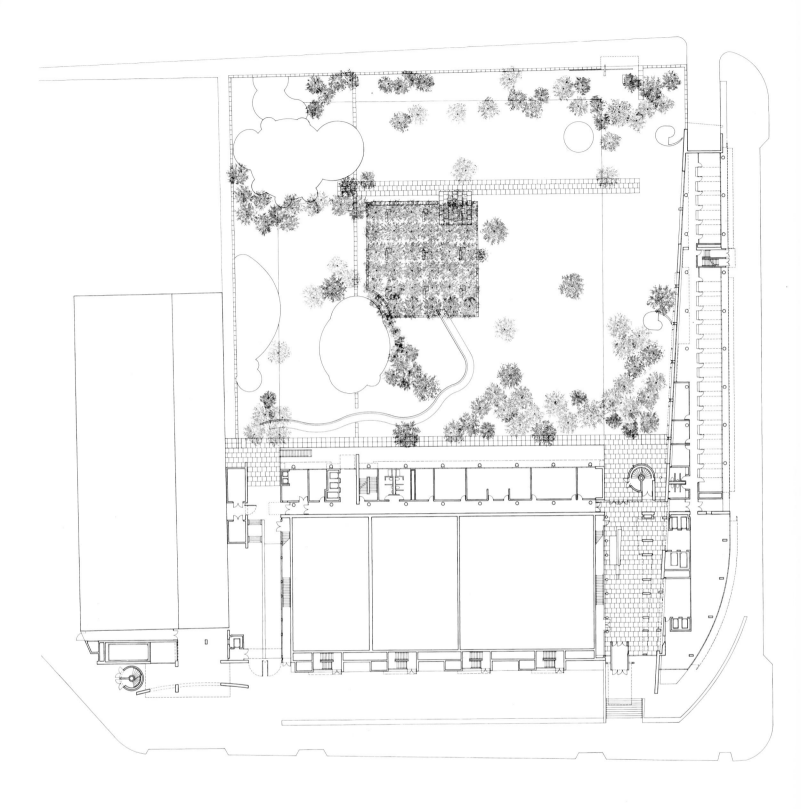

Entry floor plan

237

Rachofsky House

Dallas, Texas
1991–1996

The Rachofsky House blurs the distinction between domestic and exhibition space. Commissioned to be both home and gallery, the approximately eleven-thousand-square-foot house has one bedroom. Located on a main north-south thoroughfare in Dallas, the house assumes a public posture toward the street, with a bold front facade of white porcelain-enamel metal panels that recalls the main facade of the Museum of Contemporary Art in Barcelona. Likewise, the house sits on a podium of black granite that extends to the pool pavilion in back. The entry sequence leads through a gallery up to a double-height living area on the piano nobile. This complex space contains discrete volumes for gym and office, providing access to the backyard below and the gym above, and opens volumetrically to the

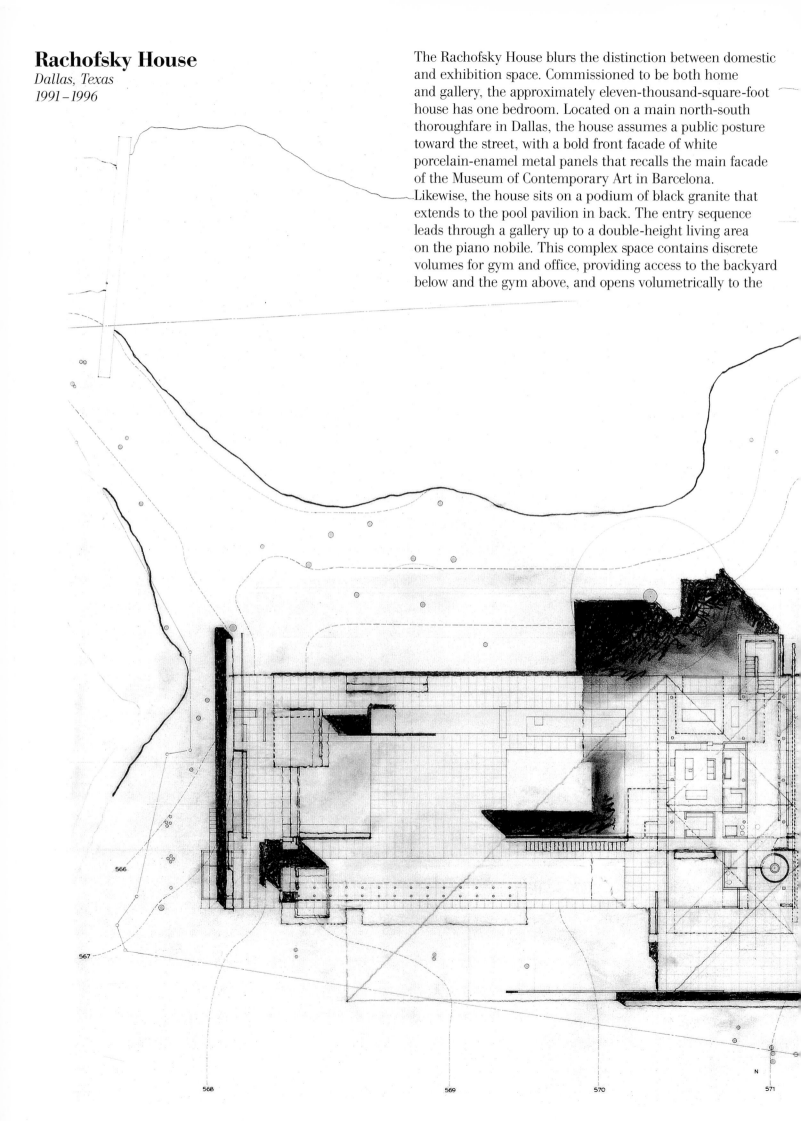

566

567

568

569

570

571

N

gallery on the ground floor. Mullions divide the large spans of glass into a stark asymmetrical composition. Light filters in through clerestories and glazing along the floor. In several rooms, exterior planes of metal panels are placed parallel to window glazing to serve as screening devices, eliminating the need for other window treatments. Outside, Meier sharply differentiates the meticulously composed granite pool area from the site's natural setting and the gently winding stream along its northern edge. The house in effect comprises many elements of Meier's late-1990s work: a program to exhibit art, a clearly delineated relationship to site, interpenetrating spaces, unexpected emissions of light, and multiple layering of wall planes and glass.

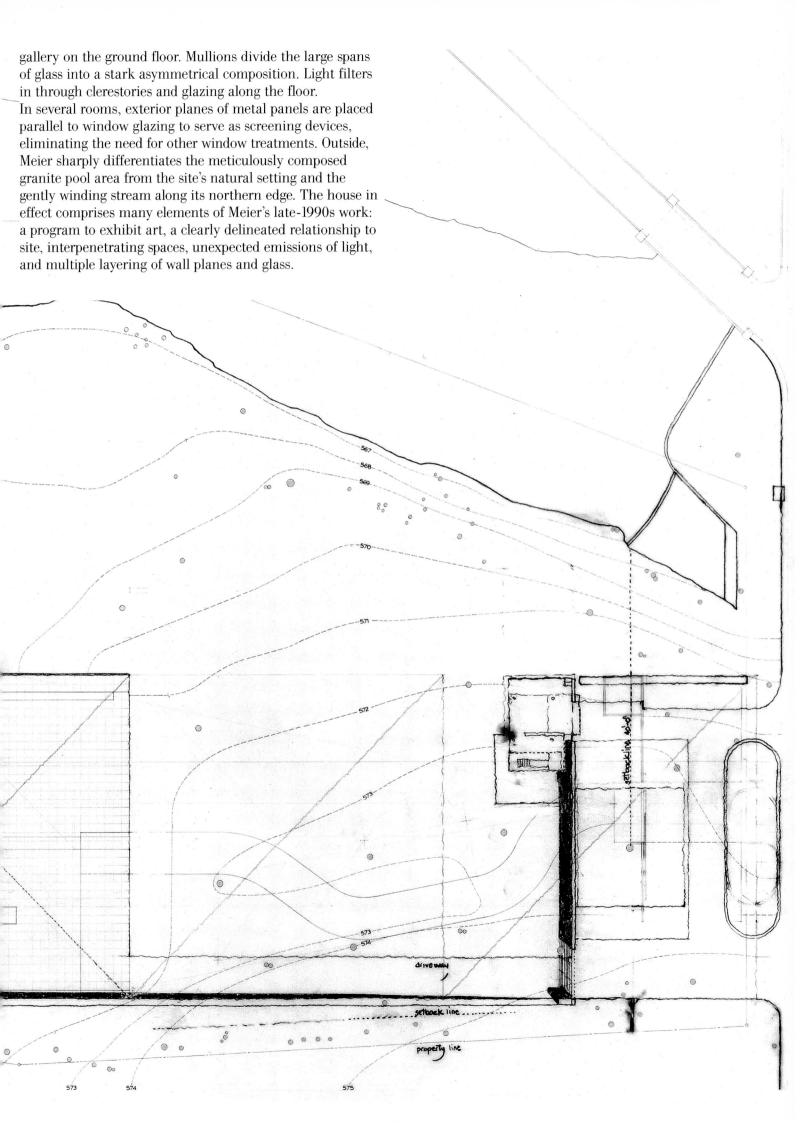

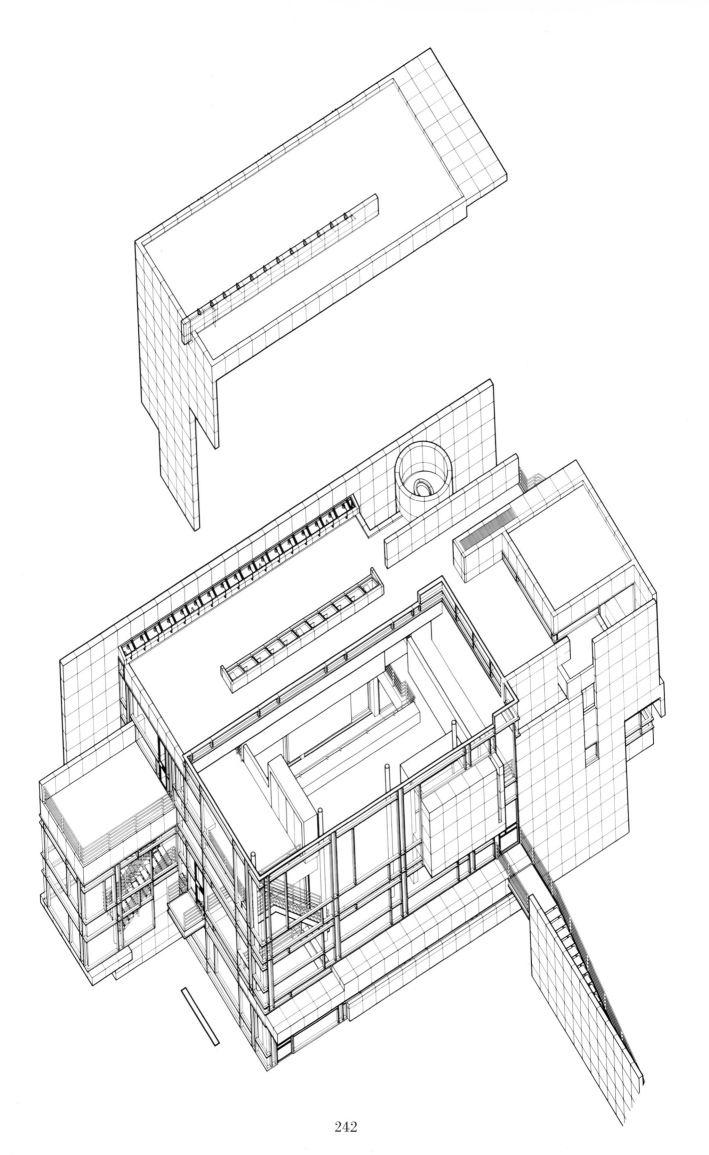

Ground floor plan

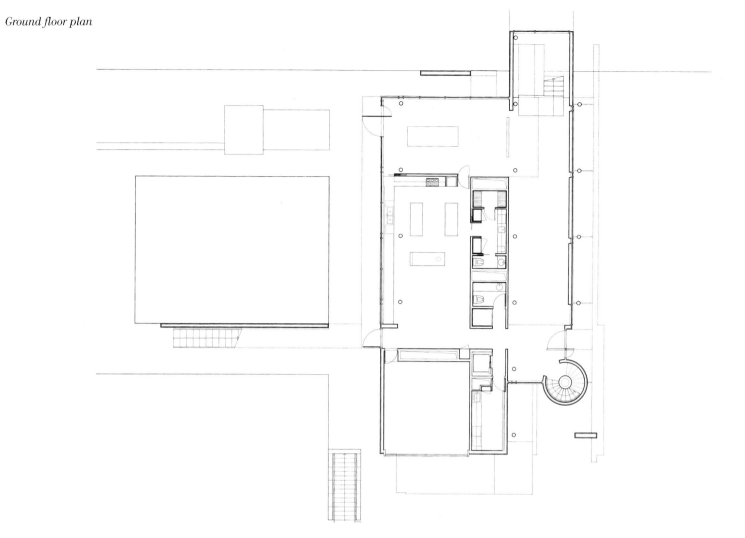

Second floor plan

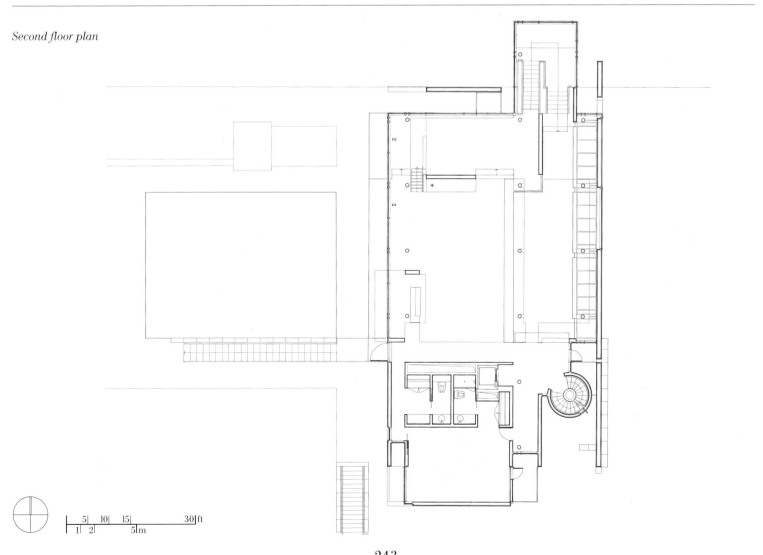

5 10 15   30 ft
1 2   5 m

243

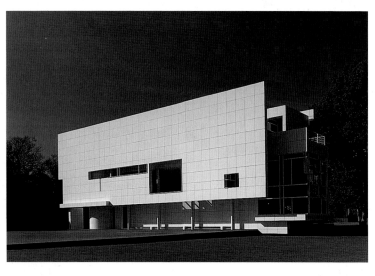

Federal Building and
United States Courthouse
Islip, New York
1993–1999

In the early 1990s, the General Services Administration (GSA)
revised its selection procedures to raise the level of public
architecture in the United States. Under this Design Excellence
initiative, the GSA has hired leading and emerging architects
for new federal buildings around the country, including
Pei Cobb Freed, Cesar Pelli, and Robert A. M. Stern. The GSA
selected Meier for two commissions: federal buildings and
courthouses in Islip, New York, and Phoenix, Arizona.
The two buildings provide an ideal case study for examining
how Meier adapts his design methods to divergent contextual
and climatic conditions. The site in Islip on New York's
Long Island is adjacent to county court facilities and a state
parkway and features panoramic views of the Great South Bay
and the Atlantic Ocean. To define the civic space, Meier
placed the building on a stone podium that becomes
an abstract landscape of low walls, reflective pools, and
geometric plantings. The main facade—a curtain wall
covered by a horizontal brise-soleil—provides sunlight
for public corridors and views of the ocean and front plaza.
The building's grand formal gesture—an extruded conical
drum projecting in front of a rectilinear block—contains the
entry rotunda. The rotunda leads to an eleven-story atrium,
through which is access to courtrooms, library, offices, and
a ceremonial courtroom. Integral to the building's highly
logical plan is an ingenious circulation diagram with distinct
routes for visitors, judges, staff, and prisoners.

Ground floor plan

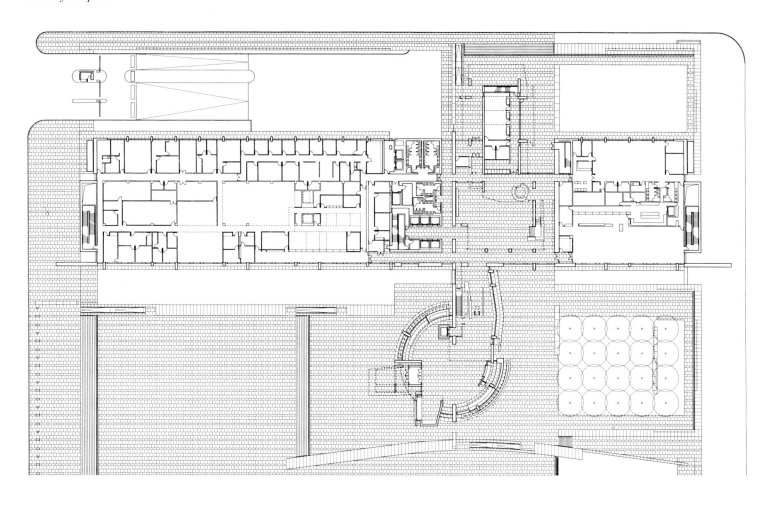

South elevation

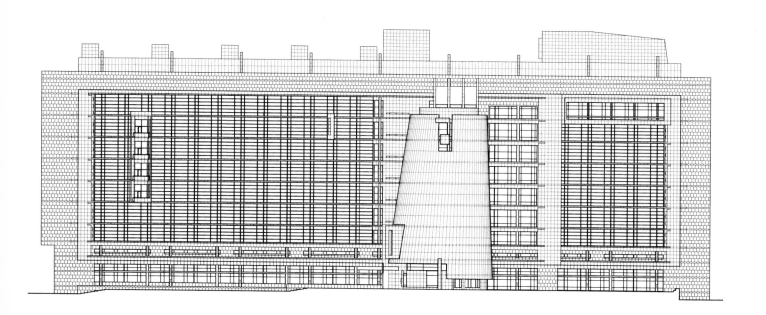

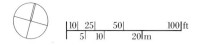

250

Section through rotunda

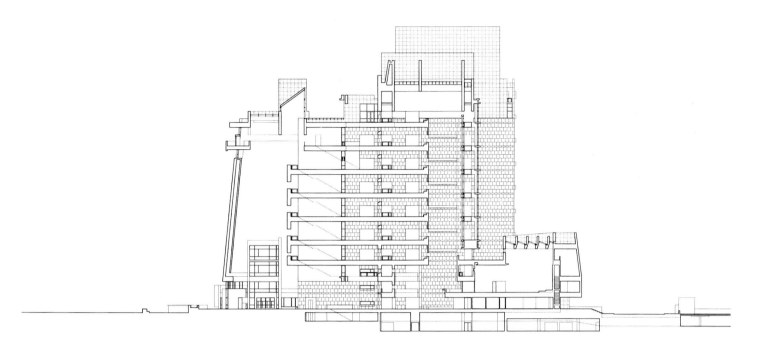

West elevation

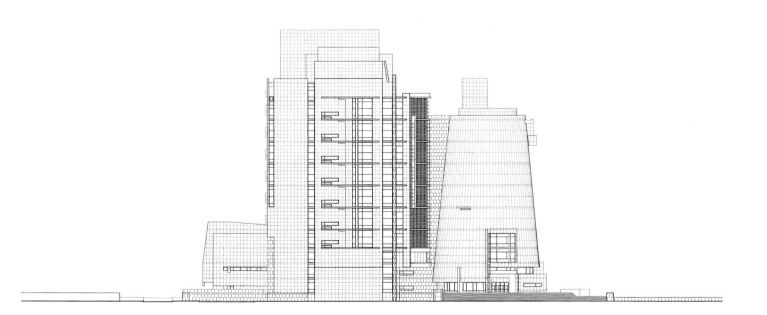

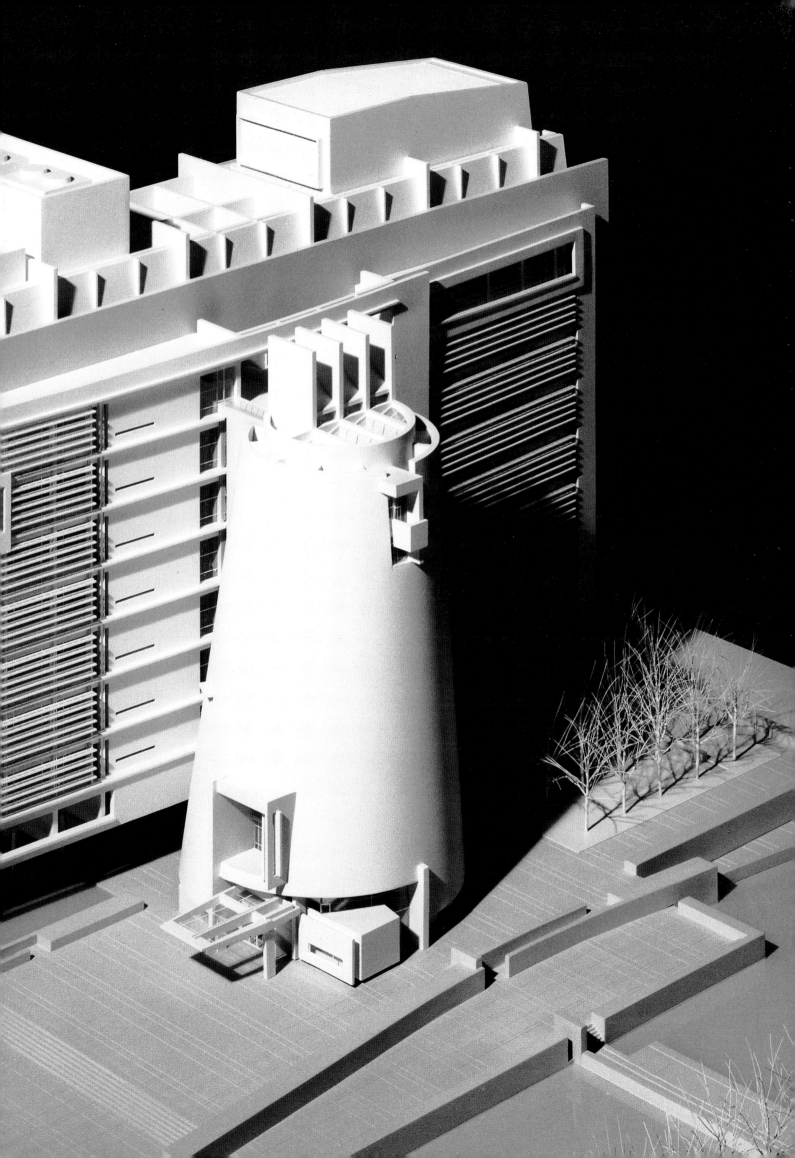

Neugebauer House
Naples, Florida
1995–1998

The Neugebauer House further demonstrates the evolution
of Meier's thinking about residential architecture. His first
single-story house since 1963, this vacation retreat is a direct
statement of transparency and structural clarity in the
tradition of Mies van der Rohe's Farnsworth House of 1946
and Paul Rudolph's Florida beach houses of the 1950s.
Situated in a beachfront area of Naples, the house reflects
Meier's idea that gentle climates allow "extremely simple
and immediate movement between inside and outside."
The plan is accordingly straightforward. Placed on a raised
plinth of Spanish limestone, the house is ordered by
a rectangular module; the only curvilinear element is a
detached garage. Behind a limestone-clad front facade,
a skylit corridor runs the length of the plan. The house is
organized into twelve bays, with portions of two bays left
open to the sky, dividing public from private spaces and
further separating the master bedroom. A reflecting pool
and swimming pool form a narrow band of water that
foregrounds views to Doubloon Bay. The inverted butterfly
roof—a novel response to the community's roof pitch
requirements—brings in abundant sunlight and serves
as a metaphor for air flow engineered into the house.
Like the Phoenix Federal Building, the house is designed
for year-round self-ventilation with an open structure, low
windows, and high ventilation grilles. Brise-soleils and
climate-sensitive building orientation further mitigate heat
gain, and in front of the bedroom wing, a row of trees
provides shade and privacy.

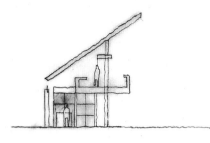

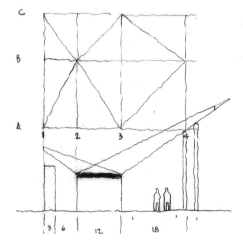

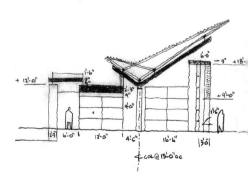

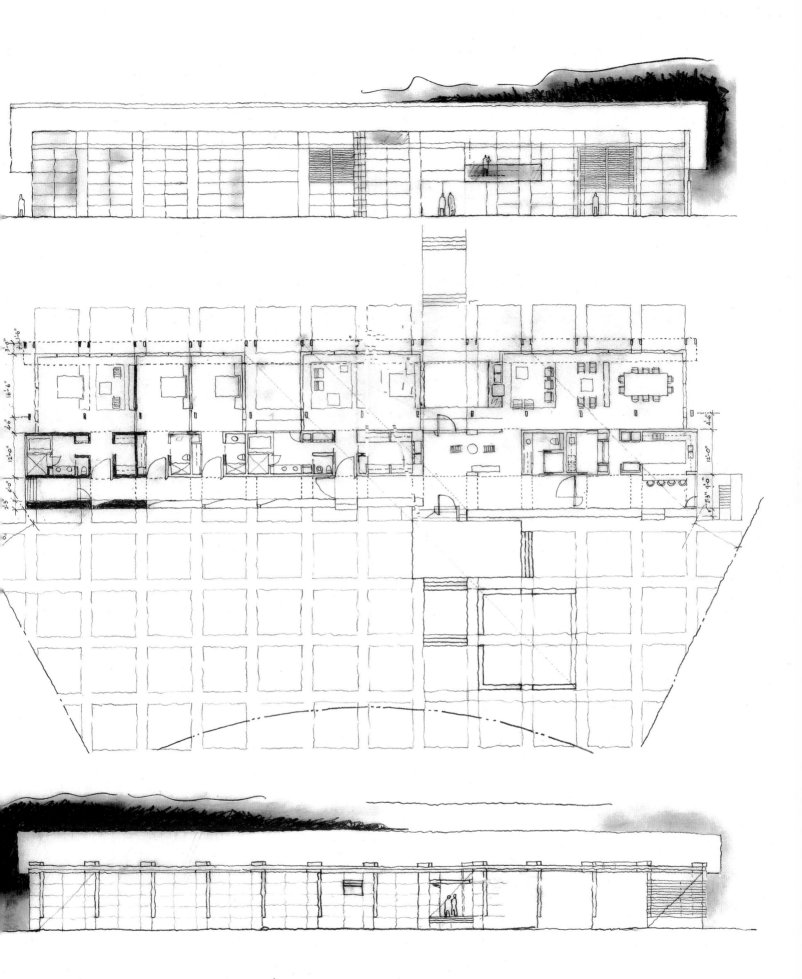

House for Dr. & Mrs. Klaus Neugebauer in Naples, Florida
28 March 1995

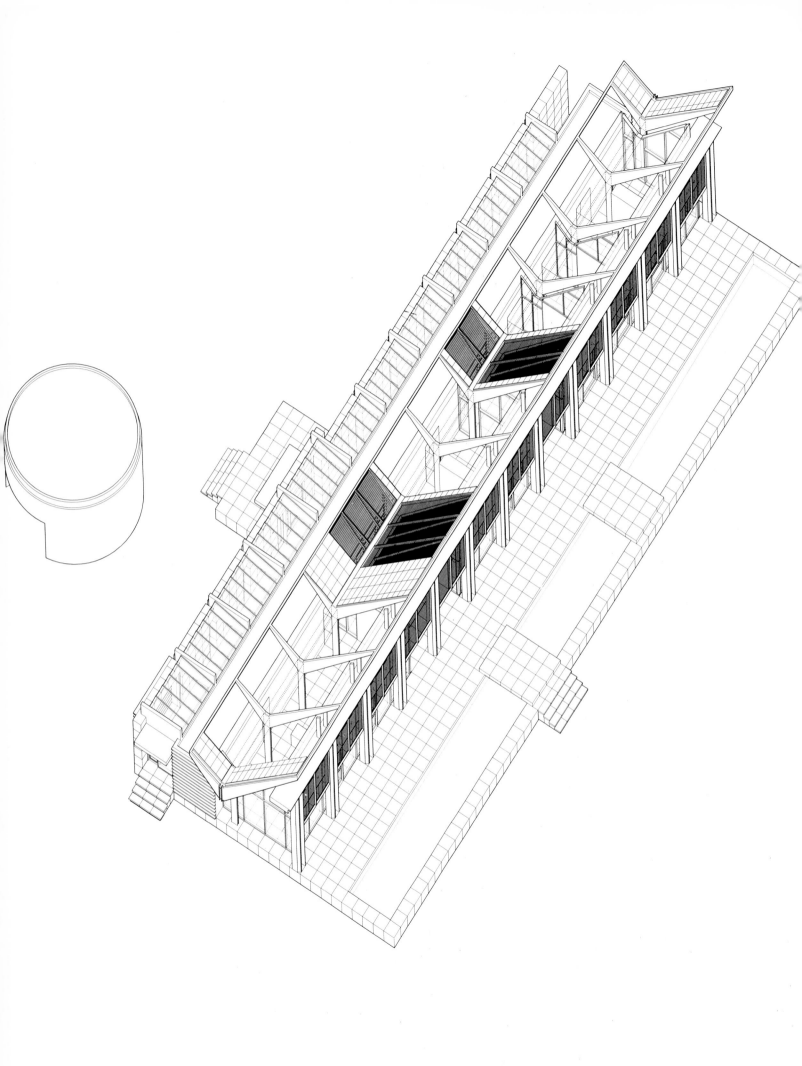

Floor plan

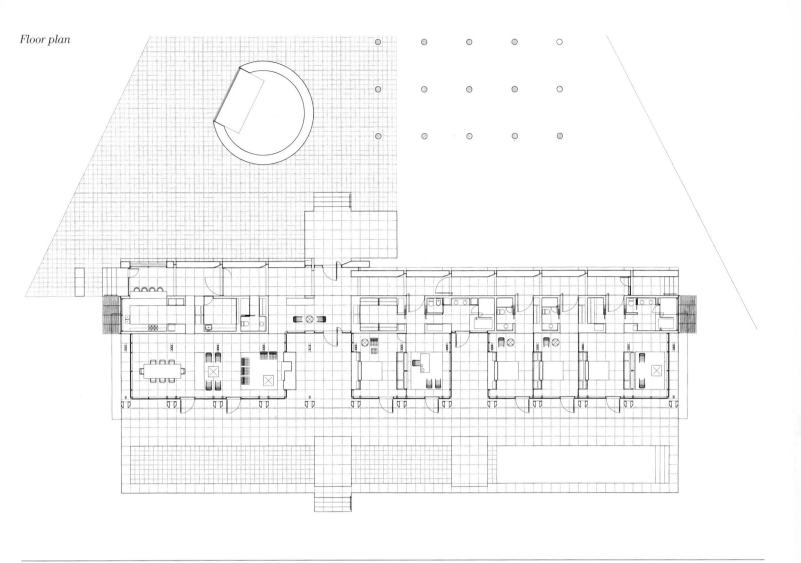

West elevation

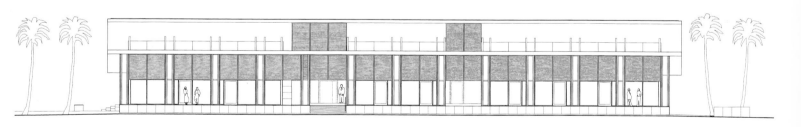

Federal Building and
United States Courthouse
Phoenix, Arizona
1995–1999

In contrast to the Islip Federal Building's outdoor
civic plaza, Meier conceived of the Phoenix Federal Building
and United States Courthouse as a great civic room.
Located downtown, the building's monumental glass hall
—roughly one hundred feet high and a city block long—
literally becomes an oasis in the Sonoran desert.
State-of-the-art climate control and a sophisticated use
of ventilation and daylight demonstrate a keen sensitivity
to the desert. Each facade is designed specifically for its
orientation. The office portion of the building is constructed
of cast-in-place concrete, and the glass hall has a steel space
frame on custom-fabricated steel columns, with aluminum
curtain walls of clear and fritted low-emissivity glass.
The giant atrium uses a simple evaporative cooling system,
engineered by Ove Arup and Partners, that provides
a highly economical way to maintain a comfortable interior
environment year-round. As air heats under skylights
and aluminum solar-control devices, it rises through roof
vents and is replaced by air that is humidified as it enters
through the curtain wall, sending misted updrafts through
the vast space. Like that in Islip, the Phoenix Federal Building
masterfully and clearly organizes its program—district and
magistrate courtrooms, judge chambers, offices, library, café,
child-care facility, health center, and public space—
by security zones. The ceremonial courtroom, an exterior
feature in Islip, is expressed as a circular space contained
within the glass hall.

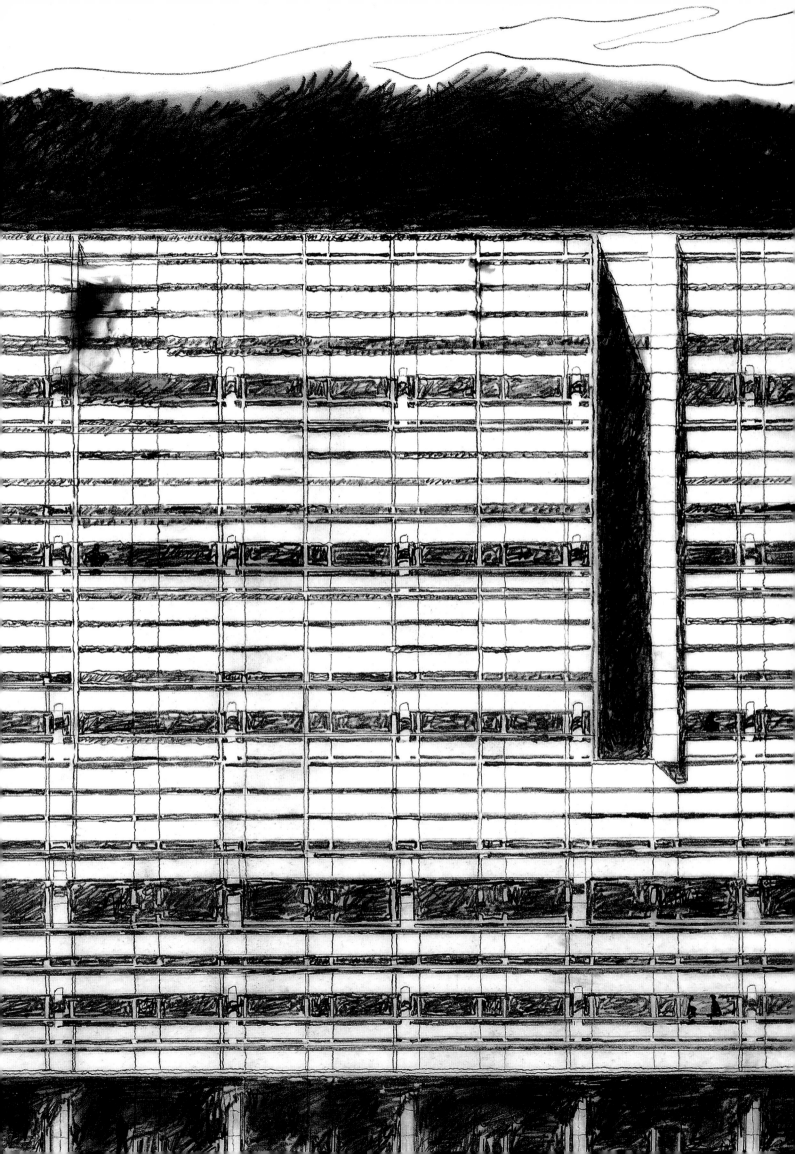

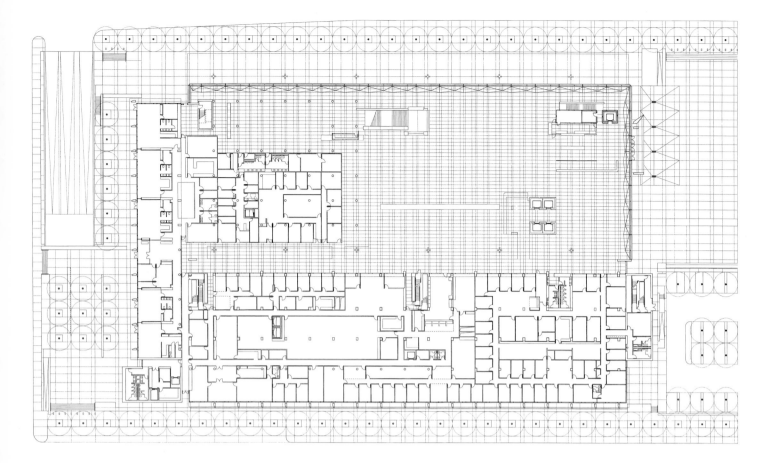

Ground floor plan

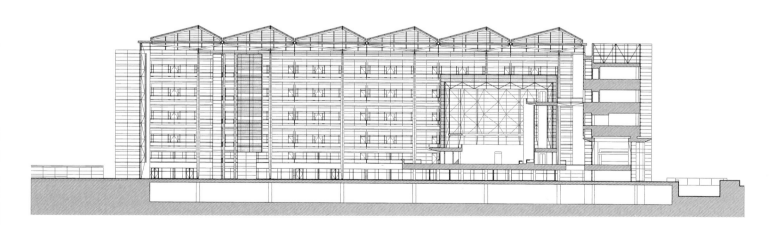

Section facing south

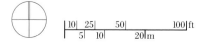

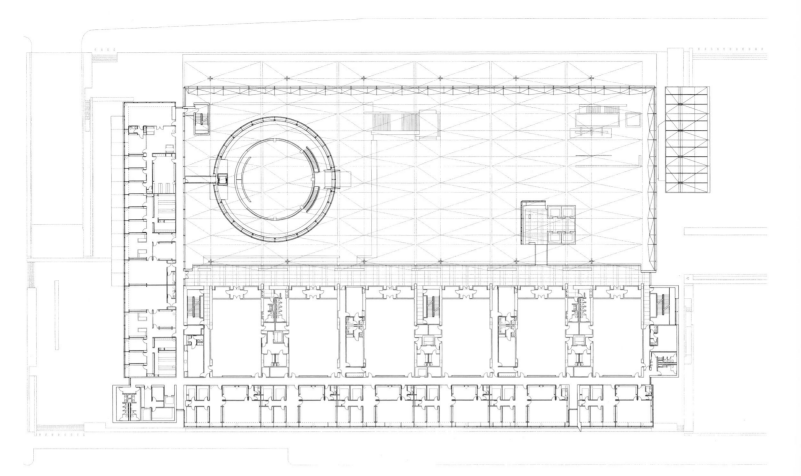

Fifth floor plan

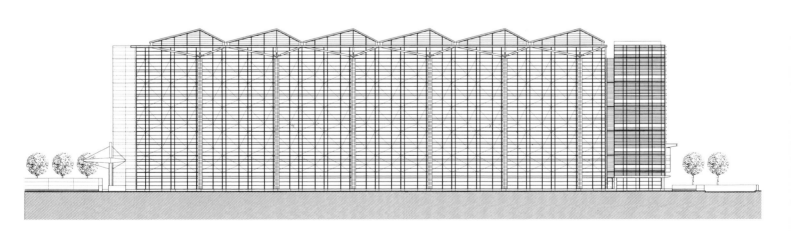

North elevation

Church of the Year 2000

Rome, Italy
1996–2000

In 1996, Meier won the design competition for the Church of the Year 2000. With this award, he became the only foreign architect to participate in the building campaign to construct new churches throughout Italy for the Roman Catholic Jubilee in 2000. Meier's first commission for a religious building since the Hartford Seminary in 1978, the church in Rome demonstrates a considerably different approach toward sacred space. (Meier has also designed the visitor's center for the Crystal Cathedral Ministry in Garden Grove, California, adjacent to Philip Johnson's cathedral.) Meier engages the site—located in the Tor Tre Teste district on the east side of the city—by organizing the church around a public courtyard to one side. Like many of his projects, the church simultaneously corresponds to the urban context and creates a singular sense of place through

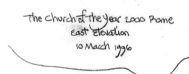

The church of the Year 2000 Rome
East Elevation
10 March 1996

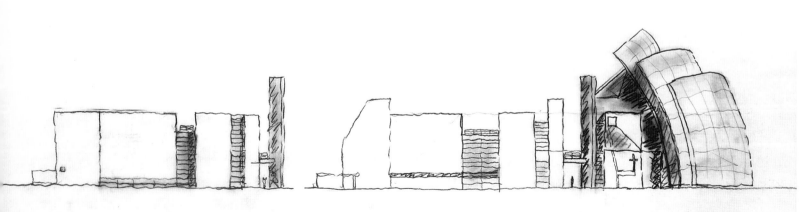

The church of the Year 2000 Rome
West Elevation
12 March 1996

site planning and the form of the design itself. The building's plan denotes the two functions of the church—a community center and a sanctuary. To the east, the L-shaped plan of the community center frames a rectilinear courtyard. To the west, the curvilinear sanctuary is a radical departure from both the rest of the building and Meier's work to date. Sculptural concrete shells—in plan, fragmentary arcs of three intersecting circles—enclose the chapel, with interstices that form skylights and windows. At night, indirect lighting —an integral building material for Meier—transforms the simple geometric shapes into a glowing organic chamber.

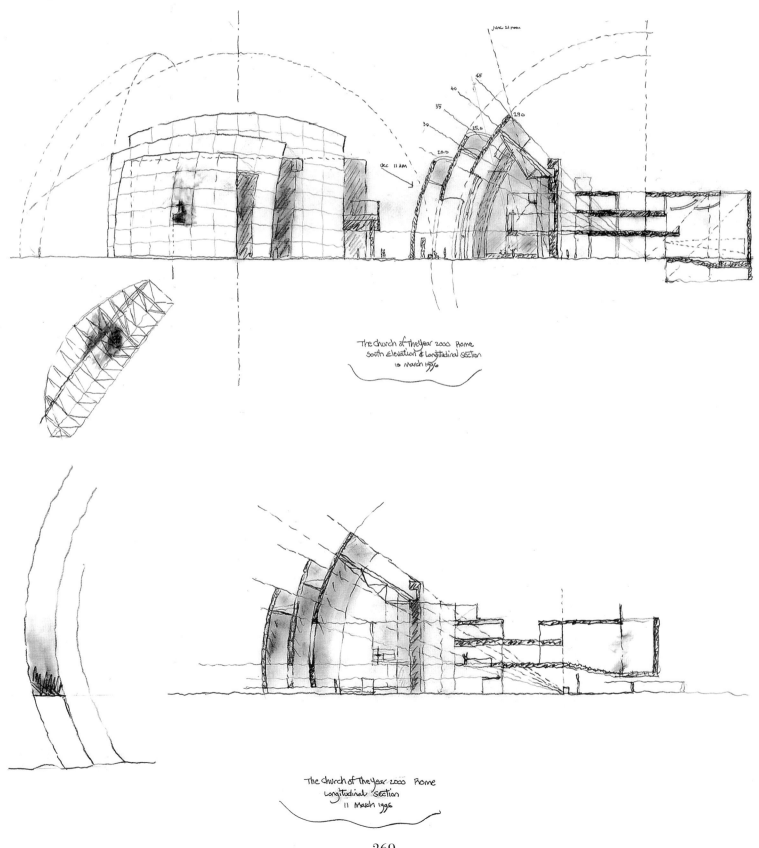

The Church of the Year 2000 Rome
South Elevation & Longitudinal Section
10 March 1996

The Church of the Year 2000 Rome
Longitudinal Section
11 March 1996

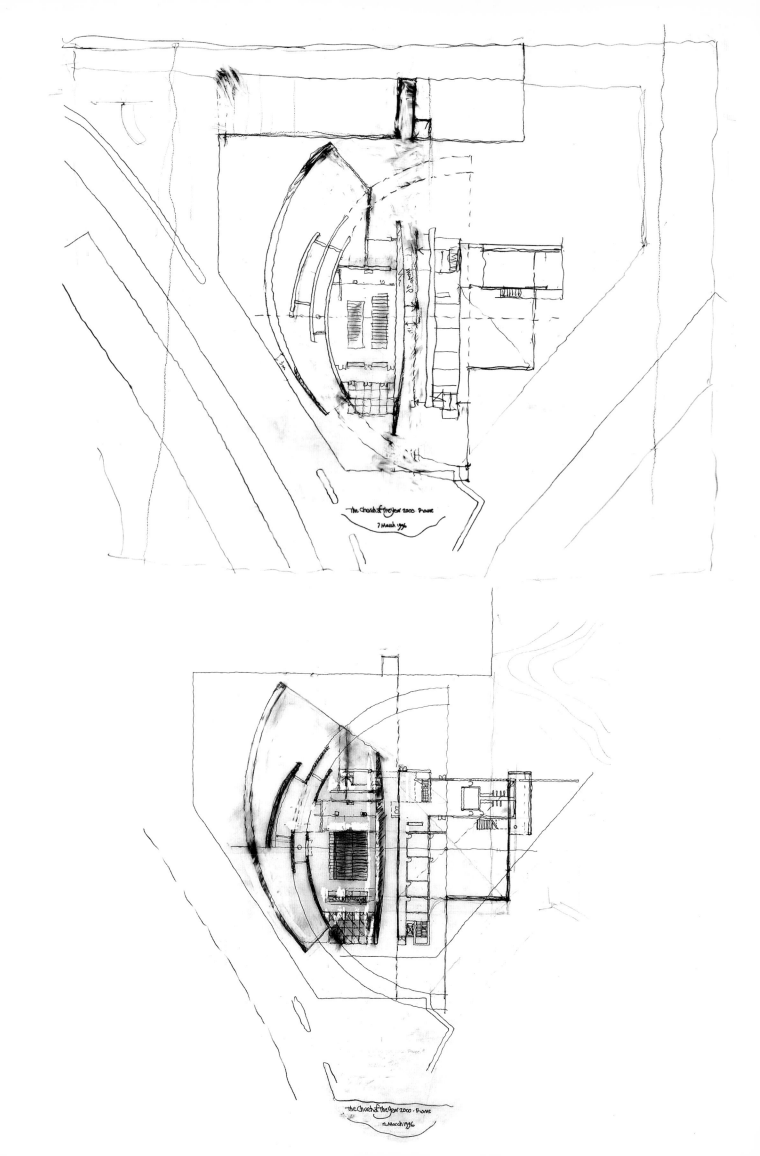

the Church of the Year 2000 - Rome
7 March 1996

the Church of the Year 2000 - Rome
12 March 1996

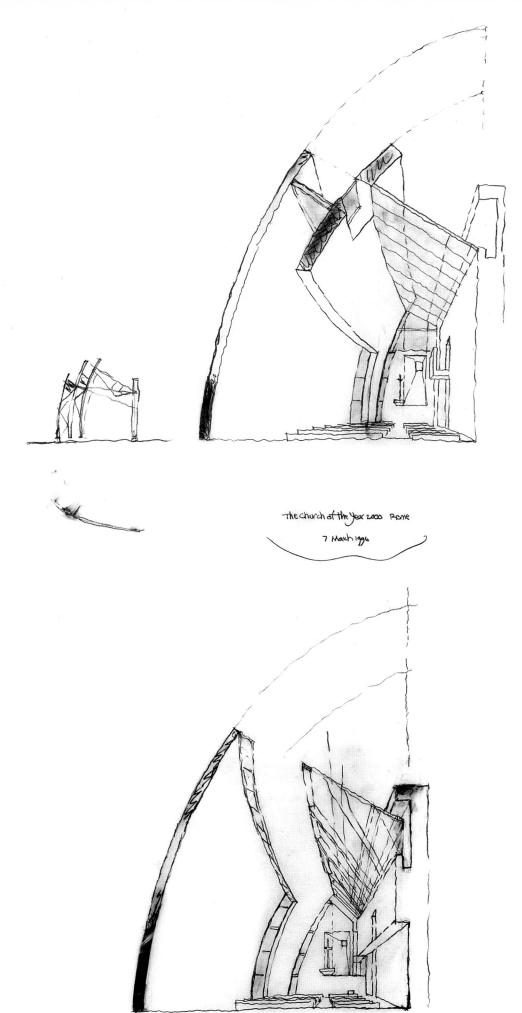

The church of the year 2000   Rome

7 March 1996

The church of The year 2000   Rome

7 March 1996

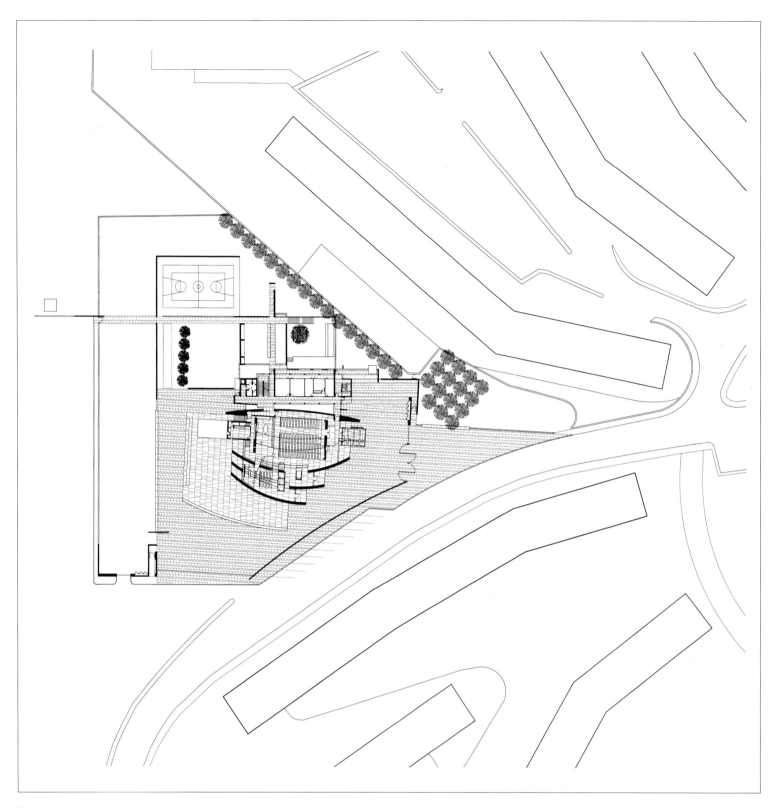

Site plan

East elevation

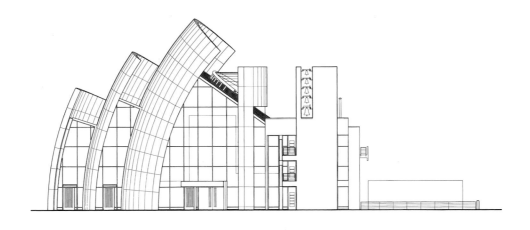

East section

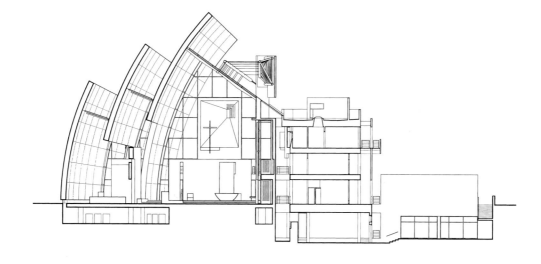

South section

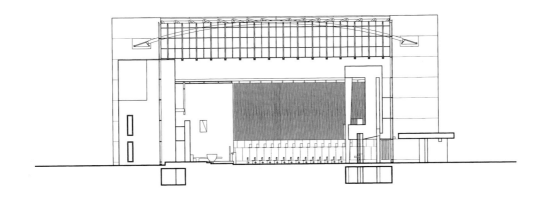

25 50 100   200 ft
10   20   40 m

273

The Richard Meier Archive

Lisa J. Green

The contents of the Richard Meier Archive is a treasure trove of surprises. It contains the entire professional history of Richard Meier and his firm in drawings, sketches, photographs, models, publications, and project files. In addition, the archive encompasses Meier's personal life and includes his collages, paintings, sculptures, private book and art collection, correspondence, and personal photographs. It should come as little surprise to anyone familiar with Meier's work that the rigor and clarity of his architecture extends to the organization of his office and his archives. An exhibition and catalogue such as this would never have been possible without the archive, currently housed in the New York office of Richard Meier & Partners.

An architectural archive in a working office is different from one housed in a university or museum: it is a much more fluid enterprise, with an aim to serve both current and future pursuits. It documents current projects and provides material for myriad public activities of the firm such as publications, exhibitions, lectures, award submissions, and new business proposals. It also preserves and organizes the work for research by future scholars.

The collection is strongest in original sketches from the 1980s and 1990s. In the early years of the office, it was probably difficult to recognize the importance of archiving, and many significant sketches from the 1960s and 1970s unfortunately were lost. But what remains ranges from alternative schemes for the Atheneum to plan studies of the Getty Research Institute worked over during meetings between the architect and the client. One of my personal favorites is a sketch of the Madison Square Garden Site Redevelopment drawn on an $8\,^1/_2$ x 11 sheet of paper and faxed to the office from Los Angeles. The small sketches on that page are essentially the design that was finally presented to the client.

Photographs are as important a part of the archives as the sketches. In addition to the great number of professional photographs by Ezra Stoller and others, Meier's own images—mostly unpublished—are an integral part of the collection. Meier, a gifted photographer, understands the power of the medium to convey the image of architecture and has documented almost all of his own buildings. Seeing how he has chosen to photograph his buildings is important to understanding the architect's intention.

Meier's travel slides—more than five thousand of them—are also part of the archives. These are a fascinating record of the architect's eye: where he went, what buildings he chose to document, the camera angles he used. There are many slides of his first extended trip to Europe from 1959–60, where he visited Aalto and Le Corbusier buildings, among other things. New York's Lower East Side is represented in a series also dating from 1959: we see the discovery of the rich fabric of the city through the eye of a recent college graduate. In addition, slides from his seminal 1962 trip to Frank Lloyd Wright's Fallingwater punctuate the period during which he was designing the house for his parents.

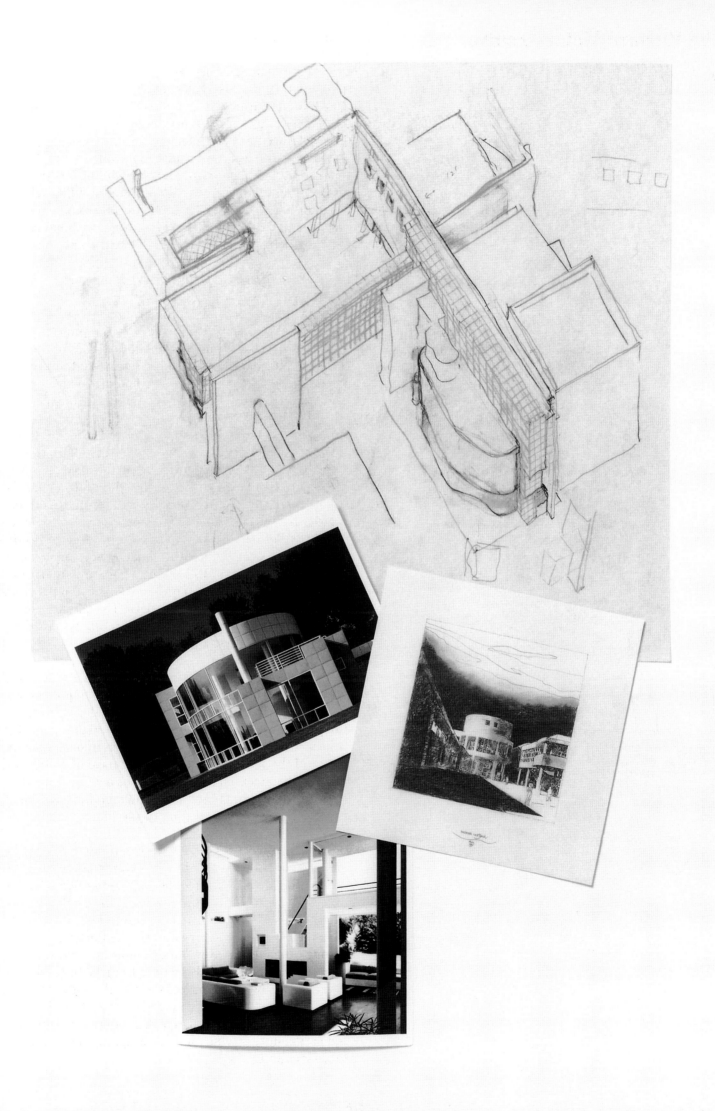

Meier, an avid bibliophile, owns thousands of books and periodicals—another part of the archives. Most of these are kept in his apartment, where he refers to them constantly. The books, primarily volumes on architecture or art, are organized alphabetically by architect or artist; the overflow is stacked precisely in mini-towers on stools and the floor. Meier often seeks out first editions and out-of-print books while traveling and is well known in most antiquarian book shops. He tries to fill gaps in the collection: I once overheard him lamenting to Joseph Rykwert that he was unable to find the first issue of *Arquitectura Bis* and that otherwise he would have every volume—and Rykwert quickly informed him that he had the complete set. There are also rare folios, including a series on Tony Garnier's designs for the Paris Opéra. While uncatalogued, the books constitute one of the most extensive private collections of twentieth-century architecture books in the United States.

The Richard Meier Archive is not only the history of a person but also the history of a certain period in the history of architecture in New York. For instance, for the last thirty years a group of architects has been meeting informally a few times a year to discuss issues relevant to the current practice of architecture. Initially these meetings were held in the home of writer Arthur Cohen and his wife, graphic designer Elaine Lustig Cohen. As the size of these meetings grew they were moved to their current setting, the Century Club. Meier was instrumental in organizing these meetings from their beginning and the Richard Meier Archive is the only place to find a list of participants— a veritable who's who, or who was who, of contemporary architecture.

The archive is full of hidden jewels that await future generations of scholars. For a period of time in the mid-1970s and again in 1984, the members of the original New York Five—Peter Eisenman, Michael Graves, Charles Gwathmey, John Hejduk, and Meier—met again to discuss and critique each other's current work. These meetings were intended to be private in order to give the architects a place to openly give and receive criticism. The archive houses cassette tapes, never transcribed, of these important private discussions.

Every effort has been made to keep the archive together rather than portioning off individual projects to separate institutions. Few exceptions to this have been made: the Atheneum model and sketches were donated to the Museum of Modern Art in New York in 1984, and several sketches of the Barcelona Museum of Contemporary Art were donated to that institution when it opened in 1995. The final disposition of the Richard Meier Archive is still uncertain. One only hopes that an appropriate institution will step forward at the necessary time to acquire it. Preserving the archive intact and keeping it accessible to researchers will be a valuable asset to the history of twentieth-century architecture.

Buildings and Projects 1960–1999

Franklin Delano Roosevelt Memorial
Competition entry (with George Nelson and Michael Graves)
Washington, D.C.
1960

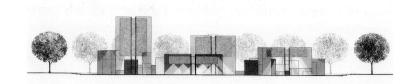

Lambert House
Fire Island, New York
1961–62

Exhibition, Design and Organization
Recent American Synagogue Architecture
The Jewish Museum
New York, New York
1963

Meier House
Essex Fells, New Jersey
1963–65

Monumental Fountain
Competition entry (with Frank Stella)
Benjamin Franklin Parkway
Philadelphia, Pennsylvania
1964

Dotson House
Ithaca, New York
1964–66

Renfield House
(with Elaine Lustig Cohen)
Chester, New Jersey
1964–66

"Sona" Shop for the Handicrafts and Handlooms
Exports Corporation of India
(with Elaine Lustig Cohen)
New York, New York
1965–67

Studio and Apartment for Frank Stella
New York, New York
1965

Smith House
Darien, Connecticut
1965–67

University Arts Center
Competition entry (with John Hejduk and Robert Slutzky)
University of California
Berkeley, California
1965

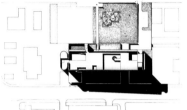
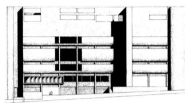

Rubin Loft Renovation
New York, New York
1966

Mental Health Facilities
West Orange, New Jersey
Jewish Counseling and Service Agency
1966

Hoffman House
East Hampton, New York
1966–67

Westbeth Artists' Housing
New York, New York
J. M. Kaplan Fund and the National Council on the Arts
1967–70

Saltzman House
East Hampton, New York
1967–69

Health and Physical Education Building
State University College
Fredonia, New York
New York State University Construction Fund
1968

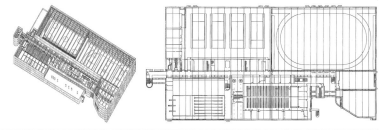
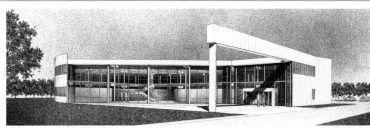

Charles Evans Industrial Buildings
Fairfield, New Jersey, and Piscataway, New Jersey
1969

Bronx Redevelopment Planning Study
New York City Housing and Development Administration and
The New York City Planning Commission
1969

House in Pound Ridge
Pound Ridge, New York
1969

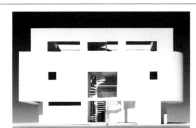

House in Old Westbury
Old Westbury, New York
1969–71

Monroe Developmental Center
(with Todd & Giroux Associates Architects)
Rochester, New York
Facilities Development Corporation for the
New York State Department of Mental Hygiene
1969–74

Twin Parks Northeast Housing
The Bronx, New York
New York State Urban Development Corporation
1969–74

Robert R. Young Housing
New York, New York
General Properties Corporation
1969

The Bronx Developmental Center
Bronx, New York
Facilities Development Corporation for the
New York State Department of Mental Hygiene
1970–77

Maidman House
Sands Point, New York
1971–76

Douglas House
Harbor Springs, Michigan
1971–73

Olivetti Branch Office Prototype
Irvine, California; Kansas City,
Missouri; Minneapolis, Minnesota;
Boston, Massachusetts; Brooklyn, New York;
Patterson, New Jersey
Olivetti Corporation of North America
1971

Modification of the Olivetti Branch Office Prototype
Riverside, California; Albuquerque, New Mexico; Tucson,
Arizona; Fort Worth, Texas; Portland, Maine; Memphis,
Tennessee; Roanoke, Virginia
Olivetti Corporation of North America
1971

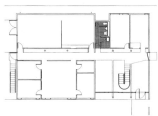

Dormitory for the Olivetti Training Center
Tarrytown, New York
Olivetti Corporation of North America
1971

Olivetti Headquarters Building
Fairfax, Virginia
Olivetti Corporation of North America
1971

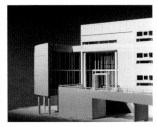

East Side Housing
(with Emery Roth, Architects)
New York, New York
Tishman Realty and Construction Corporation
1972

Shamberg House
Chappaqua, New York
1972–74

Paddington Station Housing
New York, New York
1973

Museum of Modern Art at the Villa Strozzi
Florence, Italy
Comune di Firenze
1973

Condominium Housing
Yonkers, New York
H Development Corporation
1974

 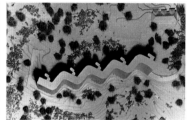

Cornell University Undergraduate Housing
Ithaca, New York
1974

Commercial Building and Hotel
Springfield, Massachusetts
Mondev International Corporation
1975

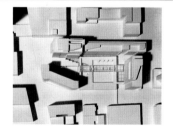

Wingfield Racquet Club
Greenwich, Connecticut
H Development Corporation
1975

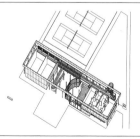

The Warehouse Rehabilitation for the Bronx Psychiatric Center
Bronx, New York
Facilities Development Corporation for the
New York State Department of Mental Hygiene
1975–78

The Atheneum
New Harmony, Indiana
Historic New Harmony, Inc.
1975–79

The Theatrum
New Harmony, Indiana
Historic New Harmony, Inc.
1975

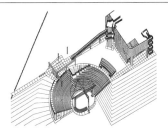

Sarah Campbell Blaffer Pottery Studio
New Harmony, Indiana
The Robert Lee Blaffer Trust
1975–78

Alamo Plaza
Colorado Springs, Colorado
Mondev International Corporation
1976

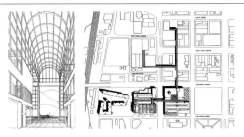

Suburban House Prototype
Concord, Massachusetts
1976

Weber-Frankel Gallery
New York, New York
1976

Opening Exhibition, Cooper-Hewitt Museum
New York, New York
1976

Manchester Civic Center
Manchester, New Hampshire
Mondev International Corporation
1977

New York School Exhibition Design
State Museum
Albany Mall, New York
State of New York Office of General Services
1977

Aye Simon Reading Room
Solomon R. Guggenheim Museum
New York, New York
1977–78

Suarez Apartment
New York, New York
1977–78

House in Palm Beach
Palm Beach, Florida
1977–78; addition 1993–95

Furniture Designs for Knoll
1978–82

Clifty Creek Elementary School
Columbus, Indiana
Batholomew Consolidated School Corporation
1978–82

The Hartford Seminary
Hartford, Connecticut
1978–81

Irwin Union Bank and Trust Company
Columbus, Indiana
1979

House in Pittsburgh
Pittsburgh, Pennsylvania
1979–83

Museum for the Decorative Arts
Frankfurt am Main, Germany
Stadt Frankfurt am Main
1979–85

East 67th Street Housing
New York, New York
Sheldon Solow
1980

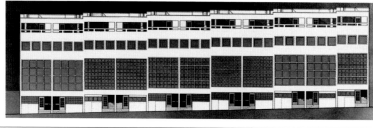

Somerset Condominiums
Beverly Hills, California
The Somerset Company
1980

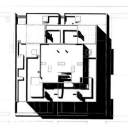

High Museum of Art
Atlanta, Georgia
Atlanta Arts Alliance
1980–83

Coffee and Tea Service for Alessi Design
1980

Meier/Stella Collaboration
1980

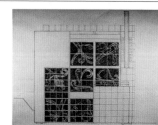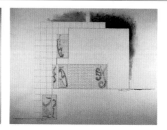

Renault Administrative Headquarters
Boulogne-Billancourt, France
Le Régie Nationale des Usines Renault
1981

Internationale Bauausstellung Housing
Berlin, Germany
1982

Parc de la Villette
Competition entry
Paris, France
1982

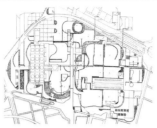

Des Moines Art Center Addition
Des Moines, Iowa
Edmundson Art Foundation
1982–85

Siemens Corporate Headquarters
Munich, Germany
1983–99

Lingotto Factory Conversion
Competition entry
Turin, Italy
Fiat S.p.A.
1983

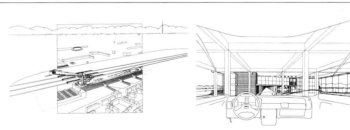

Opéra Bastille
Competition entry
Paris, France
1983

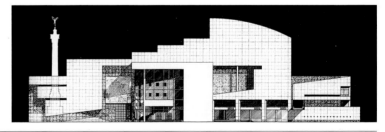

Designs for Swid Powell
1983–present

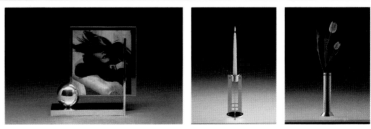

Westchester House
Westchester County, New York
1984–86

Helmick House
Des Moines, Iowa
1984

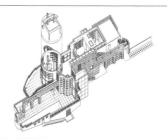

Siemens Office and Laboratory Complex
Munich, Germany
1984–99

Ackerberg House
Malibu, California
1984–86; addition 1992–94

Bridgeport Center
Bridgeport, Connecticut
People's Bank
1984–89

Barnum Museum
Bridgeport, Connecticut
1984–89

The Getty Center
Los Angeles, California
The J. Paul Getty Trust
1984–97

Grotta House
Harding Township, New Jersey
1985–89

Office, Richard Meier & Partners
New York and Los Angeles
1986

Supreme Court Building
Competition entry
Jerusalem, Israel
1986

Progetto Bicocca
Competition entry
Milan, Italy
Pirelli, S.p.A.
1986

Exhibition and Assembly Building
Ulm, Germany
City of Ulm
1986–93

City Hall and Central Library
The Hague, The Netherlands
Algemeen Burgerlijk Persioenfonds
1986–95

Eye Center
Portland, Oregon
Oregon Health Sciences University
1986

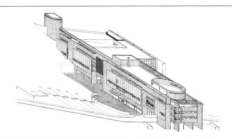

Rachofsky House I
Dallas, Texas
1986

Progetto per Napoli
Naples, Italy
University of Naples
1987

National Investment Bank
The Hague, The Netherlands
1987

Santa Monica Beach Hotel
Competition entry
Santa Monica, California
Four Fifteen Development Corporation
1987

Madison Square Garden Site Redevelopment
Competition entry
New York, New York
Olympia & York Companies (USA)
1987

Weishaupt Forum
Schwendi, Germany
Max Weishaupt, GmbH
1987–92

Royal Dutch Paper Mills Headquarters
Hiversum, The Netherlands
Koninklijke Nederlandse Papierfabrieken
1987–92

Museum of Contemporary Art
Barcelona, Spain
1987–95

Cornell University Alumni and Admissions Center
Ithaca, New York
1988

Apartment Interior
Chicago, Illinois
1988

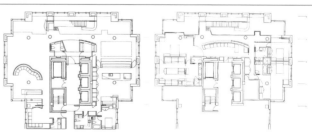

Canal+ Headquarters
Paris, France
1988–92

Espace Pitôt
Montpellier, France
URBAT
1988–93

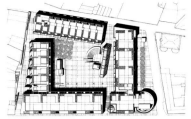

Administrative and Maritime Center Master Plan
Antwerp, Belgium
EPMC
1988

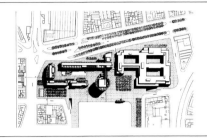

Edinburgh Park Master Plan
Edinburgh, Scotland
Enterprise Edinburgh
1988

Lighting Designs for Baldinger
1988–present

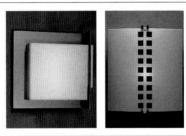

Daimler-Benz Research Center
Ulm, Germany
1989–93

Office Building
Frankfurt, Germany
Harald Quandt Holding
1989

Bibliothèque de France
Competition entry
Paris, France
1989

Fox Studio Expansion and Renovation
Los Angeles, California
1989

CMB Corporate Headquarters
Antwerp, Belgium
1989

Hypolux Bank Building
Luxembourg
Hypo Bank International, S.A.
1989–93

Museum of Ethnology
Frankfurt am Main, Germany
Stadt Frankfurt am Main
1989

Sextius Mirabeau Master Plan
Competition entry
Aix-en-Provence, France
Bouyges
1990

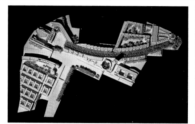

Arp Museum
Rolandseck, Germany
Foundation Hans Arp
1990–2001

Euregio Office Building
Basel, Switzerland
Credit Suisse
1990–98

Camden Medical Center
Singapore
Pontiac Land Private Limited
1990–99

Rachofsky House
Dallas, Texas
1991–96

Office Building
Berlin, Germany
Beteiligungen GmbH & Co.
1991

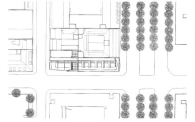

Plateau Tercier Master Plan
Nice, France
Setom
1991

Swissair North American Headquarters
Melville, New York
1991–95

Potsdamer-Platz Master Plan
Competition entry
Berlin, Germany
Daimler Benz, AG
1992

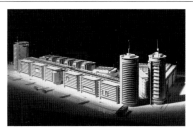

House in Wiesbaden
Wiesbaden, Germany
1992

Glass Designs for Steuben
1992

Office Furniture
Stow Davis
1992

Federal Building and United States Courthouse
(with Spectorgroup Architects)
Islip, New York
General Services Administration
1993–99

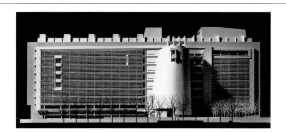

Administrative Building
Marckolsheim, France
Jungbunzlauer, S.A.
1993

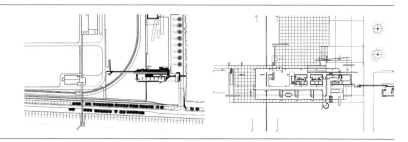

Museum of Television & Radio
Beverly Hills, California
1994–96

Compaq Computer Adminstrative, Manufacturing, and Distribution Center Master Plan
Houston, Texas
1994

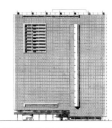

Gagosian Gallery
Beverly Hills, California
1994–95

Berliner Volksbank Headquarters
Competition entry
Berlin, Germany
1994

Federal Building and United States Courthouse
(with Langdon Wilson Architects)
Phoenix, Arizona
General Services Administration
1995–99

Neugebauer House
Naples, Florida
1995–98

Swiss RE Headquarters
Competition entry
Kingston, New York
1995

Grand Piano
Rud. Ibach Sohn
1995

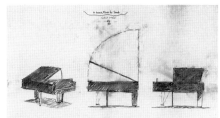

Ara Pacis Museum
Rome, Italy
Comune di Roma
1996–2000

Church of the Year 2000
Rome, Italy
Vicariato di Roma
1996–2000

Kolonihavehus
Copenhagen, Denmark
1996–2000

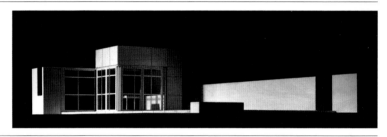

Crystal Cathedral Visitor's Center
Garden Grove, California
1996

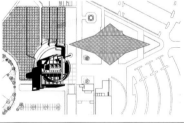

Coordinated Street Furniture
New York, New York
Adshel Inc.
1996

House in Kuala Lumpur
Kuala Lumpur, Malaysia
1997–99

Glasgow Exhibition House
Glasgow, Scotland
Wimpey Homes Holdings, Ltd.
1997

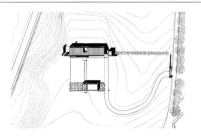

Tag McLaren Headquarters
Woking, Surrey, England
1997

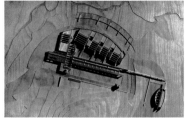

Indoor/Outdoor Seating
MABEG Kreuschner GmbH
1997

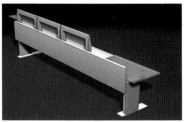

Westwood Promenade
Los Angeles, California
Christina Development Corporation
1998

Deutsche Post Building
Competition entry
Bonn, Germany
1998

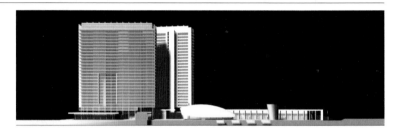

Peek & Cloppenburg Department Store
Düsseldorf, Germany
1998–2001

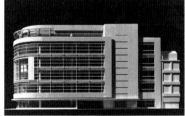

Bayer AG Headquarters
Competition entry
Leverkusen, Germany
1998

Scottish Parliament
Competition entry
Edinburgh, Scotland
The Foreign Office
1998

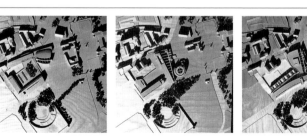

Cittadella Bridge
Alessandria, Italy
Comune di Alessandria
1998–2000

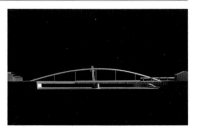

Office Building
Tokyo, Japan
1998–2001

Rickmers Headquarters
Hamburg, Germany
1998–2000

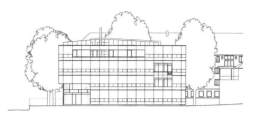

Friesen Residence
Los Angeles, California
1998–99

San Jose Civic Center
San Jose, California
San Jose Redevelopment Authority
1998–2003

Malibu House
Malibu, California
1999–2001

Selected Bibliography

Books and Special Issues—General

Blaser, Werner. *Richard Meier: Building for Art*. Basel: Birkhäuser Verlag, GmbH, 1990.

Blaser, Werner. *Richard Meier Details*. Basel: Birkhäuser Verlag, GmbH, 1996.

Cassarà, Silvio. *Richard Meier*. Bologna: Zanichelli Editore S.p.A., 1995. Reprinted in German. Basel: Birkhäuser Verlag, GmbH, 1996. Reprinted in Spanish. Barcelona: Editorial Gustavo Gili, S.A., 1997.

Ciorra, Pippo, ed. *Richard Meier*. Includes "Richard Meier o la rappresentazione della modernità" by Livio Sacchi. Milan: Electa, 1993.

Costanzo, Michele, Vincenzo Giorgi, and Maria Grazia Tolomeo, eds. *Richard Meier /Frank Stella: Arte e Architettura*. Exhibition catalogue. Includes "All Time is Unredeemable" by Franco Purini; "The Work of Richard Meier: Origins and Influences" by Roberto Einaudi; "Volumes Under Light" by Michele Costanzo; "The Principle of Settlement" by Vincenzo Giorgi; "Richard Meier and Frank Stella: A Conversation between Architect and Artist" edited by Peter Slatin; "A Relationship in the Industry of Excellence" by Earl Childress. Milan: Electa, 1993.

Fernandez-Galiano, Luis, ed. *Arquitectura Viva Monografias 59: Richard Meier in Europe*. Includes "Houses and Museums: Meier in America" by Jorge Sainz; "A European America" by Alexander Tzonis and Liane Lefaivre; "Modern or Contemporary" by Joseph Giovannini; "Transparency and Perspective" by Stephan Barthelmess. May/June 1996.

Five Architects: Eisenman/Graves/Gwathmey/Hejduk/Meier. Introductions by Kenneth Frampton and Colin Rowe. New York: Wittenborn, 1972, pp. 11–13, 111–34. Reprinted in Spanish. Barcelona: Editorial Gustavo Gili, S.A., 1976. Reprinted in Italian. Rome: Officina Edizioni, 1976.

Five Architects/Twenty Years Later. Includes "The Five After Twenty-Five: An Assessment" by Kenneth Frampton; introduction by Steven W. Hurtt; "Recollections" by Ralph Bennett. College Park, Md.: University of Maryland, 1992.

Flagge, Ingeborg, and Oliver Hamm, eds. *Richard Meier in Europe*. Berlin: Ernst & Sohn, 1997.

Haito, Masahiko, and Midori Nishizawa, eds. *Richard Meier and Frank Stella: Architecture and Art*. Exhibition catalogue. Includes "Meier's Toad and Stella's Garden" by David Galloway; "Ecstasy of the Artificer: On the Architecture of Richard Meier" by Seiken Fukuda. Tokyo: Akira Ikeda Corporation, 1996.

Izzo, Ferruccio, and Alessandro Gubitosi, eds. *Richard Meier Architetture /Projects 1986–1990*. Exhibition catalogue. Naples: Palazzo Reale, June 21–July 21, 1991. Includes essays by Vittorio Magnago Lampugnani, Alberto Izzo, Camillo Gubitosi, Ferruccio Izzo. Florence: Centro Di, 1991.

Jodidio, Philip. *Richard Meier*. Cologne: Benedikt Taschen Verlag, 1995.

Nesbitt, Lois. *Richard Meier: Collages*. Includes "The Art of Abstraction" interview with Richard Meier by Clare Farrow. New York: St. Martin's Press, 1990.

Nesbitt, Lois. *Richard Meier Sculpture: 1992–1994*. New York: Rizzoli, 1994.

Papadakis, Andreas C., ed. *The New Modern Aesthetic*. Includes "Richard Meier and the City in Miniature" by Kenneth Frampton; "The Tate Gallery Discussion" with Richard Meier, Charles Jencks, Daniel Libeskind, and Conrad Jameson; transcript of lecture given by Richard Meier at "The Annual Architecture Forum," London: Art and Design, 1990, pp. 10–19, 30–31, 45–46.

Richard Meier. Includes introduction by Kenneth Frampton; "Le 'allusioni' di Richard Meier" by Francesco Dal Co; "La 'memoria' del movimento moderno nell'opera di Richard Meier" by Gianni Pettena. Venice: Marsilio, 1981.

Richard Meier. Includes "Romantic Modernist" by Michael Webb. *Korean Architects*, no. 153, May 1997, pp. 60–161.

Richard Meier Architect. Includes preface by Richard Meier; introduction by Joseph Rykwert; postscript by John Hejduk. New York: Rizzoli, 1984.

Richard Meier Architect 2. Includes preface by Richard Meier; "Works in Transition" by Kenneth Frampton; "The Second Installment" by Joseph Rykwert; postscript by Frank Stella. New York: Rizzoli, 1991.

Richard Meier Architect 3. Includes preface by Richard Meier; "Three Tropes in the Later Work of Richard Meier" by Kenneth Frampton; "The Third Installment" by Joseph Rykwert; postscript by Arata Isozaki. New York: Rizzoli, 1999.

Richard Meier, Architect: Buildings and Projects 1966–1976. Includes introduction by Kenneth Frampton; postscript by John Hejduk. New York: Oxford University Press, 1976.

Richard Meier: Buildings and Projects 1979–1989. Includes "Richard Meier and the City in Miniature" by Kenneth Frampton; "Richard Meier Interviews 1980–1988" by Charles Jencks; "RIBA Royal Gold Medal Address 1988" by Richard Meier. London: Academy Editions, 1990. Reprinted in German. Stuttgart: Deutsche Verlags-Anstalt GmbH, 1990.

Richard Meier Houses. Includes "The Dance of Composition" by Paul Goldberger; "Richard Meier's Ideal Villas" by Sir Richard Rogers. New York: Rizzoli, 1996. Reprinted in Italian. Milan: RCS Libri & Grandi Opere S.p.A., 1996. Reprint, London: Thames & Hudson, 1996.

Spatial Structure of Richard Meier. Includes "Lyricism in Whiteness" by Arata Isozaki; "My Statement" by Richard Meier; "Analysis: Richard Meier's Work" by Mario Gandelsonas; "Recent Work of Richard Meier" by Rosemarie Bletter; "Meier's Whiteness" by Ching-Yu Chang; *A+U*, April 1976.

Special Feature: Recent Works of Richard Meier. Includes "A Heightened Urbanity: The Recent Works of Richard Meier" by David Galloway. *A+U*, March 1988.

Vaudou, Valerie, ed. *Richard Meier/Monographies*. Includes foreword by Richard Meier; "La Modernité comme seuil" by Hubert Damisch; "Radieuse modernité" by Henri Ciriani; "Sur Richard Meier" by Diane Lewis; "La Capture du regard" by Jean Mas. Paris: Electa Moniteur, 1986. Reprinted in Italian. Milan: Electa, 1986.

White Existence: Richard Meier, 1961–77. Includes "A Word from Richard Meier"; "Dialogue: On Architecture" by Richard Meier and Fumihiko Maki; "A Personal View on R. Meier" by Yukio Futagawa; "Expression Crisis— The Implications of the Formation of Richard Meier" by Yuzuru Tominaga; "Architecture of Pleasure" by Hiromi Fujii; "Works: Private Buildings and Projects"; "Richard Meier's Works Chronologically Scanned." *Space Design*, January 1978.

Books and Special Issues—Specific Projects

Ackerberg House + Addition. Includes introduction by Richard Meier. New York: The Monacelli Press, 1996.

Blaser, Werner. *Weishaupt Forum/Richard Meier*. Includes introduction by Richard Meier; essay by Claudia Rudeck. Schwendi: Max Weishaupt GmbH, 1993.

Brawne, Michael. *Architecture in Detail: The Getty Center*. London: Phaidon Press Ltd., 1998.

Brawne, Michael. *Architecture in Detail: Museum für Kunsthandwerk*. London: Phaidon Press Ltd., 1992.

Der Dialog als Program die Hypobank in Luxemburg. Includes "Die Hypolux und die Ästhetik des städtischen" by David Galloway. Luxembourg: Hypobank International S.A., 1993.

Flagge, Ingeborg. *Richard Meier: Daimler Benz*. Stuttgart: Gerd Hatje, 1994.

Futagawa, Yukio, ed. "Collage and Study Sketches for the Atheneum"; "Meier's Atheneum" by Kenneth Frampton; "Richard Meier, an American Architect" by Arthur Cohen; "The Atheneum, New Harmony, Ind. (First Scheme)"; "The Atheneum (Executed Scheme)." *GA Document 1*, 1980.

Futagawa, Yukio, ed. "Douglas House, Harbor Springs, Michigan. 1974." Text by Paul Goldberger. *Global Architecture 34*, 1975. Reprinted in *Global Architecture Book 3: Modern Houses*. Tokyo: A.D.A. Edita Co., 1981.

The Getty Center. Includes "A Citadel for Los Angeles and an Alhambra for the Arts" by Kurt Foster; "Richard Meier's Getty Center" by Henri Ciriani. *A+U*, November 1992.

The Getty Center Design Process. Includes introduction by Harold Williams; "The Architect Selection and Design" by Bill Lacy; "The Architectural Program" by Stephen D. Rountree; "The Design Process" by Richard Meier. Los Angeles: J. Paul Getty Trust, 1991.

Making Architecture. Includes introduction by Harold Williams; "The Clash of Symbols" by Ada Louise Huxtable; "A Concert of Wills" by Stephen D. Rountree; "A Vision for Permanence" by Richard Meier. Los Angeles: J. Paul Getty Trust, 1997.

New Buildings by Richard Meier. Includes "Is Richard Meier Really Modern?" and "Sculptural Sanctum" by Joseph Giovannini; "Aloof Abstraction" by Peter Buchanan; "The Getty Gets Ready" by Martin Filler; "Swiss Precision" by Reed Kroloff; "Dutch Modern" by Colin Davies; "Meier's White Turns Green" by Raul Barreneche. *Architecture*, February 1996.

The New Getty. Includes "Shining City on a Hill" by Nicolai Ouroussoff; "His Defining Moment" by Steve Proffitt. *Los Angeles Times Magazine*, special issue, December 7, 1997.

Richard Meier: Barcelona Museum of Contemporary Art. Includes "Urban Promenade as Architectural Promenade" by Dennis L. Dollens; "Designing the Barcelona Museum of Contemporary Art" by Richard Meier; "A Big White Mass Shines over a Plaza" by Federico Correa. New York: The Monacelli Press, 1997.

Richard Meier: Stadthaus Ulm. Includes "Richard Meier and the Urban Context" by David Galloway; "The Urbanization of Architecture" by Stephan Barthelmess. Ulm: International Creative Management, 1993.

Sack, Manfred. *Richard Meier Stadthaus Ulm*. Stuttgart: Axel Menges, 1994.

Staal, Gert. *KNP Corporate Office Hilversum*. Netherlands: KNP, June 1992.

Stadhuis Bibliotheek: The City Hall/Library Complex by Richard Meier in The Hague. Includes interview with Richard Meier; "The Quest for the City Hall" by Fred Feddes; "The City Hall as a Pivot of Urban Renewal" by Victor Freijser; "A Public Library in a Prominent Place" by Olof Koekebakker; "The Atrium, Livable Climate and Technology" by Ed Melet. Rotterdam: NAi Publishers, 1995.

Vigtel, Gudmund, Richard Meier, Anthony Ames. *High Museum of Art. The New Building: A Chronicle of Planning, Design and Construction*. Atlanta: High Museum of Art, 1983.

Writings by Richard Meier

Arata Isozaki 1960/1990. Includes "On Arata Isozaki" by Richard Meier. Tokyo: Executive Committee for *Arata Isozaki Architecture 1960/1990* exhibition catalogue, 1991, p. 26.

Cobb, Henry N., and Richard Meier. "Richard Meier's Museum für Kunsthandwerk." *Express*, April 1981, p. 7.

Dante O. Benini: Intuition and Precision. Includes introduction by Richard Meier. Milan: l'Arca Edizioni, 1998, pp. 6–7.

Deal, Joe. *Between Nature and Culture: Photographs of the Getty Center*. Includes preface by Richard Meier. Los Angeles: Getty Trust Publications, 1999.

Five Houses 1976–1986: Anthony Ames, Architect. Includes postscript by Richard Meier. Princeton: Princeton Architectural Press, 1987, p. 130.

Frank Stella: Shards. Exhibition catalogue. Includes "Thoughts on Frank Stella" by Richard Meier. London and New York: Petersburg Press, 1983, pp. 1–4.

Henri Ciriani. Includes foreword by Richard Meier. Rockport, Mass.: Rockport Publishers, 1997, p. 6.

Meier, Richard. *Building the Getty*. New York: Alfred A. Knopf Inc., 1997.

Meier, Richard. "Cultural Congress." *Skyline*, April 1983, p. 7.

Meier, Richard. "Design Strategies: Eight Projects by Richard Meier and Associates—Systematic Self-Description of the Compositional Process." *Casabella*, May 1974, pp. 17–38.

Meier, Richard. "Essay." *Perspecta 24*. New York: Rizzoli, 1988, pp. 104–5.

Meier, Richard. "Guest Speaker: On the Spirit of Architecture." *Architectural Digest*, June 1981, pp. 156, 160, 162, 164.

Meier, Richard. "Lecture in Japan." *Spazio*, December 20, 1976, supplement.

Meier, Richard. "Les Heures Claires." In "Le Corbusier: Villa Savoye, Poissy, France, 1929–31." Edited by Yukio Futagawa. *Global Architecture 13*, 1973, pp. 2–7.

Meier, Richard. "On the Road Again." *Architecture, Shaping the Future*. San Diego: University of California, 1990, pp. 25–35.

Meier, Richard. "Planning for Jerusalem." *Architectural Forum*, April 1971, pp. 56–57.

Meier, Richard. "Remembering Breuer." *Skyline*, October 1981, p. 11.

Meier, Richard. *Richard Meier: On Architecture*. Eliot Noyes Lecture. Cambridge, Mass.: Harvard University Graduate School of Design, 1982.

Meier, Richard. "Thoughts on Alberto Sartoris." *Space Design*, September 1987, p. 93.

Meier, Richard, ed. *Recent American Synagogue Architecture*. Includes introduction by Richard Meier. New York: The Jewish Museum, 1963.

Meier, Richard, and Arata Isozaki. "Dialogue." *A+U*, August 1976, pp. 21–38.

Piero Sartogo/Nathalie Grenon: Architecture in Perspective. Includes foreword by Richard Meier. New York: The Monacelli Press, 1998, pp. 7–8.

Stamberg Aferiat Architecture. Includes contribution by Richard Meier. New York: Rizzoli, 1997, pp. 20–21.

Wilmotte: Réalisations et projets. Includes foreword by Richard Meier. Paris: Le Moniteur, 1993, p. 9.

Interviews with Richard Meier

Diamonstein, Barbaralee. "Richard Meier." In *American Architecture Now*. New York: Rizzoli, 1980, pp. 105–22.

Diamonstein, Barbaralee. "Richard Meier." In *American Architecture Now II*. New York: Rizzoli, 1985, pp. 161–68.

Flagge, Ingeborg. "Interview: Richard Meier." *Lufthansa Bordbuch*, No. 6/91, November/December 1991, pp. 24–28, 30.

Futagawa, Yukio, ed. *GA Document Extra 08: Richard Meier*. Includes interview with Richard Meier. Tokyo: A.D.A. Edita Co., 1997.

Henning, Larson, et al. "Interview with Richard Meier." *Skala*, August 1987, pp. 11–15.

James, Warren. "Interview: Richard Meier." *Arquitectura*, July/August 1990, pp. 138–53.

Keens, William. "Dialogue and Fantasy in White: An Interview with Richard Meier." *American Arts*, September 1983, pp. 16–21.

"Meier's Museums: A Tale of Two Cities." *The Journal of Art*, April 1989, pp. 50–53.

"The Met Grill: Interview with Richard Meier." *Metropolitan Home*, September 1986, p. 24.

Rudolph, Karen. "Light is a Transient Medium." *ERCO Lichtbericht 52*, August 1996, pp. 10–11.

Slatin, Peter. "Interview: Richard Meier." *Omni*, September 1993, pp. 69–70, 86, 88, 92–94.

Selected Articles

Adam, Peter. "Ein Meister der Moderne." *Ambiente*, July 1987, pp. 44–52.

Allen, Gerald. "Traditional Image for Olivetti." *Architectural Record*, February 1974, pp. 117–24.

Andersen, Kurt. "A City on a Hill." *New Yorker*, September 29, 1997, pp. 66–72.

Andersen, Kurt. "A Grand New Getty." *Time*, October 21, 1991, p. 100.

Bächer, Max. "The Stadthaus at Ulm and the Cathedral Square," *Domus*, February 1995, pp. 7–22.

Balfour, Alan. "High Museum, Atlanta, Georgia." *Architectural Review*, February 1984, pp. 26–27; project documentation, pp. 20–25.

Banham, Reyner. "Who's the King of the Mountain?" *California*, August 1984, pp. 94–103, 120–21.

Barthelmess, Stephan N. "Richard Meier's Stadthaus Project at Ulm." *Journal of Architectural Education*, Spring 1990, pp. 2–19.

Beaudouin, Laurent. "Canal+ Building in Paris." *A+U*, January 1993, pp. 46–71.

"Bronx Developmental Center." Includes "Bronx Developmental Center" by Paul Goldberger; "A Comparative Study—Bronx Developmental Center and Gunma Prefectural Museum of Modern Art" by Arata Isozaki; "The Modern Language of Architecture and Richard Meier" by Francesco Dal Co. *A+U*, November 1977, pp. 3–29.

Castellano, Aldo. "The Church of the Year 2000." *l'Arca*, September 1996, pp. 12–17.

Ciorra, Pippo. "Richard Meier and Peter Eisenman. Talent and Ideas." *Casabella*, December/January 1997, pp. 106–7.

Cohen, Stuart. "Physical Context/Cultural Context: Including It All." *Oppositions 2*, 1974, pp. 14–21, 30–37.

Colacello, Bob. "Meier's Moment." *Vanity Fair*, April 1997, pp. 332–39, 376–79.

Dal Co, Francesco. "The 'Allusions' of Richard Meier." *Oppositions 9*, 1977, pp. 6–18.

Dietsch, Deborah. "Howard's House." *Architecture*, July 1997, pp. 72–79.

Eisenman, Peter. "Letter to the Editor: Meier's Smith House." *Architectural Design*, August 1971, p. 52.

Filler, Martin. "Eminent Domain." *House & Garden*, April 1987, pp. 162–69. Reprinted in French as "Precision au Sommett." *Vogue Decoration*, September 1987, pp. 114–17, 212.

Forgey, Benjamin. "Getty's Big Address." *Washington Post*, December 14, 1997, sect. G, pp. 1, 4.

Forster, Kurt. "Carácter corporativo: Nuevo sede de Canal+ en Paris." *Arquitectura Viva*, May/June 1993, pp. 90–95.

Forster, Kurt. "Stella televisia sul palcoscenico urbano." *Domus*, September 1992, pp. 29–41.

Frampton, Kenneth. "High Museum of Art at Atlanta." *Casabella*, November 1982, pp. 50–61.

Frampton, Kenneth. "Progetti in Europa di Richard Meier & Partners." *Casabella*, December 1990, pp. 4–10.

Frampton, Kenneth. "Twin Parks as Typology." *Architectural Forum*, June 1973, pp. 56–61.

Galloway, David. "Richard Meier, Master Builder." *Inter Nations German-American Cultural Review*, October 6, 1993, pp. 40–47.

Galloway, David. "Richard Meier: Style in Context." *Art in America*, January 1995, pp. 40–47.

"The Getty Center" special issue. Includes "Art vs. Architecture" by Allan Schwartzman; "Faulty Towers" by Aaron Betsky; "Ready for Art?" by Dave Hickey. *Architecture*, December 1997.

Goldberger, Paul. "Can the Getty Buy Design Happiness?" *New York Times*, October 13, 1991, sect. 2, pp. 1, 31.

Goldberger, Paul. "The People's Getty." *New Yorker*, February 23/March 2, 1998, pp. 178–81.

Goldberger, Paul. "A Short Skyscraper with a Tall Assignment." *New York Times*. March 26, 1989, p. 32.

Goldberger, Paul. "Twin Parks, an Effort to Alter the Problem of Public Housing." *New York Times*, December 27, 1973, p. 39.

Grasso, Giacomo. "The Church of the Year 2000." *L'Architettura*, July 1996, pp. 68–80.

Gruber, Michael. "A Look at Making in the Meier-Getty Model Shop." *Architecture California*, 1994, pp. 32–41.

Hines, Thomas. "Bridging the Public and Private Realms in a Dallas House." *Architectural Digest*, April 1997, pp. 118–25, 214.

Hollenstein, Roman. "Eine Alhambra für Los Angeles." *Neue Zurcher Zeitung*, November 15, 1991, p. 65.

Hoyet, Jean-Michel. "Made in U.S.A.: Trois Conceptions récentes de Richard Meier & Associés." *Techniques & Architecture*, November 1982, pp. 140–47.

Hoyt, Charles. "4 Projects by Richard Meier: Change and Consistency," *Architectural Record*, March 1975, pp. 111–20.

Hughes, Robert. "Architecture: Richard Meier." *Architectural Digest*, October 1987, pp. 152–59.

Hughes, Robert. "Bravo! Bravo!" *Time*, November 3, 1997, pp. 98–105.

James, Warren. "Casa en Westchester, Nueva York 1984–87." *Arquitectura*, November/December 1987, pp. 80–89.

Jodidio, Philip. "La Quadrature du cercle," *Connaissance des Arts*, December 1994, pp. 96–105.

Ketcham, Diana. "No Garland for Getty Garden." *San Francisco Examiner*, December 17, 1997, sect. B, pp. 1, 6.

Kieran, Kevin, et al., eds. "The Getty Trust and the Process of Patronage." *Harvard Architecture Review*, no. 6, 1987, pp. 122–31.

Lampugnani, Vittorio Magnago. "Des Moines Art Center Addition." *Domus*, April 1986, pp. 37–43.

Lampugnani, Vittorio Magnago. "The Jewel with All Qualities." *Lotus International* 28, 1980, pp. 34–41.

Maxwell, Robert. "Modern Master." *Building Design*, September 16, 1988, p. 28.

McGuigan, Cathleen. "A Place in the Sun." *Newsweek*, October 13, 1997, pp. 72–74.

McGuigan, Cathleen, with Emily Yoffe. "A Lavish Place in the Sun." *Newsweek*, October 21, 1991, p. 64.

"Meier's Magic Mountain." Includes "Getty Genesis" by Ivor Richards; "Playing to the Gallery" by Michael Brawne. *Architectural Review*, February 1998, pp. 30–51.

Metz, Tracy. "A Circle in the Square." *Architectural Record*, October 1995, pp. 90–99.

Moneo, Rafael. "Proyectos no realizados para Olivetti." *Arquitecturas Bis*, July 1975, pp. 10–14.

Muschamp, Herbert. "Architecture of Light and Remembrance." *New York Times*, December 15, 1996, sect. B, pp. 1, 44.

Muschamp, Herbert. "A Mountaintop Temple Where Art's Future Worships Its Past." *New York Times*, December 1, 1997, sect. A, pp. 1, 18.

Muschamp, Herbert. "On a Clear Day, You Can Watch Television." *New York Times*, February 7, 1993, sect. B, p. 32.

Muschamp, Herbert. "A Reason to Rubberneck on the Expressway." *New York Times*, February 26, 1995, sect. B, p. 42. Reprinted in Italian. "Un cigno tra le anatre."*Casabella*, October 1995, pp. 63–65.

Pearson, Clifford. "Working Couple." *Architectural Record*, March 1993, pp. 52–61.

"Meier's Canal+." Includes "The Message in the Medium" by Jean-Louis Cohen; "Bien Venue" by Thomas Vonier. *Progressive Architecture*, December 1992, pp. 44–53.

Reese, Thomas. "The Architectural Politics of the Getty Center for the Arts." *Lotus 85*, 1995, pp. 6–43.

Reese, Thomas, and Carol McMichael Reese. "Richard Meier's New Getty Center in Los Angeles." *A+U*, January 1998, pp. 6–69.

"Richard Meier: Museum für Kunsthandwerk." Includes "Décalages et Dynamisme: An Interview with Richard Meier," by Henri Ciriani and Jacques Lucan; "Le Musée de Francfort; 'Apprendre à voir l'architecture,'" by Jacques Lucan. *AMC*, December 1985, pp. 20–33.

Richards, Ivor. "Heart of the Hague." *Architectural Review*, January 1996, pp. 40–49.

Richards, Ivor. "Interactive Languages." *Architectural Review*, April 1993, pp. 22–37.

Riding, Alan. "A Modern 'Pearl' Inside Old Barcelona." *New York Times*, May 10, 1995, sect. C, p. 13.

Rykwert, Joseph. "Acropolis with Hover-Tram." *Times* (London) *Literary Supplement*, January 9, 1998, pp. 15–16.

Rykwert, Joseph. "Richard Meier: Two New Houses in USA." *Domus*, March 1987, pp. 29–45.

Stein, Karen D. "The Getty Center, Los Angeles, California." *Architectural Record*, November 1997, pp. 72–105.

Stephens, Suzanne. "Malibu Modernism." *Progressive Architecture*, December 1987, pp. 94–101.

Tafuri, Manfredo. "'European Graffiti': Five x Five = Twenty-Five." *Oppositions 5*, 1976, pp. 35–74.

Tafuri, Manfredo. "L'Architecture dans le Boudoir." *Oppositions 3*, 1974, p. 52.

Vidler, Anthony. "Architecture as Spectacle." *Los Angeles Times*, May 3, 1998, sect. M, pp. 1, 6.

Vidler, Anthony. "Deconstructing Modernism." *Skyline*, March 1982, pp. 21–23.

Von Eckardt, Wolf. "Taking on an Imperial Task." *Time*, November 12, 1984, p. 111.

Zardini, Mirko. "Il Bianco e Il grigio." *Casabella*, July/August 1985, pp. 4–10.

Zevi, Bruno. "Richard Meier and the Language of Baalbek." *L'Architettura*, November 1993, pp. 754–55.

Zevi, Bruno. "Richard Meier in Bramante's Place." *L'Architettura*, July 1996, pp. 66–67.

Other Media

Concert of Wills: Making the Getty Center. Documentary film by Susan Froemke and Bob Eisenhardt with Albert Maysles. 100 min. J. Paul Getty Trust, 1997.

Mas, Jean, ed. *Richard Meier Architect*. CD-ROM. Includes commentary by Henri Ciriani, Kenneth Frampton, Andre Rousselet, Frank Stella, Ezra Stoller. Lugano: Victory Interactive Media S.A., 1995.

Richard Meier. Documentary film by Michael Blackwood. 58 min. Michael Blackwood Productions Inc., 1984. Narration by Suzanne Stephens. Produced and directed by Michael Blackwood.